Data-Driven Computational Methods

Parameter and Operator Estimations

Modern scientific computational methods are undergoing a transformative change; big data and statistical learning methods now have the potential to outperform the classical first-principles modeling paradigm. This book bridges this transition, connecting the theory of probability, stochastic processes, functional analysis, numerical analysis, and differential geometry. It describes two classes of computational methods to leverage data for modeling dynamical systems. The first is concerned with data fitting algorithms to estimate parameters in parametric models that are postulated on the basis of physical or dynamical laws. The second is on operator estimation, which uses the data to nonparametrically approximate the operator generated by the transition function of the underlying dynamical systems.

This self-contained book is suitable for graduate studies in applied mathematics, statistics, and engineering. Carefully chosen elementary examples with supplementary MATLAB® codes and appendices covering the relevant prerequisite materials are provided, making it suitable for self-study.

John Harlim is a Professor of Mathematics and Meteorology at the Pennsylvania State University. His research interests include data assimilation and stochastic computational methods. In 2012, he received the Frontiers in Computational Physics award from the *Journal of Computational Physics* for his research contributions on computational methods for modeling Earth systems. He has previously co-authored another book, *Filtering Complex Turbulent Systems* (Cambridge, 2012).

Data-Driven Computational Methods

Parameter and Operator Estimations

JOHN HARLIM

The Pennsylvania State University

CAMBRIDGE
UNIVERSITY PRESS

University Printing House, Cambridge CB2 8BS, United Kingdom

One Liberty Plaza, 20th Floor, New York, NY 10006, USA

477 Williamstown Road, Port Melbourne, VIC 3207, Australia

314–321, 3rd Floor, Plot 3, Splendor Forum, Jasola District Centre, New Delhi – 110025, India

79 Anson Road, #06–04/06, Singapore 079906

Cambridge University Press is part of the University of Cambridge.

It furthers the University's mission by disseminating knowledge in the pursuit of education, learning, and research at the highest international levels of excellence.

www.cambridge.org
Information on this title: www.cambridge.org/9781108472470
DOI: 10.1017/9781108562461

First published 2018

Printed in the United Kingdom by TJ International Ltd. Padstow Cornwall

A catalogue record for this publication is available from the British Library.

ISBN 978-1-108-47247-0 Hardback

This book is dedicated to the joys of my life,
my wife, Leonie, and my son, Kelvin.

I also dedicate this book to my parents, Gemiati and Siang Jong,
who have made my childhood dream to become a student forever come true.

Contents

Preface

Stochastic modeling of dynamical systems has been instrumental in various applied fields, including material sciences, atmospheric and ocean sciences, biology, chemistry, etc. With the rapid advancement in data collection, an important emerging scientific discipline is to leverage this new information to improve modeling and prediction of complex dynamical systems. While the theory of stochastic processes is a well-established field, the development of the data-driven computational tools for their practical implementation has emerged to become an important new discipline in applied mathematics and engineering science. The aim of this book is to provide a survey of such computational tools. In particular, the book covers computational methods for stochastic modeling of dynamical systems.

In general, there are two classes of mathematical/statistical modeling: parametric and nonparametric paradigms. Arguably, one can merge these two classes and invent a semi-parametric paradigm. Parametric modeling of complex dynamical systems usually involves proposing a model based on some physical laws (such as Newtonian, conservation laws, etc.), inferring the model parameters from the available observed data, and verifying the results against the observables. In contrast, one can also use the data to build nonparametric models with minimal assumptions on the underlying dynamics. In such an approach, the notion of nonparametric modeling follows from the standard statistical literature which makes no assumption either about how the dynamics should behave or about the distribution of the underlying dynamics. Instead, we let the data determine the dynamics.

In this book, we discuss computational methods both for the parametric approach and for the non-parametric approach. For the parametric approach, our choice will be to employ parameter estimation methods with Bayesian inference, which have been widely used in many applications. For this topic, we cover two basic approaches. The first one is the Markov-Chain Monte Carlo (MCMC) method in Chapter 2, which aims to estimate the distribution of the hidden parameters of dynamical systems from the noisy data. The second method is the ensemble Kalman filter (EnKF) in Chapter 3, which has been successfully used in numerical weather forecasting applications. EnKF is complementary to MCMC in the sense that it estimates only the first- and second-order moments of the hidden parameters of dynamical systems from the noisy data. In this book, we will neglect the non-Bayesian parameter estimation techniques.

For the nonparametric modeling of dynamical systems, we will provide a rigorous treatment of a recently developed computational method, the so-called diffusion forecasting model, which allows one to approximate the solution operator corresponding to the Fokker–Planck equation of the Itô diffusion completely from the data. One of the main emphases of this book is the intention to show readers that this nonparametric approach is a natural generalization of the central idea in uncertainty quantification (UQ), namely the representation of random variables with a linear superposition of polynomial basis functions of appropriate Hilbert space. In the traditional UQ approach, one usually chooses the polynomial basis functions by assuming that the random variables that are to be represented belong to a certain class of known distributions on some Euclidean domain. The diffusion forecast generalizes this idea by representing the semigroup operator generated by the transition function of the Itô drifted diffusion processes with basis functions that are purely constructed from the data that lies on a (possibly non-Euclidean) manifold. We shall see that the diffusion forecasting approach is indeed a spectral Galerkin method that uses the data-driven basis functions to represent the Fokker–Planck equation nonparametrically. To facilitate this generalization viewpoint, we give a brief review of a basic non-data-driven UQ approach, namely the stochastic spectral method with polynomial chaos expansion in Chapter 4. Since the construction of the data-driven basis functions relies on a kernel-based manifold learning method, namely the so-called diffusion maps algorithm, we provide a review of the classical Karhunen–Loève expansion in Chapter 5. The key point is to show that proper orthogonal decomposition (POD), which is a popular linear manifold learning algorithm, is an application of the Karhunen–Loève expansion that exploits Mercer's theorem. The theoretical discussion in this chapter, which ties together the eigenfunctions of kernel-based integral operators and the orthonormal basis functions of a Hilbert space, will become handy in understanding the construction of the diffusion maps algorithm. These two chapters are included to give more solid understanding of the operator estimation technique discussed in Chapter 6.

This book is designed for applied mathematicians and engineers ranging from first-year graduate students to senior researchers interested in leveraging data to model stochastic dynamics. Selected elementary examples, together with the MATLAB® scripts (in the supplementary material), are provided to help readers' self-study. While we expect readers to be familiar with basic probability theory, stochastic processes, and differential geometry language, they are not essential. In fact, we provide three appendices reviewing these basic materials.

Acknowledgments

Parts of this book are summaries based on the author's joint works with Andrew Majda, Tyrus Berry, Dimitris Giannakis, Xiantao Li, Adam Mahdi, Haizhao

Yang, Shixiao Jiang, and Yicun Zhen. The author thanks these colleagues for their explicit and implicit contributions to this material. The author also thanks Tyrus Berry, Nan Chen, Wen Shen, Xin Tong, He Zhang and anonymous reviewers for reading through the manuscript and their suggestions.

Special thanks are due to Juliani and Guy Vachon for their hospitality. A large part of this book was written during my stay at their home in Asheville, North Carolina.

The author gratefully acknowledges the generous support from the Office of Naval Research through Reza Malek-Madani and Scott Harper and from the National Science Foundation through Leland Jameson. These research funds made this book a reality. Special thanks are due to the students in the graduate course MA597E Uncertainty Quantification Methods in Fall 2015 at Pennsylvania State University, who motivated the author to assemble this text. The author also thanks the undergraduate students in the REU program in Summer 2016 who worked on a few of the examples in this book.

John Harlim
University Park, PA

1 Introduction

In applied science and engineering applications, modeling effort requires both physical insight in order to choose the appropriate mathematical models and computational tools for parameter inference and model validation. Insofar as the physical intuition is concerned, one usually proposes a mathematical model based on a certain physical law or observed mechanism. Unfortunately, the resulting models are typically subject to errors, be they of a systematic type due to incomplete physical understanding or of statistical nature due to uncertainties in the initial conditions, boundary conditions, model parameters, numerical discretization, etc. Since the ultimate goal of modeling dynamical systems is to predict the future states, it is important to compare the model-based predictions with the actual observables. It is also equally important to provide uncertainties associated with the predictions. As a consequence, the demand for computational methods that involve data fitting and uncertainty quantification is increasing.

Traditionally, statistical science is the leading and established field that analyzes data and develops such computational tools. The focus of this book to a large extent is on surveying recent data-driven methods for modeling dynamical systems. In particular, we survey numerical methods that leverage observational data to estimate parameters in a dynamical model when the parametric model is available and to approximate the model nonparametrically when such a parametric model is not available. These topics were developed through interaction between certain areas of mathematics and statistics such as probability, stochastic processes, numerical analysis, spectral theory, applied differential geometry, Bayesian inference, Monte Carlo integrals, and kernel methods for density and operator estimations. Even with such a wide spectrum of interdisciplinary areas, the coverage here is far from complete. Nevertheless, we hope that the selected topics in this book can serve as a foundation for the data-driven methods in modeling stochastic dynamics.

1.1   The Role of Data in Parametric Modeling

Consider modeling dynamical systems in the form of differential equations,

$$\frac{dx}{dt} = f(x, \theta), \tag{1.1}$$

where $x(t; \theta)$ is the variable of interest and the vector field f defines the "law" that determines how x changes with time. Here, the differential equations can be either deterministic or stochastic. When the dependence of f on state variables x and parameters θ is given (or imposed), we call such a representation *parametric modeling*.

To make this dynamical model useful for predicting the future state, $x(t; \theta), t > t_i$, one needs to specify the parameters θ as well as the initial condition, $x(t_i)$, which reflects the current state. This inverse problem can naturally be solved with a Bayesian approach (Dashti & Stuart 2017). This parameter estimation problem is the first main topic of this book. We will neglect the non-Bayesian approach in this book.

Now, let us describe the basic idea of the Bayesian approach. In practice, we often observe noisy discrete-time data,

$$y_i = h(x(t_i; \theta^\dagger, x_0)) + \eta_i, \tag{1.2}$$

where the subscript i denotes a discrete time index, h denotes the observation operator, and $x(t_i; \theta^\dagger, x_0)$ denotes the solutions of (1.1) at time t_i with hidden parameters $\theta^\dagger$ and initial condition $x(t_0) = x_0$. In (1.2), the terms η_i denote unbiased independent and identically distributed (i.i.d.) noises, representing measurement error. Depending on the distribution of the observation error η_i, one can define the likelihood function of (θ, x_0) via the conditional distribution, $p(y_i|x_0, \theta) = p(y_i - h(x(t_i; \theta, x_0))) = p(\eta_i)$, where x_0 can also be estimated when it is not known. In this book, we will survey two popular Bayesian computational methods to estimate the conditional density for θ given the measured observations in (1.2).

1.1.1   Markov-Chain Monte Carlo

Let's denote $y = \{y_1, \dots, y_n\}$ and $p(y|\theta) = \prod_{i=1}^n p(y_i|\theta)$ and assume that the initial condition x_0 is given. The objective of this Bayesian inference is to estimate $p(\theta|y)$ by applying Bayes' rule,

$$p(\theta|y) \propto p(\theta)p(y|\theta), \tag{1.3}$$

where $p(\theta)$ denotes the prior density of the parameter. Here, the prior acts as a regularization term to overcome ill-posedness in the inverse problems (Dashti & Stuart 2017). From the estimated posterior density $p(\theta|y)$, one can deduce statistical quantities, such as the mean as a point estimator for $\theta^\dagger$ and the covariance, to quantify the uncertainty of the mean estimate.

A popular method to sample the posterior density $p(\theta|y)$ in (1.3) is the Markov-chain Monte Carlo (MCMC) method, which will be discussed in Chapter 2. We will give a brief survey of the mathematical theory behind MCMC to give readers a solid understanding of this sampling procedure. Briefly, this method constructs a Markov chain with the posterior $p(\theta|y)$ as the limiting or target distribution. While the MCMC approach for solving Bayes' formula in (1.3) is a "gold standard," this objective is computationally demanding and may not be feasible when the underlying model in (1.1) is high-dimensional. This computational overhead is because MCMC involves an iterative procedure that requires one to solve the dynamical system in (1.1) on the proposed parameters in each iteration. One popular way to avoid this expensive calculation is with a surrogate modeling (Marzouk & Xiu 2009), which will be discussed in Section 2.5. In Example 1.1, we give a brief illustration of the expected product of the MCMC implemented with the underlying dynamics as well as with a surrogate model constructed using a polynomial expansion (which is discussed in detail in Chapter 4).

Example 1.1 Consider estimating two parameters D, F of a system of a five-dimensional Lorenz-96 model (Lorenz 1996),

$$\frac{dx_j}{dt} = x_{j-1}(x_{j+1} - x_{j-2}) - Dx_j + F, \qquad j = 1, \ldots, J,$$

$$x_j(0) = \sin\left(\frac{2\pi j}{5}\right),$$

(1.4)

from a given set of discrete-time observations, $\Delta t = t_i - t_{i-1} = 0.05$, $i = 1, \ldots, 10$,

$$y_j(t_i) = x_j(t_i) + \eta_i, \quad \eta_i \sim \mathcal{N}(0, 0.01).$$

(1.5)

In (1.5), the observations of state $x(t_i)$ are corrupted with i.i.d. Gaussian noises, η_i.

In Figure 1.1, we show the resulting posterior density estimate from the MCMC with the underlying model in (1.4) as well as with a surrogate modeling constructed using a polynomial expansion that avoids integrating the system of differential equations in (1.4). Notice that the true parameter values are within the posterior density estimates.

1.1.2   The Ensemble Kalman Filter

The second Bayesian inference method we will discuss is the ensemble Kalman filter. In particular, define $\mathcal{Y}_i = \{y_j, j \leq i\}$. Here, we consider applying Bayes' formula sequentially to approximate the posterior distribution of both the state and the parameters,

$$p(\theta_i, x_i | \mathcal{Y}_i) \propto p(\theta_i, x_i | \mathcal{Y}_{i-1}) p(y_i | x_i, \theta_i),$$

(1.6)

as the new observation y_i becomes available. At each time step, we need to specify an initial density, $p(\theta_i, x_i | \mathcal{Y}_{i-1})$.

Faithful solutions to the Bayesian filtering in (1.6) have been proposed, such as the particle filter or sequential Monte Carlo (Doucet *et al.* 2001), which represents the prior density with a point measure. However, clever sampling algorithms are needed to mitigate the curse of dimensionality of the classical particle filter (Bengtsson *et al.* 2008, Bickel *et al.* 2008). In the world of applied science and engineering, a popular choice to approximate this Bayesian filtering problem is

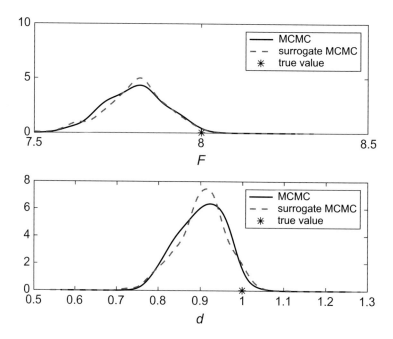

Figure 1.1 Standard MCMC density of each parameter (black), surrogate MCMC density (dashes), and the true parameter value (asterisk).

to use algorithms that are based on the celebrated Kalman filter (Kalman & Bucy 1961). One of the most successful schemes that has been used in many applications, including numerical weather predictions, is the ensemble Kalman filter (EnKF) (Evensen 1994). The EnKF is a clever extension to the Kalman filter on nonlinear problems, without which the Kalman filter is impractical for high-dimensional problems. Since the Kalman filter formula is derived under strict assumptions, namely linearity and Gaussianity, it is clear that the EnKF, which represents the prior density, $p(\theta_i, x_i | \mathcal{Y}_{i-1})$, with a Gaussian measure, will not produce a meaningful estimate of the posterior density $p(\theta_i, x_i | \mathcal{Y}_i)$ in nonlinear and non-Gaussian problems. Nevertheless, what is interesting is that often the ensemble solutions can track the true initial conditions, x_i, and parameter values, $\theta^\dagger$. In Chapter 3, we will discuss recent theoretical results that justify the accuracy of the EnKF as a state estimation method, which has also been observed in many applications. The main emphasis of this chapter will be on the application of the EnKF in estimating both the state x_i and the parameters θ in (1.1). In particular, we will focus on two parameter estimation methods. The first technique is a simple application of the EnKF to estimate parameters θ of the deterministic terms in the model. The second technique is on adaptive covariance estimation schemes that can be used in tandem with the EnKF to estimate parameters θ which represent the amplitudes of additive white noise forcings. In particular, we will discuss two recently developed methods that have been tested in many parameter estimation problems; the Berry–Sauer scheme

(Berry & Sauer 2013) and the classical Belanger scheme (Belanger 1974) which was recently adapted to the EnKF (Harlim *et al.* 2014).

While fitting data to a dynamical model is a central topic of Chapters 2 and 3, constructing a model with accurate statistical prediction in the presence of model errors remains a challenging problem. In other words, constructing a model that can reproduce the marginal statistics (or observables) of the hidden dynamics is a nontrivial problem in general. In Section 3.3, we discuss this problem in the context of reduced-order modeling. Here, we survey the Mori–Zwanzig formalism (Mori 1965, Zwanzig 1961, 1973) as an idealistic concept for reduced-order modeling. Our goal with this discussion is to elucidate the difficulty of this problem. Subsequently, we will discuss a Markovian approximation for the generalized Langevin equation (GLE) derived from the Mori–Zwanzig formalism. Here, we will demonstrate the potential of using the parameter estimation scheme surveyed in this chapter to calibrate statistically accurate reduced-order Markovian dynamics. In Example 1.2, we give a brief illustration of the expected product from the parameter estimation method discussed in Chapter 3, implemented on a reduced-order model of a multiscale dynamical system.

Example 1.2   Consider the two-layer Lorenz-96 model (Lorenz 1996), whose governing equations are a system of $N(J + 1)$-dimensional ODEs given by

$$\frac{dx_i}{dt} = x_{i-1}(x_{i+1} - x_{i-2}) - x_i + F + h_x \sum_{j=(i-1)J+1}^{iJ} y_j,$$

$$\frac{dy_j}{dt} = \frac{1}{\epsilon}\big(ay_{j+1}(y_{j-1} - y_{j+2}) - y_j + h_y x_{\mathrm{ceil}(i/J)}\big). \tag{1.7}$$

Let $\vec{x} = (x_i)$ and $\vec{y} = (y_j)$ be vectors in $\mathbb{R}^N$ and $\mathbb{R}^{NJ}$, respectively, where the subscript i is taken modulo N and j is taken modulo NJ. In this example, we set $N = 8, J = 32, \epsilon = 0.25, F = 20, a = 10, h_x = -0.4$, and $h_y = 0.1$. In this regime the timescale separation is small.

Suppose that we are given the following set of noisy observations:

$$\vec{v}_m = h(\vec{x}(t_m)) + \eta_m, \quad \eta_m \sim \mathcal{N}(0, R),$$

where $R = 0.1\mathcal{I}_M$. In our experiment below, we will take observations only at every other grid point ($M = 4$). That is, $h(\vec{x}) = H\vec{x}$ is a linear observation function where $H \in \mathbb{R}^{4 \times 8}$ and $H(i, 2(i - 1) + 1) = 1$ and zero everywhere else.

Consider the single-layer N-dimensional stochastically forced Lorenz-96 model (Berry & Harlim 2014) as the reduced-order model

$$\frac{d\tilde{x}_i}{dt} = \tilde{x}_{i-1}(\tilde{x}_{i+1} - \tilde{x}_{i-2}) - \tilde{x}_i + F - \alpha\tilde{x}_i(t) + \sigma\dot{W}_i(t), \tag{1.8}$$

where the $\dot{W}_i(t)$ denote white noises. Our goal is to estimate parameters α and σ such that the reduced-order model in (1.8) can reproduce the statistics of the slow components of (1.7). Here, we estimate these parameters with an EnKF in tandem with the Berry–Sauer adaptive covariance method discussed

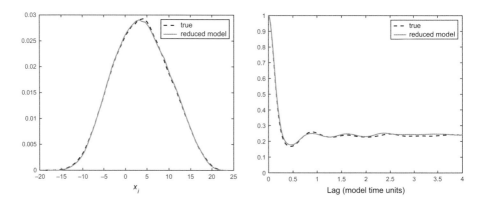

Figure 1.2 Comparison of the marginal density (left) and the time correlation (right) predicted by the reduced-order model in (1.8) (gray solid) compared with the corresponding true statistics (black dashes) of (1.7).

in Chapter 3. For this example, see Berry & Harlim (2014) for more detailed implementation and comparisons with other methods. In Figure 1.2, we show the resulting statistical solutions of the reduced-order model in (1.8) compared with the statistics of the true solutions of (1.7). Notice that the reduced-order model is able to accurately reproduce the marginal density and autocorrelation function of the slow component, x_i, of the full dynamics in (1.7).

1.2   Nonparametric Modeling

The second main topic of this book concerns an operator estimation method for *nonparametric* modeling of dynamical systems. Our notion of nonparametric modeling follows directly from the standard statistical literature (see for example Härdle *et al.* (2012)). That is, we do not make any strong assumption about how the vector field f in (1.1) depends on the state variables x and parameters θ. However, the method still contains parameters. For example, a histogram is a nonparametric approach for estimating density functions, and it contains parameters, namely the bin size and the number of bins. Kernel density estimation is another nonparametric approach for estimating density functions, and it also has a parameter, namely the kernel bandwidth parameter. In fact, the kernel density estimate is usually implemented with a specific choice of kernel function, such as the Gaussian kernel, Epanechnikov kernel, etc. However, it is still considered nonparametric modeling in the sense that it does not make any a-priori assumption about the distributions that are being estimated, and the resulting estimate is independent with respect to the choice of kernel functions. In contrast, a parametric model for estimating densities imposes that the data be sampled from a certain distribution, such as the Gaussian, exponential, gamma, etc.

An example of nonparametric modeling of dynamical systems is the *analog forecast*, which finds states in the historical time series that are very similar to the current state (it identifies analogs) and hopes that the history repeats itself (Lorenz 1969). Although this approach is less susceptible to model errors, it is difficult to identify the analog if the data space is high-dimensional, even if the underlying dynamical systems are low-dimensional (Zhao & Giannakis 2016). Furthermore, it is not so clear whether one can use this method for uncertainty quantification.

In Chapter 6, we discuss a *nonparametric probabilistic modeling* technique, the so-called *diffusion forecast* (Berry *et al.* 2015, Berry & Harlim 2016*a*). This data-driven method rigorously approximates the solutions of the corresponding Fokker–Planck partial differential equations without knowing the differential operator. Since the solutions of the Fokker–Planck PDEs characterize the evolution of the distribution of the underlying dynamics, one can compute the corresponding time-dependent statistics to predict the future states and quantify uncertainties of the predictions. In a nutshell, the diffusion forecast is a method to solve a set of differential equations without knowing the equations.

Our aim here is to show readers that the diffusion forecast is a natural extension of the central idea in uncertainty quantification (UQ), namely representation of random variables with a linear superposition of polynomial basis functions of appropriate Hilbert space. The main difference is that the diffusion forecast does not make any assumption on the distribution of the random variables, which usually determines the polynomial basis functions as in the standard UQ. Instead it learns the basis functions from the data using a kernel-based nonlinear manifold learning method, the so-called *diffusion maps* algorithm (Coifman & Lafon 2006, Berry & Harlim 2016*d*). We shall see that the diffusion forecast is a spectral Galerkin representation of the semigroup solution of the Fokker–Planck equation corresponding to the underlying dynamics with the data-driven basis functions.

With this intention, we include the following two related topics: the stochastic spectral method, which has nothing to do with data, and the Karhunen–Loève expansion, whose applications include a linear manifold learning algorithm. Our main intention in including these two chapters is to demonstrate the transitional ideas in passing from the non-data-driven methods that are usually used in a parametric modeling context to a purely data-driven nonparametric modeling technique in the diffusion forecasting method. Readers who are familiar with these two topics can skip them and go directly to Chapter 6.

1.2.1   Stochastic Spectral Method

Given a parametric model as in (1.1), a popular subject known as uncertainty quantification (UQ) (Xiu 2010, Le Maître & Knio 2010) is concerned with estimating the following statistical quantities:

$$\mathbb{E}[A(x)](t) = \int_{\mathcal{M}} A(x(t;\theta))p(\theta)d\theta. \tag{1.9}$$

Here the parameters θ are assumed to be a realization of a random variable Θ with distribution $p(\theta)d\theta$ over the parameter domain $\mathcal{M}$. We also assume that $A \circ x \in L^1(\mathcal{M}, p)$. The standard forward UQ technique imposes a certain assumption on the distribution of Θ and subsequently represents functions of Θ with a linear superposition of the orthogonal basis functions $\varphi_j(\theta)$ of the corresponding Hilbert space $L^2(\mathcal{M}, p)$. For example, $\varphi_j(\theta)$ is the Hermite polynomial of degree j if p is a Gaussian or Legendre polynomial of degree j if p is uniformly distributed.

Given these basis functions, if x is smooth as a function of θ, one can approximate it as

$$x(t; \theta) \approx \sum_{k=1}^{N} x_k(t)\varphi_k(\theta), \tag{1.10}$$

where the time-dependent expansion coefficients, $x_k(t) = \langle x(t; \cdot), \varphi_k \rangle_p$, are to be determined. With this approximation, one can estimate the integral in (1.9) for $A(x) = x^2$ as

$$\mathbb{E}[x^2](t) \approx \sum_{k,\ell=1}^{N} x_k(t)x_\ell(t) \int_{\mathcal{M}} \varphi_k(\theta)\varphi_\ell(\theta)p(\theta)d\theta = \sum_{k=1}^{N} x_k^2(t),$$

thanks to the orthogonality property. In Chapter 4, we will discuss several approaches to compute the coefficients, $x_k(t)$, which may or may not involve deriving new equations based on the dynamics in (1.1).

As we mentioned before, this polynomial representation is non-data-driven. In fact, it chooses the basis functions by imposing certain assumptions on the distribution and the domain of the parameters. Since the representation idea is mathematically elegant, we would like to extend it nonparametrically. That is, our aim is to use the data to find the basis functions without making any assumption on the sampling distribution and the data manifold. Subsequently, we approximate the smooth densities of the Itô drifted diffusions with functions of a finite-dimensional subspace spanned by the resulting data-driven basis functions on $\mathcal{M}$. This is the central idea of the diffusion forecasting method. In contrast to the usual parametric approach, here we let the data determine the basis functions via the diffusion maps algorithm (Coifman & Lafon 2006, Berry & Harlim 2016d). In fact, if the sampling measure of the data is Gaussian on the real line, then the resulting data-driven basis functions obtained via the diffusion maps algorithm are precisely the Hermite polynomials that are usually used in the orthogonal polynomial expansion for representing a one-dimensional Gaussian random variable. Therefore, the data-driven basis that is used in the diffusion forecasting method is a natural generalization of the orthogonal polynomial basis on the data manifold.

1.2.2 Karhunen–Loève Expansion

The polynomial basis functions described in Chapter 4 can also be deduced from solving appropriate Sturm–Liouville eigenvalue problems with appropriate boundary conditions. This is an eigenvalue problem of a self-adjoint second-order differential operator on a compact domain (Andrews & Askey 1985). This classical theory gives us an intuition behind the construction of the data-driven basis functions. Namely, our aim is to approximate a self-adjoint second-order differential operator on the compact manifold where the data lie, solve the corresponding eigenvalue problem, and set the resulting eigenvectors to be the discrete estimators of the basis functions. The diffusion maps algorithm (Coifman & Lafon 2006) is a method that was designed to perform these tasks on nonlinear data manifolds.

To provide a self-contained exposition, we briefly review the Karhunen–Loève (KL) expansion in Chapter 5. Our emphasis is to understand the KL expansion as an application of Mercer's theorem that ties together the eigenfunctions of kernel-based integral operators and orthonormal basis functions of a Hilbert space. In an example, we will show that sometimes it is more convenient to transform the eigenvalue problem associated with an integral operator in the KL expansion into an eigenvalue problem of a second-order elliptic differential operator. We shall see that the diffusion maps algorithm is designed in exactly the opposite way. This method is a kernel-based algorithm which approximates a weighted Laplacian operator on the data manifold with an integral operator. So, it approximates an eigenvalue problem of a differential operator by solving the eigenvalue problem of an appropriate integral operator.

While the basic theory of the KL expansion assumes the availability of the autocovariance function, one can also employ the KL expansion with an empirically estimated autocovariance function from the data. Intuitively, this approach represents the data in terms of the directions in which the data have the largest variance. The resulting method is a linear manifold learning algorithm which bears many names depending on the field of applications, including proper orthogonal decomposition (POD), principal component analysis (PCA), the empirical orthogonal function (EOF), etc. By linear manifold learning, we refer to the fact that PCA represents data by a linear projection on a set of basis functions of a linear manifold, namely the ellipsoid. Specifically, the basis functions, which are usually called the principal components, are the axes of the ellipsoid. On the other hand, the diffusion maps algorithm (which will be discussed in Chapter 6 in detail) is a nonlinear manifold learning algorithm since it provides basis functions on an arbitrary data manifold embedded in a Euclidean space.

To clarify the distinction between linear and nonlinear manifold learning, we compare the principal components obtained from the POD and the basis functions obtained from the diffusion maps on a trivial yet illuminating example.

Example 1.3 Consider uniformly sampled data, $x_i = (\cos(\theta_i), \sin(\theta_i))^\top$, $i = 1, \ldots, N$, on a unit circle S^1 embedded in $\mathbb{R}^2$. Here, θ_i denotes the ith sample on the intrinsic coordinate of the circle, S^1. For clarity of exposition, in our numerical test on this artificial example below we generate "very nice" samples, with uniformly spaced $\theta_i = 2\pi i/N$. In practice, we usually don't have such a nice data set, and the accuracy of the estimates will depend on the samples. Denote $X = [x_1, x_2, \ldots, x_N] \in \mathbb{R}^{2 \times N}$.

Loosely speaking, the goal of manifold learning is to find (basis) functions $\varphi(x)$ that can describe the data $x \in \mathcal{M}$. In particular, POD describes the data in terms of principal components, which are defined as follows. The kth principal component (of POD) is defined as a functional $\psi_k(x) = w_k^\top x$, where w_k solves the symmetric positive-definite eigenvalue problem $(1/N)XX^\top w_k = \lambda_k w_k$. For this trivial circle example, $k = 1, 2$, and

$$\frac{1}{N}XX^\top \longrightarrow A = \begin{pmatrix} 1/2 & 0 \\ 0 & 1/2 \end{pmatrix},$$

as $N \to \infty$. In this case, the limit can be estimated analytically as follows:

$$A_{ij} = \frac{1}{2\pi} \int_0^{2\pi} x^i(\theta)x^j(\theta)d\theta = \frac{1}{2}\delta_{ij}.$$

Here, the notation $x^j(\theta)$ denotes the jth component of $x \in \mathbb{R}^2$; that is,

$$x^j(\theta) = \begin{cases} \cos(\theta) & \text{if } j = 1, \\ \sin(\theta) & \text{if } j = 2. \end{cases}$$

Since the standard bases $e_1, e_2 \in \mathbb{R}^2$ are eigenvectors of A, the principal components are nothing but $\psi_1(x) = e_1^\top x = x^1$ and $\psi_2(x) = e_2^\top x = x^2$. Essentially, each component of the given data (or each row of matrix X) is the principal component. To clarify this assertion, we plot the principal components (in color) as functions of the data in Figure 1.3. Notice that the first principal component identifies the data in the horizontal direction (the function values increase from -1 to 1). On the other hand, the second principal component identifies the data in the vertical direction. These two axes correspond to the principal axes of the unit circle. In general, the principal components of POD correspond to the principal axes of an ellipsoid that is fitted to the data even if the data do not lie on an ellipsoid (see the example in Chapter 5).

On the other hand, the diffusion maps algorithm solves the eigenvalue problem $\Delta_\theta \varphi_k(\theta) = \lambda_k \varphi_k(\theta)$, where the Laplace–Beltrami operator is numerically estimated using a matrix as a discretization of a kernel-based integral operator. For this example, since the embedding function (or the Riemannian metric) is known, it is clear that the Laplace–Beltrami operator is simply a one-dimensional derivative with respect to the intrinsic coordinate. The explicit solutions of this eigenvalue problem are the Fourier series $\varphi_k(\theta) = e^{ik\theta}$, which form a basis for $L^2(S^1)$. In Figure 1.4, we compare the discrete estimates of the first four Fourier modes obtained from the diffusion maps algorithm applied on the data $\{x_i\}_{i=1,\ldots,N}$, where $N = 1000$, with the corresponding analytical solutions.

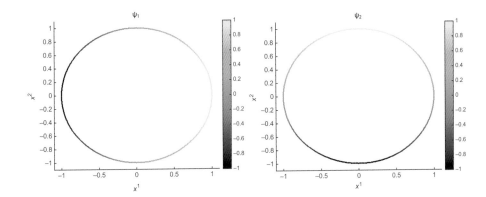

Figure 1.3 The principal components (color) as functions of the data.

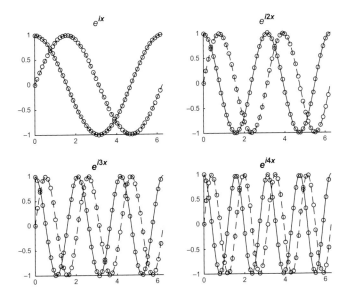

Figure 1.4 Discrete estimates of the eigenfunctions e^{ikx}, for $k = 1, \ldots, 4$, evaluated on the training data manifold (circles) compared with the analytical solutions. In each panel, we show the cosine (solid) and sine (dashes) components.

In summary, the diffusion maps algorithm produces orthonormal basis functions of a Hilbert space $L^2(S^1)$, where each component $\varphi_k \colon \mathcal{M} \to \mathbb{R}$ is a nonlinear map. In contrast, the principal components of POD are the first Fourier mode in this example, where each principal component is a linear function of the data manifold.

In the next example, we show the application of the diffusion maps algorithm on a data set with a complicated manifold corresponding to solutions of a chaotic dynamical system. The key point is that we don't have any knowledge of the embedding (or the Riemannian metric) for the following example. As a consequence, we don't have an analytical expression for differential operators on this data manifold whose components are samples of the invariant measure of the dynamical systems. In this situation, the diffusion maps algorithm is a powerful tool that approximates the weighted Laplacian operator on this complicated data manifold, where the weight is defined with respect to the sampling measure of the data.

Example 1.4 Consider the famous three-dimensional chaotic Lorenz model (Lorenz 1963), which is a truncated approximation to the Navier–Stokes equations. This toy model has been found to be useful to describe laser physics (Haken 1975) and it is well known as the first example of a simple deterministic dynamical system with solutions that are sensitive to initial conditions; this behavior has been called deterministic chaos or simply chaos. The governing equation of the Lorenz-63 model is given as

$$\begin{aligned} \frac{dx}{dt} &= \sigma(y-x), \\ \frac{dy}{dt} &= \rho x - y - xz, \\ \frac{dz}{dt} &= xy - bz, \end{aligned} \tag{1.11}$$

with the parameter set (σ, b, ρ), where, in its original derivation (Lorenz 1963, Solari *et al.* 1996), σ is called the Prandtl number and ρ is the Rayleigh number.

In Figure 1.5, we show the nonparametric estimates of the basis functions obtained via the diffusion maps algorithm, implemented with variable-bandwidth kernels (which will be discussed in Chapter 6). These eigenfunctions are generated using solutions (x_i, y_i, z_i) of (1.11) at 5000 discrete time instances, with time step $t_{i+1} - t_i = \Delta t = 0.5$ (see Berry *et al.* (2015) for the computational detail). In each of these panels, we depict the discrete estimate of the eigenfunction evaluated on each training data point, $\varphi_j(x_i, y_i, z_i)$.

From these two examples, we can view the diffusion maps algorithm as a numerical method to estimate generalized Fourier bases (or orthogonal polynomials) of Hilbert space on the data manifold. Next, we will give a brief description of the diffusion forecasting method using these data-driven basis functions.

1.2.3   Diffusion Forecasting

Suppose that $x(t) \in \mathcal{M} \subset \mathbb{R}^n$ denotes a time-dependent Itô diffusion, which satisfies a system of differential equations

$$dx = a(x)dt + b(x)dW_t, \tag{1.12}$$

where $a(x)$ and $b(x)$ denote the drift and diffusion terms, respectively. Here, dW_t denotes white noises.

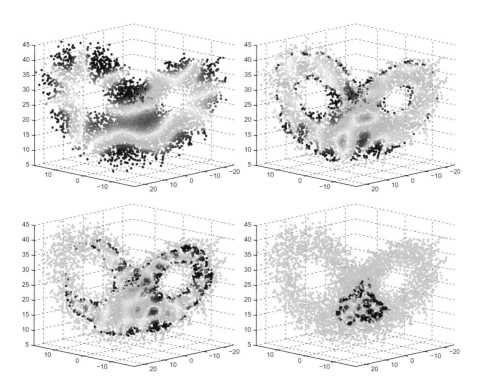

Figure 1.5 Discrete estimates of the eigenfunctions $\varphi_{40}, \varphi_{500}, \varphi_{1500}$, and φ_{4000} evaluated on the training data manifold.

Assume that the model in (1.12) is unknown, which means that the corresponding Fokker–Planck (or Liouville if (1.12) is deterministic) equation,

$$\frac{\partial p}{\partial t} = \mathcal{L}^* p, \tag{1.13}$$

is also unknown. Instead we are given only a set of time series $X = \{x_i, i = 1, \ldots, N\}$ from measurements; here $x_i = x(t_i)$ are the solutions of (1.12) given an initial condition x_0. We assume that N is finite but large enough that all configurations of the dynamics (or points in $\mathcal{M}$) are sufficiently close to some components in X. Given such practical constraints, the diffusion forecasting method uses these data to train a nonparametric probabilistic model whose solutions approximate the probability density function of x at any time t. The key idea of this method is to represent an approximation of the semigroup solutions of the generator of (1.12) with data-adapted basis functions $\varphi_j(x_i)$, obtained via the diffusion maps algorithm (Coifman & Lafon 2006, Berry & Harlim 2016d). In particular, we will represent the solutions of (1.13) as

$$p(x, t) = e^{t\mathcal{L}^*} p(x, 0) = \sum_j \langle e^{t\mathcal{L}^*} p(x, 0), \varphi_j \rangle_{p_{\text{eq}}} \varphi_j(x) p_{\text{eq}}(x), \tag{1.14}$$

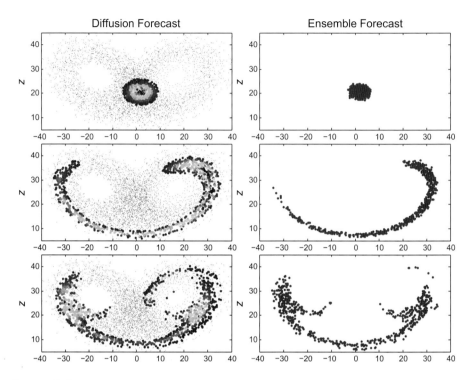

Figure 1.6 Probability densities (as functions of $x + y$ and z) from the equation-free diffusion forecasting model (left column) and an ensemble forecasting model (right column) at times $t = 0$ (first row), $t = 0.5$ (second row), and $t = 2$ (third row). In the column on the left, the color spectrum ranging from red to blue is to denote high to low values of density.

where $p_{\mathrm{eq}}(x)$ denotes the equilibrium measure of the dynamical system in (1.12), such that $\mathcal{L}^* p_{\mathrm{eq}} = 0$. Subsequently, we employ a nonparametric approximation to the time-evolving coefficients $\langle e^{t\mathcal{L}^*} p(x, 0), \varphi_j \rangle_{p_{\mathrm{eq}}}$ such that we don't need to know $\mathcal{L}^*$. Since the diffusion map algorithm is a kernel-based method, one can interpret the diffusion forecast as an extension of the kernel density estimation method to estimate operators of Markovian dynamical systems. This is the topic of Chapter 6. In the next example, we give a brief illustration of the expected product of the diffusion forecast applied on time series of a chaotic dynamical system, the famous Lorenz-63 model.

Example 1.5   In Figure 1.6, we show snapshots of the probability density at various times, obtained from the diffusion forecasting method, on the three-dimensional Lorenz-63 model in (1.11). For qualitative comparison, we also show the Monte Carlo approximation of the evolution of the density (or ensemble forecasting), assuming that the full Lorenz-63 model is known. Here, the Monte Carlo initial conditions are prescribed by sampling the Gaussian density used in the diffusion forecasting method (as shown in the first row in Figure 1.6).

In each panel of this figure, we show the density as a function of $x + y$ and z (corresponding to the three components of the Lorenz model) at different instances. In the left column, we also show the data set that is used for training the diffusion model (smaller dots). Notice that, even at a long time $t = 2$ (which is longer than the doubling time of this model, 0.78), the densities obtained from the two forecasting methods are still in good agreement. From these time-evolving density functions, one can compute statistical quantities for state estimation as well as uncertainty quantification nonparametrically.

While the example above assumes that the initial density is given, it is important to stress that in practice the initial density is not known. Usually, one is interested in predicting the future states with initial configurations, x_j, that are not in the training data set X. Therefore one needs to specify the corresponding initial densities, $p(x|x_j)$, to be used for predictions. In Chapter 6, we will also discuss the Nyström extension and a Bayesian filtering method to specify these initial distributions for noiseless and noisy data, respectively.

2 Markov-Chain Monte Carlo

In this chapter, we discuss how to leverage data for modeling dynamical systems. In particular, we will focus our discussion on the density estimation of the hidden parameters of dynamical systems using a class of Markov-chain Monte Carlo (MCMC) method, known as the Metropolis–Hastings method. We begin by giving a brief review of the relevant properties of Markov processes. Subsequently, we discuss the basic idea behind the Metropolis–Hastings scheme and its application as a parameter estimation method. We close the chapter by discussing the polynomial chaos-based surrogate models to reduce the computational cost in the Metropolis scheme. For readers who are not familiar with the basic concepts of probability theory and stochastic processes, we provide an elementary review of these topics in Appendices A and B.

2.1 A Brief Review of Markov Processes

The goal of this section is to give a quick introduction to MCMC. In particular we want to clarify the difference between MCMC and the standard Monte Carlo method. To explain this, we give a very brief review of the discrete-time continuous-state Markov chain. For more elaborate discussions on Markov chains, we refer readers to excellent introductory texts such as Lawler (2006) and Karlin (2014).

Let $X_i \colon \Omega \to E$, $i \geq 0$, be a discrete time chain. Here, Ω denotes the sample space of the probability space and E denotes the state space of the chain. We say that this chain is Markovian when its probability law satisfies

$$\mathbb{P}(X_{i+1} \in A | X_i = x_i, X_{i-1} = x_{i-1}, \ldots, X_0 = x_0) = \mathbb{P}(X_{i+1} \in A | X_i = x_i),$$

for $A \in \mathcal{G}$, where $\mathcal{G}$ denotes the σ-algebra of E. This Markovian condition states that the probability of the future state depends only on the current state. When the process is time-homogeneous, we can define a transition function

$$P(x, A) := \mathbb{P}(X_{i+1} \in A | X_i = x), \quad i \geq 0,$$

which is also known as the transition kernel. This function is defined such that, for all $x \in E$, $P(x, \cdot)$ is a probability distribution on E and, for all $A \subset \mathcal{G}$, we can evaluate $x \mapsto P(x, A)$. Let the nth iterate of the chain, starting from x_0, be defined as

$$P^n(x_0, A) = \mathbb{P}(X_n \in A | X_0 = x_0).$$

We define π to be the stationary (or invariant) distribution of the chain with time-homogeneous transition probability kernel P if

$$\pi(A) = \int_E P(x, A)\pi(x)dx,$$

for all $A \in \mathcal{G}$. Suppose that P admits a density $p(x, y)$ such that

$$P(x, A) = \int_A p(x, y)dy.$$

Then we can write

$$\int_A \pi(y)dy = \int_E \int_A p(x, y)\pi(x)dy\, dx = \int_A \int_E p(x, y)\pi(x)dx\, dy,$$

which gives an alternative expression for the stationary condition:

$$\pi(y) = \int_E p(x, y)\pi(x)dx, \tag{2.1}$$

for almost every y. Unfortunately, sometimes it is difficult to use the condition in (2.1) to check that π is stationary. Instead, we can use the following sufficient condition.

Lemma 2.1 *A sufficient condition for π to be the stationary distribution is the detailed balance condition, $\pi(x)p(x, y) = \pi(y)p(y, x)$.*

Proof

$$\int_E \pi(x)p(x, y)dx = \int_E \pi(y)p(y, x)dx = \pi(y)\int_E p(y, x)dx = \pi(y).$$

$\square$

We call the stationary distribution π the limiting distribution of the chain if, for almost every $x \in E$,

$$\lim_{n \to \infty} P^n(x, A) = \pi(A), \quad \text{for all} A \in \mathcal{G}. \tag{2.2}$$

Now, we briefly review the technical conditions for the stationary distribution π to be the limiting distribution of the chain in the sense of (2.2).

Definition 2.2 The transition kernel P is π-irreducible if $\pi(E) > 0$ and for each $x \in E$ and for all $A \in \mathcal{G}$, with $\pi(A) > 0$, there exists an $n \geq 1$ such that $P^n(x, A) > 0$.

Definition 2.3 A π-irreducible transition kernel P is periodic if there exists $d \geq 2$ and disjoint nonempty subsets $A_1, \ldots, A_d \in \mathcal{G}$ with $\pi(A_i) > 0$, such that $P(x, A_{i+1}) = 1$ for all $x \in A_i$, where $i \in \{1, \ldots, d-1\}$ and $P(x, A_1) = 1$, for all $x \in A_d$. If $d = 1$, the kernel is aperiodic.

Definition 2.4   A π-irreducible chain X_i with a stationary distribution π is recurrent if, for all $A \in \mathcal{G}$, with $\pi(A) > 0$, $\mathbb{P}(X_n \in A \text{ i.o.}|X_0 = x) > 0$ for all x, and $\mathbb{P}(X_n \in A \text{ i.o.}|X_0 = x) = 1$ for almost every x. The chain is Harris recurrent if $\mathbb{P}(X_n \in A \text{ i.o.}|X_0 = x) = 1$, for all x. Here, the notation $\{A_n \text{ i.o.}\}$ means A_n occurs infinitely often, that is, $\sum_n 1_{A_n} = \infty$. A recurrent kernel P with a finite invariant measure π is called positive recurrent, otherwise it is null recurrent.

Given these definitions, we can now formally state the conditions for the stationary distribution π to be the limiting distribution (Nummelin 1984).

Theorem 2.5   *Let P be a π-irreducible transition kernel with a stationary distribution π, then P is positive recurrent and π is the unique stationary distribution. If P is also aperiodic, then, for almost every x,*

$$\|P^n(x, \cdot) - \pi(\cdot)\|_{TV} \to 0,$$

where $\|\mu - \mu'\|_{TV} = \frac{1}{2} \int_E |\rho(x) - \rho'(x)| dx$ denotes the total variation norm defined on probability measures $\mu, \mu' \in (E, \mathcal{G})$ with densities ρ, ρ', respectively. If the chain is Harris recurrent, then the convergence holds for every x.

A Markov chain that has a unique stationary distribution is called an ergodic Markov chain. This key result suggests that one way to sample a distribution is to generate an ergodic Markov chain. In particular, if one devises a Markov chain with a transition kernel P that has a stationary distribution π and satisfies all of the hypotheses above, namely by being (Harris) recurrent and aperiodic, then, starting at (any) almost any x, the distribution of the chain converges to π for sufficiently many iterations. Although these samples (or realizations of the corresponding chain) are not independent, one can nonetheless still use them to approximate integrals, relying on the following ergodic theorem.

Theorem 2.6   *Let X_i be an ergodic Markov chain with stationary distribution $\pi(x)$. We denote X as the random variable with distribution $\pi(x)$. For any integrable function $f(X)$, as $n \to \infty$,*

$$\frac{1}{n} \sum_{i=1}^{n} f(X_i) \overset{\text{a.s.}}{\to} \int_E f(x)\pi(x)dx := \mathbb{E}_\pi[f(X)].$$

Basically, this theorem suggests that one can use realizations of an appropriate Markov chain to estimate an integral in contrast to the usual Monte Carlo integral that uses i.i.d. samples of π. So, the main practical question is how to generate such a Markov chain (which satisfies all of the conditions in Theorem 2.5 above). In the next section, we will discuss a popular technique known as the Metropolis–Hastings method.

2.2   The Metropolis–Hastings Method

The key idea of the Metropolis–Hastings (MH) method is to generate an ergodic Markov chain with stationary measure as the target distribution to be sampled. Since the sequence is Markovian, it is not i.i.d. but, by the ergodicity theorem discussed above, we can compute a Monte Carlo integration by averaging over these samples, ignoring their dependence. Of course one can also reduce the dependence of these samples by subsampling.

Consider a Markov transition kernel density $q \colon E \times E \to \mathbb{R}^+$ such that $\int_E q(x,y)dy = 1$, for all $x \in E$. The MH method generates samples $\{x_i\}$ of a target density $\pi(x)$, as follows.

1. Given x_{i-1}, draw a proposal $u \sim q(x_{i-1}, \cdot)$.
2. Accept the proposal, $x_i = u$ with probability $\min(\alpha(x_{i-1}, u), 1)$. Otherwise set $x_i = x_{i-1}$. Here,

$$\alpha(x_{i-1}, u) = \frac{\pi(u)q(u, x_{i-1})}{\pi(x_{i-1})q(x_{i-1}, u)}. \tag{2.3}$$

Practically, we don't need to know the normalization constant for π since only the ratio of π is needed to determine the acceptance rate in (2.3). Numerically, this step can be realized by drawing a sample of the standard uniform distribution, $z \sim U[0,1]$, and then setting

$$x_i = \begin{cases} u, & \text{if } z < \alpha(x_{i-1}, u), \\ x_{i-1}, & \text{otherwise.} \end{cases}$$

First, let's investigate why we should believe that the x_i constructed via these two steps are realizations of the chain with stationary density $\pi(x)$. First of all, let x_i be a Markov chain with transition density $p(x_{i-1}, x_i)$. We want to show that π is the stationary density. That is, we want to show that the chain generated by the MH method above satisfies the detailed balance condition in Lemma 2.1. Notice that, using the MH method, we can write the transition kernel $p(x_{i-1}, u)$, which quantifies the probability of accepting u at the ith step given the realization x_{i-1} at the $(i-1)$th step, as a product of the probability of proposing u and the probability of accepting u,

$$p(x_{i-1}, u) = q(x_{i-1}, u) \min(\alpha(x_{i-1}, u), 1).$$

Thus,

$$\begin{aligned} \pi(x_{i-1})p(x_{i-1}, u) &= \pi(x_{i-1})q(x_{i-1}, u) \min\left(\frac{\pi(u)q(u, x_{i-1})}{\pi(x_{i-1})q(x_{i-1}, u)}, 1\right) \\ &= \pi(u)q(u, x_{i-1}) \min\left(1, \frac{\pi(x_{i-1})q(x_{i-1}, u)}{\pi(u)q(u, x_{i-1})}\right) \\ &= \pi(u)q(u, x_{i-1}) \min(\alpha(u, x_{i-1}), 1) \\ &= \pi(u)p(u, x_{i-1}). \end{aligned}$$

which means that x_i generated by the MH method satisfies the detailed balance condition. By Lemma 2.1, $\pi(x)$ is the stationary density. To verify theoretically whether we obtain samples of π if we implement the MH method with sufficiently large i is simply equivalent to asking whether the chain is recurrent and aperiodic (which are the conditions in Theorem 2.5). A detailed study of the convergence rates of some Metropolis–Hastings kernel densities was reported in Tierney (1994).

We should note that, if the proposal transition density q is chosen to be symmetric, $q(x, y) = q(y, x)$, then the resulting method is known as the Metropolis scheme, with acceptance rate

$$\alpha(x_{i-1}, u) = \frac{\pi(u)}{\pi(x_{i-1})}.$$

Intuitively, this rate compares the probability of the proposal u with that of the previous chain value, x_{i-1}. A popular choice of symmetric proposal density is Gaussian, which yields the random-walk Metropolis proposal

$$q(x_{i-1}, u) = q(u|x_{i-1}) = \mathcal{N}(x_{i-1}, C),$$

for some proposal covariance matrix C. Numerically, we realize the sample as

$$u = x_{i-1} + C^{1/2}\xi_i, \quad \xi_i \sim \mathcal{N}(0, \mathcal{I}).$$

Next, we will discuss a parameter estimation method using the MH scheme.

2.3   Parameter Estimation Problems

Consider a time-dependent state variable $x(t; \theta)$, which implicitly depends on the parameters θ through the following initial value problem:

$$\dot{x} = f(x, \theta), \quad x(0) = x_0, \tag{2.4}$$

where, for any fixed θ, f is a vector field. Here, we are interested in the problem of estimating the conditional distribution of θ, given discrete-time noisy observations

$$y_i = x_i^\dagger + \eta_i, \quad i = 1, \ldots, n, \tag{2.5}$$

where $x_i^\dagger := x(t_i; \theta^\dagger)$ are solutions of (2.4) for a specific hidden parameter $\theta^\dagger$ and η_i denote unbiased and i.i.d. noises representing the measurement error.

Let $x_i = x(t_i; \theta) = \varphi_i(\theta)$ be the solutions of the initial value problem in (2.4) at time t_i with initial condition x_0, where we have suppressed the dependence on x_0 in our notation. With this notation, it is clear that $\varphi_i(\theta^\dagger) = x_i^\dagger$. We should note that evaluating $\varphi_i(\theta)$ requires solving the initial value problem in (2.4), which can be very expensive for some high-dimensional problems, especially when the explicit solutions are not available. With this notation, the observation in (2.5) is equivalent to

$$y_i = \varphi_i(\theta^\dagger) + \eta_i, \quad i = 1, \ldots, n,$$

and the classical inverse problem is to estimate the hidden parameter $\theta^\dagger$. Below, we will use the MCMC method to determine the conditional distribution of θ given $y = \{y_1, \ldots, y_n\}$ and use the corresponding statistic as an estimator of $\theta^\dagger$.

Suppose that the distribution of the i.i.d random noises η_i can be characterized by the density function $p(\eta_i)$. Then we can define a likelihood function of θ as a conditional density of $y = \{y_1, \ldots, y_n\}$ given θ,

$$p(y|\theta) := \prod_{i=1}^{n} p(\eta_i) = \prod_{i=1}^{n} p(y_i - \varphi_i(\theta)).$$

For example, if we assume that $\varphi_i \in \mathbb{R}$ and $\eta_i \sim \mathcal{N}(0, \sigma^2)$, then the likelihood function is given by

$$p(y|\theta) \propto \exp\left(-\frac{\sum_{i=1}^{n}(y_i - \varphi_i(\theta))^2}{2\sigma^2}\right). \tag{2.6}$$

We should mention that this is not the only way to construct likelihood functions. For example, one can use the Girsanov formula to determine the likelihood functions of the parameters of stochastic differential equations (see Pavliotis (2014)).

Given a prior density, $p_0(\theta)$, Bayes' theorem allows one to estimate a posterior distribution as

$$p(\theta|y) \propto p(y|\theta)p_0(\theta).$$

The essence of Bayesian inference is to estimate this conditional distribution. If one is interested in point estimation of the parameter θ, one can use the mean as an estimator. If one is interested in the uncertainty of the mean as a point estimator, one can quantify the uncertainty with the variance statistic. Another popular estimator is the mode, which is defined as

$$\theta_{\mathrm{MAP}} = \arg\max_{\theta} p(\theta|y),$$

where θ_{MAP} is known as the maximum a-posteriori (MAP) estimate. A related, routinely used estimate is the so-called *maximum likelihood estimate* (MLE), which is the MAP estimate with an uninformative prior density, $p_0(\theta)$, that is,

$$\theta_{\mathrm{MLE}} = \arg\max_{\theta} p(y|\theta).$$

Statisticians refer to the MLE as a frequentist (as opposed to Bayesian) approach, where the estimate, θ_{MLE}, is viewed as the parameter value that makes the observed output most likely. In the Bayesian point of view, θ_{MAP} corresponds to the most likely parameter value based on the given data y.

In the remainder of this chapter, we will discuss how to use MCMC to sample the posterior density $p(\theta|y)$. While this approach is a gold standard, numerically it can be very expensive for high-dimensional problems. In particular, the complexity depends on the cost in evaluating $\varphi_i(\theta)$. In Chapter 3, we will discuss an alternative parameter estimation method that can be scaled to higher-dimensional problems, the ensemble Kalman filter.

2.4   Parameter Estimation with the Metropolis Scheme

The key idea of parameter estimation with the Metropolis scheme is to construct a Markov chain such that its limiting distribution is the conditional density $p(\theta|y)$, replacing π in Section 2.2. Given $\theta_0 \sim p(\theta_0|y) > 0$, the Metropolis algorithm consists of the following steps.

1. Sample $\theta^* \sim q(\theta_{i-1}, \theta^*)$. For example, use the random-walk Metropolis algorithm to generate proposals

$$\theta^* = \theta_{i-1} + C^{1/2}\xi, \quad \xi \sim \mathcal{N}(0, \mathcal{I}), \tag{2.7}$$

   where C, the proposal covariance, is a tunable nuisance parameter. In this case, the proposal kernel density is symmetric, $q(\theta_{i-1}, \theta^*) = q(\theta^*, \theta_{i-1})$.
2. Accept the proposal, $\theta_i = \theta^*$ with probability $\min(\alpha(\theta_{i-1}, \theta^*), 1)$, otherwise set $\theta_i = \theta_{i-1}$. Here,

$$\alpha(\theta_{i-1}, \theta^*) = \frac{p(\theta^*|y)}{p(\theta_{i-1}|y)}.$$

3. Set $i \leftarrow i + 1$ and go back to step 1.

Now, let's apply this scheme to a problem with explicit posterior solutions.

Example 2.7   Consider estimating the diffusion coefficient, $b^2 > 0$, of the linear stochastic differential equation

$$dx = -\frac{1}{2}x\,dt + b\,dW_t$$

from n i.i.d. samples x_i of the equilibrium distribution. For this problem, notice that the equilibrium density is Gaussian on variable x,

$$p(x|b^2) \propto (b^2)^{-1/2}e^{-\frac{x^2}{2b^2}}, \tag{2.8}$$

but it is an inverse-gamma distribution on the variable b^2. Recall that the density function of the inverse-gamma distribution $Y \sim \text{IG}(\alpha, \beta)$ is

$$p(y) \propto y^{-(\alpha+1)}e^{-\beta/y}.$$

Given n i.i.d. observations x_i, the likelihood function for b^2 is given by

$$p(x|b^2) = \prod_{i=1}^{n} p(x_i|b^2),$$

which is an inverse-gamma distribution on $b^2 \sim \mathrm{IG}(n/2 - 1, \frac{1}{2}\sum_{i=1}^{n} x_i^2)$. Consider a prior density $p_0(b^2)$ that is also an inverse-gamma distribution $\mathrm{IG}(\alpha, \beta)$. Applying the Bayes' formula, we obtain an inverse-gamma posterior distribution

$$p(b^2|x) \propto p_0(b^2)p(x|b^2) \sim \mathrm{IG}\left(\alpha + \frac{n}{2}, \beta + \frac{1}{2}\sum_{i=1}^{n} x_i^2\right). \tag{2.9}$$

Now, let's verify the efficacy of the random-walk Metropolis scheme in sampling this posterior density. In particular, we will infer the conditional distribution from $n = 10$ observations that are generated from very "nice" samples of (2.8) with true parameter $(b^\dagger)^2 = 5$. These very "nice" samples are constructed (to avoid sampling errors) using the inversion method on $n = 10$ equally spaced points on the interval $[0, 1]$, excluding the end points. In our numerical simulation, we set the prior parameters $\alpha = 3, \beta = 10$, initial chain $b_0^2 = 7$, and the proposal covariance $C = 0.05$. In Figure 2.1, we compare the MCMC posterior density (smoothed using a kernel density estimation method) from 300,000 MCMC samples (ignoring the first 50 samples) with the analytic posterior density. Notice that the posterior density estimate is quite accurate. Moreover, the mean statistics of the analytical and MCMC methods also coincide. For this example, the MAP estimate is simply the maximum (mode) of the posterior density in (2.9), which has an analytical expression, $(\beta + \frac{1}{2}\sum_{i=1}^{n} x_i^2)/(\alpha + n/2 + 1)$.

As a final remark on this example, we should point out that, as $n \to \infty$, both the mean and MAP estimates converge to the equilibrium variance of x, that is, $b^2 = \mathbb{E}(x^2)$, where the expectation is defined with respect to the density in (2.8). In this limiting case, the influence of the prior density diminishes and the parameter b^2 can be estimated without using MCMC. That is, if one has access to large enough ($n \gg 1$) i.i.d. samples of x, the parameter b^2 can be estimated using the empirical variance (or Monte Carlo average), $b^2 \approx (1/n)\sum_{i=1}^{n} x_i^2$.

In the synthetic example above, we choose C empirically by trial and error since we know the true posterior solution. In real applications, unfortunately, the posterior density is unknown. Furthermore, when the variance C is too large, many proposals will be rejected since they have smaller probabilities relative to that of the previous chain, $p(\theta^*|y) < p(\theta_{i-1}|y)$, and the chain does not move for a long period. On the other hand, when C is too small, the acceptance ratio will be high, $\alpha \approx 1$, and the algorithm will be slow in exploring the parameter space. So devising a proposal that avoids these two extreme regimes will be important for generation of well-mixed samples.

There are various methods to specify C. For example, one can apply the ordinary least-squares estimator, which is discussed below. One can also consider a non-static C and estimate it empirically using a weighted temporal covariance estimate from the chain. This strategy is known as the *adaptive Metropolis* scheme (e.g. see Haario *et al.* (2006)).

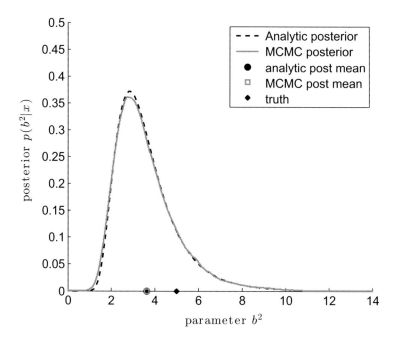

Figure 2.1 Posterior density estimate of the random walk MCMC for the problem in Example 2.7 with an analytic posterior density given by (2.9).

2.4.1   Specifying Parameters in the Proposal

A simple way to estimate C in (2.7) is to use the ordinary least-squares (OLS) estimate of the corresponding nonlinear problem. That is, we let θ_{OLS} be the OLS estimate,

$$\theta_{\mathrm{OLS}} = \arg\min_\theta \sum_{j=1}^n (y_j - \varphi_j(\theta))^2.$$

Numerically, one can use nonlinear solvers such as Levenberg–Marquardt to solve this nonlinear problem. In the case where $y_j \in \mathbb{R}$, the error variance estimate is given by

$$\tilde{\sigma}^2 = \frac{1}{n-p} R^\top R, \tag{2.10}$$

where $R_j = y_j - \varphi_j(\theta_{\mathrm{OLS}})$. By linearizing $\varphi_j(\theta)$ about the true $\theta^\dagger \in \mathbb{R}^d$, we obtain a covariance estimator

$$C \approx \sigma^2 (\chi^\top(\theta^\dagger)\chi(\theta^\dagger))^{-1} \approx \tilde{\sigma}^2 (\chi(\theta_{\mathrm{OLS}})^\top \chi(\theta_{\mathrm{OLS}}))^{-1}, \tag{2.11}$$

where $\chi(\theta) \in \mathbb{R}^{n \times d}$ with components $\chi_{ij} = \partial\varphi^i(\theta)/\partial\theta_j$. Here, $\varphi^i \colon \mathbb{R}^d \to \mathbb{R}$ denotes the ith component of the solutions of (2.4), where we have suppressed the time indices (subscript).

2.4.2   Specifying the Measurement Noise Variance

For the Gaussian likelihood function in (2.6), one can use the mean square of the residuals in (2.10) as an estimator for the unknown measurement error variance, σ^2.

Alternatively, notice that the likelihood function in (2.6),

$$p(y, \theta|\sigma^2) = (2\pi\sigma^2)^{-n/2} \exp\left(-\frac{\sum_{i=1}^{n}(y_i - \varphi_i(\theta))^2}{2\sigma^2}\right), \tag{2.12}$$

is an inverse-gamma distribution on $\sigma^2 \sim \mathrm{IG}(n/2 - 1, \frac{1}{2}\sum_{i=1}^{n}(y_i - \varphi_i(\theta))^2)$.

Now, if we define a prior to be also the inverse-gamma distribution,

$$p(\sigma^2) \propto (\sigma^2)^{-(a+1)} e^{-b/\sigma^2},$$

for some nuisance parameters a and b, we can apply Bayes' formula to obtain

$$p(\sigma^2|\theta, y) \propto p(\sigma^2)p(y, \theta|\sigma^2) \sim \mathrm{IG}\left(a + \frac{n}{2}, b + \frac{1}{2}\sum_{i=1}^{n}(y_i - \varphi_i(\theta))^2\right).$$

An empirical method (Smith 2013) for specifying the parameters a, b is to choose $b = a\sigma_s^2$, where σ_s^2 can be approximated from the ordinary least-squares estimate in (2.10), $\sigma_s^2 \approx \tilde{\sigma}^2$, or from the previous time-step estimate, $\sigma_s^2 \approx \sigma_{i-1}^2$. One can also set $a, b = 0$ to obtain an uninformative prior, the so-called Jeffrey prior, $p(\sigma^2) \propto \sigma^{-2}$.

2.4.3   Pseudo-algorithm

With the methods from Sections 2.4.1 and 2.4.2, the pseudo-algorithm for the Metropolis scheme with an adaptive estimation of σ^2 is given as follows.

1. Set parameters a, σ_s and initial conditions θ_0, σ_0^2.
2. Define the proposal kernel density. For instance, use the random walk in (2.7) with noise variance C, specified as in (2.11).
3. Iterate the following three steps for $i \geq 1$.
   - Draw a proposal with the random-walk Metropolis algorithm,

   $$\theta^* = \theta_{i-1} + C^{1/2}\xi, \quad \xi \sim \mathcal{N}(0, \mathcal{I}).$$

   - Accept the proposal $\theta_i = \theta^*$ with probability $\min(\alpha(\theta_{i-1}, \theta^*), 1)$, otherwise set $\theta_i = \theta_{i-1}$. Here, the construction of α depends on σ_{i-1}^2.
   - Draw $\sigma_i^2 \sim \mathrm{IG}(a + n/2, a\sigma_s^2 + \frac{1}{2}\sum_{i=1}^{n}(y_i - \varphi_i(\theta_i))^2)$.

In this particular scheme, there are three nuisance parameters to be tuned, a, σ_s for estimating σ and the proposal noise variance C.

Example 2.8 Consider a system of a J-dimensional Lorenz-96 model (Lorenz 1996),

$$\frac{du_j}{dt} = u_{j-1}(u_{j+1} - u_{j-2}) - u_j + F, \qquad j = 1, \ldots, J,$$

$$u_j(0) = \sin\left(\frac{2\pi j}{J}\right),$$

with a periodic boundary, that is, $u_{j+J} = u_j$. We set $J = 5$. Our goal here is to estimate the hidden parameter $F = 8$, given noisy observations,

$$v_j(t_m) = u_j(t_m) + \epsilon_{m,j}, \quad \epsilon_{m,j} \sim \mathcal{N}(0, \sigma^2), \quad m = 1, \ldots, 10,$$

where the observation noise variance, $\sigma^2 = 0.01$, is also to be estimated. Here, $u_j(t_m)$ denotes the approximate solution (with the Runge–Kutta method) at discrete times $t_m = m\,\Delta t$, where $\Delta t = 0.05$ is the integration time step.

Let $\vec{\varphi}_m(F) = \vec{u}(t_m) \in \mathbb{R}^J$ be the approximate solutions at times t_m, evaluated at the parameter F. Let's denote the proposal as $F^* = F_{i-1} + C^{1/2}\xi$, where we empirically choose $C^{1/2} = 0.3$ in our numerical simulation below. The likelihood function is defined as

$$p(V|F, \sigma^2) = \exp\left(-\frac{1}{2\sigma^2}\sum_{m=0}^{10}\|\vec{v}_m - \vec{\varphi}_m(F)\|^2\right),$$

where $V = \{\vec{v}_1, \ldots, \vec{v}_{10}\}$ and the jth component of $\vec{v}_m \in \mathbb{R}^J$ is $v_j(t_m)$. With this likelihood function, the acceptance rate is given by

$$\alpha(F_{i-1}, F^*) = \exp\left(-\frac{1}{2\sigma^2}\left[\sum_{m=0}^{10}\|\vec{v}_m - \vec{\varphi}_m(F^*)\|^2 - \sum_{m=0}^{10}\|\vec{v}_m - \vec{\varphi}_m(F_{i-1})\|^2\right]\right),$$

where an uninformative prior, p_0, is used.

In our numerical experiment, we set $a = 200$, $\sigma_s^2 = 0.01$, initial conditions $F_0 = 9$ and $\sigma_0^2 = 0.02$, and generate the chain for 5000 iterations. In Figure 2.2, we show the realization of F and σ^2 as functions of the chain iteration. Notice that, after a few iterations, the chain for F fluctuates around the true value $F = 8$, whereas, for σ^2, the chain fluctuates slightly above the true value $\sigma^2 = 0.01$. In Figure 2.3, we show the density of the chain, generated with kernel density estimate on the chain ignoring the first 1000 iterations, together with the true value and the mean estimate.

In this chapter, we only discuss the basic Metropolis–Hastings scheme. Another MCMC scheme worth mentioning is the delayed rejection adaptive Metropolis (DRAM) scheme proposed by Haario *et al.* (2006), who designed a sampling strategy that accelerates the convergence of the chain to the limiting distribution. For further study of this topic and its applications, we recommend the excellent books by Gamerman & Lopes (2006), Wilkinson (2011), and Kaipio & Somersalo (2006).

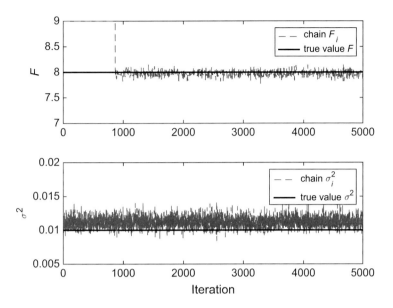

Figure 2.2 Chain realization for 5000 iterations (dashes) compared with the true parameter (solid).

2.5   MCMC with a Surrogate Model

The computational cost in practical implementations of MCMC depends significantly on the complexity in evaluating φ_j on the proposal θ^*. This computational cost becomes expensive when the dynamical systems in (2.4) are high-dimensional and when the corresponding analytical solutions are not available. Several approaches to mitigate this issue include an efficient sampling strategy (Higdon *et al.* 2003, Christen & Fox 2005) or using reduced or surrogate models (Kennedy & O'Hagan 2001, Marzouk *et al.* 2007, Marzouk & Xiu 2009). In this section, we will discuss a surrogate model approach based on polynomial chaos expansion that was introduced in Marzouk *et al.* (2007).

The main idea in Marzouk *et al.* (2007) and Marzouk & Xiu (2009) is to approximate the solutions in (2.4) with the polynomial chaos (PC) expansion. Let the parameter θ in (2.4) be a random function of Z with density p_Z. Approximate

$$\varphi_i(\theta) = x(t_i, \theta) = x(t_i, \theta(z)) \approx \sum_{\mathbf{k}} \hat{x}_{\mathbf{k}}(t_i)\Phi_{\mathbf{k}}(z) \tag{2.13}$$

on the space spanned by the orthogonal polynomials $\Phi_{\mathbf{z}} \in L^2(\mathcal{M}^d, p_Z)$. In practice, this approximation requires assumptions on the domain $\mathcal{M}^d$ as well as the density p_Z. In our practical implementation below, we will set $\mathcal{M}^d$ to be a hypercube with an appropriate boundary. We will also apply the expansion with respect to a tensor product of the Legendre polynomials, assuming that the components of Z are independent and uniformly distributed. With this PC representation, one can precompute the PC coefficients $\hat{x}_{\mathbf{k}}$ using either

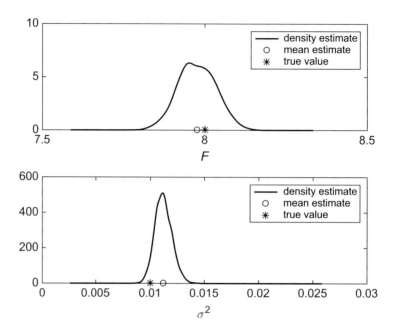

Figure 2.3 Estimated density of each parameter (line), estimated mean (circle), and the true parameter value (asterisk).

the Galerkin approximation (Marzouk *et al.* 2007) or the collocation method (Marzouk & Xiu 2009) on sparse grid points as discussed in Section 4.5.1. In the example below, we compute the coefficients $\hat{x}_{\mathbf{k}}(t_i)$ in (2.13) using the Galerkin method. This requires solving a system of coupled ODEs with a vector field that depends on coefficients that are expressed in terms of the inner product in $L^2(\mathcal{M}^d, p_Z)$ (see Example 4.9 for details). We will numerically estimate these coefficients with the Clenshaw–Curtis quadrature rule on Smolyak level-8 sparse grids (see Section 4.5.1 for detail). The computational cost of this approximation is in computing $\hat{x}_{\mathbf{k}}(t_i)$, which is done offline prior to iterating the MCMC steps. Once this training step has been done, one simply computes the likelihood function $p(y|\theta^*) = p(y|\theta(z^*))$ by evaluating (2.13) on any proposal z^* in each MCMC iteration, and thus avoids integrating the model in (2.4) at $\theta^* = \theta(z^*)$. Now we close this chapter with an example, comparing the standard MCMC and the polynomial surrogate MCMC.

Example 2.9 Consider estimating both the damping coefficient, D, and the forcing parameter, F, in the Lorenz-96 model,

$$\frac{du_j}{dt} = u_{j-1}(u_{j+1} - u_{j-2}) - Du_j + F, \qquad j = 1, \ldots, J,$$

$$u_j(0) = \sin\left(\frac{2\pi j}{J}\right).$$

As in Example 2.8, we will set $J = 5$ and consider observations

$$v_j(t_m) = u_j(t_m) + \epsilon_{m,j}, \quad \epsilon_{m,j} \sim \mathcal{N}(0, \sigma^2), \quad m = 1, \dots, 10,$$

with observation noise variance $\sigma^2 = 0.01$. Here, $u_j(t_m)$ denote the approximate solutions (with the Runge–Kutta method) at discrete times $t_m = m \, \Delta t$, where $\Delta t = 0.05$ is the integration time step.

We consider the random-walk Metropolis scheme with $C^{1/2} = 0.3$ such that the proposal is given by

$$D^* = D_{i-1} + C^{1/2}\xi,$$
$$F^* = F_{i-1} + C^{1/2}\zeta,$$

where the noises $\xi, \zeta \sim \mathcal{N}(0, 1)$ are i.i.d. samples. For simplicity, assume that σ^2 is known so that we don't need to use the method discussed in Section 2.4.2. For the surrogate model, we assume $D \sim U[0, 2]$ and $F \sim U[7, 9]$, so we can write

$$(D, F) = (1, 8) + (Z_1, Z_2),$$

where Z_1, Z_2 are independent uniformly distributed random variables on the interval $[-1, 1]$. We apply the expansion on the corresponding tensor product of the Legendre polynomials up to order $N = 15$ as in Example 4.9, which yields a total of 136 basis functions.

In Figures 2.4 and 2.5, we compare the results obtained from the standard MCMC and the surrogate model for 10,000 realizations of the chain, starting from

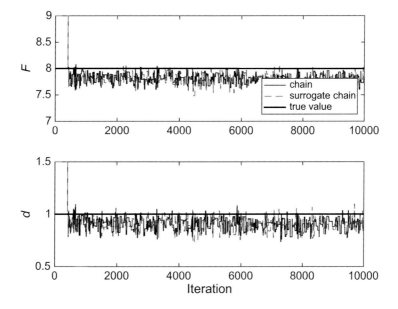

Figure 2.4 Standard MCMC chain realization for 10,000 iterations (gray) compared with the surrogate MCMC chain realization (dashes) and the true parameter (full line).

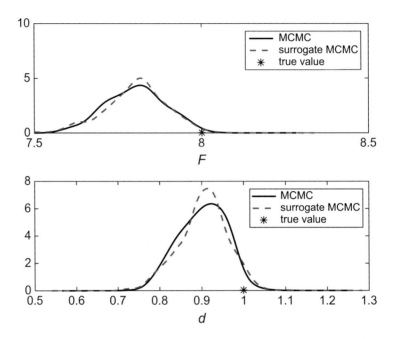

Figure 2.5 Standard MCMC density of each parameter (full line), surrogate MCMC density (dashes), and the true parameter value (asterisk).

initial conditions $D_0 = 1.5$ and $F_0 = 9$. For comparison, we apply both inversion schemes with exactly identical realizations of observations v_j as well as noises ξ, ζ in the proposal. Notice that, although the density estimates are somewhat different, they share the same compact support and the modes of the estimated densities are not very different. We should mention that the convergence of the surrogate Bayesian inversion approximation depends on the accuracy of the polynomial approximation, which was reported in the context of the collocation approach in Marzouk & Xiu (2009).

3   Ensemble Kalman Filters

In this chapter, we discuss a popular data assimilation method known as the ensemble Kalman filter (EnKF), which was invented by Geir Evensen (1994). While the EnKF is usually used to estimate initial conditions, our emphasis here will be to describe it as an alternative parameter estimation method to the MCMC method described in Chapter 2. Algorithmically, MCMC samples the parameters by fitting the model iteratively to the same set of observations, whereas the EnKF is a sequential algorithm that fits the model to new observations as they become available. From the theoretical standpoint, the EnKF, like any other Bayesian filter, does not require the posterior distribution to be ergodic or even stationary, whereas MCMC relies on the ergodicity assumption to estimate the target posterior distribution. The tradeoff, however, is that the EnKF assumes Gaussianity, so it will not estimate the posterior density accurately for nonlinear and/or non-Gaussian problems, but at least it can produce accurate state estimates with the first-order statistics. Together with adaptive covariance methods, such as those developed by Berry & Sauer (2013) and Harlim *et al.* (2014), which will be discussed in detail in this chapter, one can even obtain reasonably accurate second-order statistical estimates.

This chapter is organized as follows. We begin with a discussion on the EnKF and its relation to the classical Kalman filter for linear and Gaussian problems (Kalman & Bucy 1961). We will briefly mention several recent theoretical results on the accuracy estimation of the EnKF with finite ensemble sizes on chaotic dynamical systems (González-Tokman and Hunt 2013, Kelly *et al.* 2014, Tong *et al.* 2016, Majda & Tong 2016). These results are taken to justify the empirical successes of the EnKF as a state estimation method in various applications. Subsequently, we describe the parameter estimation with the EnKF and the adaptive covariance estimation methods. We conclude the chapter with an application of the EnKF in estimating parameters of reduced dynamical systems.

3.1   A Review of Ensemble Kalman Filters

Throughout this chapter, we consider a discrete-time filtering problem,

$$x_i = f(x_{i-1}, \theta) + \Gamma \epsilon_i, \quad \epsilon_i \sim \mathcal{N}(0, Q), \tag{3.1}$$

$$y_i = h(x_i) + \zeta_i, \quad \zeta_i \sim \mathcal{N}(0, R). \tag{3.2}$$

Here, $x_i \in \mathbb{R}^n$ denotes the hidden state variable of interest at time t_i, which evolves according to a dynamical model f and is randomly forced by an unbiased independent Gaussian noise $\epsilon_i \in \mathbb{R}^q$ with covariance matrix $Q \in \mathbb{R}^{q \times q}$. Here, the matrix $\Gamma \in \mathbb{R}^{n \times q}$ is assumed to be given. This discrete-time dynamical model is a generic representation of a discretization of continuous-time dynamical systems such as stochastically forced partial/ordinary differential equations. In some of the literature (e.g., meteorology) $\Gamma \epsilon_i$ is taken as the dynamical model error term since, in these applications, the authors typically use a deterministic model. This interpretation, however, can be misleading in general since there are various ways to account for model error besides using additive Gaussian noises, as explained in a review article (Harlim 2017). The variable y_i in (3.2) denotes the observation at time t_i with observation function $h \colon \mathbb{R}^n \to \mathbb{R}^m$ and is corrupted by an unbiased independent Gaussian noise $\zeta_i \in \mathbb{R}^m$. Let's denote $\mathcal{Y}_i = \{y_j\}_{j \leq i}$ as the set of observations up to time t_i. In this context, the goal of the filtering problem is to specify the conditional distribution $p(x_i | \mathcal{Y}_i)$ given the observation set $\mathcal{Y}_i$, dynamical operator f, parameter θ, matrix Γ, observation model function h, and covariance matrices Q and R. Later in this chapter, we will discuss methods to specify Q and R when they are not available and also the parameter θ in f, or in an approximate model $\tilde{f}$ when the underlying f is unknown. For now, let's keep it simple by assuming that they are all available.

The basic idea of filtering is to find the posterior density $p(x_i | \mathcal{Y}_i)$ by applying Bayes' formula sequentially,

$$p(x_i | \mathcal{Y}_{i-1}, y_i) \propto p(x_i | \mathcal{Y}_{i-1}) p(y_i | x_i), \quad i = 1, 2, \dots . \tag{3.3}$$

Here, $p(y_i | x_i)$ denotes the likelihood function of x_i knowing observation y_i. It is also a conditional density function for y_i given x_i. Specifically, for the observation model in (3.2), we have $p(y_i | x_i) = \mathcal{N}(h(x_i), R)$, which means

$$p(y_i | x_i) \propto \exp\left(-(y_i - h(x_i))^\top R^{-1} (y_i - h(x_i)) \right). \tag{3.4}$$

In (3.3), $p(x_i | \mathcal{Y}_{i-1})$ denotes the prior density at time t_i. It describes a distribution of x_i prior to (or before accounting for) the observation y_i. In practice, the prior density is determined by the dynamical model through a transition kernel corresponding to the dynamics in (3.1). For example, if the model in (3.1) is a discretization of an Itô stochastic process with densities that solve a Fokker–Planck equation with operator $\mathcal{L}^*$ (see Appendix B), then, given a posterior density at the previous time t_{i-1}, the prior density at time t_i is given by

$$p(x_i | \mathcal{Y}_{i-1}) = e^{\tau \mathcal{L}^*} p(x_{i-1} | \mathcal{Y}_{i-1}), \tag{3.5}$$

where $\tau = t_i - t_{i-1}$ and $e^{\tau \mathcal{L}^*}$ is the semigroup of the Fokker–Planck operator. In practice, solving (3.5) is not feasible when n is large. An alternative popular approach is to draw a finite number of samples from the posterior density $x_{i-i}^{k,+} \sim p(x_{i-1} | \mathcal{Y}_{i-1})$, where the superscript $k = 1, \dots, K$ denotes the kth sample and the "+" sign denotes a sample of posterior densities, and take the solutions of

$$x_i^{k,-} = f(x_{i-1}^{k,+}, \theta) + \Gamma \epsilon_i^k, \quad \epsilon_i^k \sim \mathcal{N}(0, Q), \quad k = 1, \ldots, K,$$

as the samples of the prior density in (3.5). Here, the "−" sign denotes a sample of prior densities.

Given these samples, there are at least several approaches to approximate the prior density function. One way is to use a point measure, that is,

$$p(x_i) \approx \frac{1}{K} \sum_{k=1}^{K} \delta(x_i - x_i^{k,-}).$$

This approach is known as the particle filter or sequential Monte Carlo method (Doucet *et al.* 2001, Bain & Crisan 2009). The challenge with this approach is to overcome high-dimensionality (Bengtsson *et al.* 2008, Bickel *et al.* 2008), which is currently an active research problem, see, e.g., van Leeuwen (2015), Chorin *et al.* (2016), Poterjoy (2016), and Lee & Majda (2016). The ensemble Kalman filter assumes a Gaussian approximate density,

$$p(x_i) \approx \frac{1}{Z} \exp \left(- (x_i - \bar{x}_i)^\top P_i^{-1} (x_i - \bar{x}_i) \right), \tag{3.6}$$

with an empirical estimation of the mean and covariance matrix,

$$\bar{x}_i = \frac{1}{K} \sum_{k=1}^{K} x_i^{k,-}, \tag{3.7}$$

$$P_i = \frac{1}{K-1} X_i X_i^\top, \tag{3.8}$$

where the matrix $X_i = [x_i^{1,-} - \bar{x}_i, \ldots, x_i^{K,-} - \bar{x}_i]$ is defined such that the kth column denotes the deviation of the kth ensemble member from its empirical mean in (3.7). If we consider x_i as a random variable[1] and define the random variable $e_i := x_i - \bar{x}_i$, then P_i is an approximation to the mean square error of the prior mean $\bar{x}_i$ in estimating x_i, that is, $\mathbb{E}[e_i e_i^\top] \approx P_i$, where the expectation is defined with respect to the underlying distribution of x_i.

Taking the product of the likelihood function in (3.4) and (3.6), we have

$$p(x_i | \mathcal{Y}_{i-1}, y_i) \propto \exp \left(- J(x_i) \right),$$

where

$$J(x_i) = (y_i - h(x_i))^\top R^{-1}(y_i - h(x_i)) + (x_i - \bar{x}_i)^\top P_i^{-1}(x_i - \bar{x}_i). \tag{3.9}$$

Here, we basically want to find the maximum a-posteriori estimate for $p(x_i | \mathcal{Y}_{i-1}, y_i)$, or equivalently, to minimize $J(x_i)$. To guarantee an explicit

---

[1] Throughout this chapter, we use the same lowercase notation for the realization of a random variable and the random variable itself. For example, x_i is simultaneously used to denote the solutions (or sample path) of (3.1) and a random variable. Depending on the context, it should be clear to the reader which one we are referring to.

solution, one can apply Taylor's approximation to the nonlinear observation function,

$$h(x_i) \approx h(\bar{x}_i) + \nabla_{x_i} h(\bar{x}_i)(x_i - \bar{x}_i).$$

With this approximation, we have a quadratic cost function to minimize,

$$J(x_i) \approx (y_i - h(\bar{x}_i) - H_i(x_i - \bar{x}_i))^{\top} R^{-1}(y_i - h(\bar{x}_i) - H_i(x_i - \bar{x}_i)) \\ + (x_i - \bar{x}_i)^{\top} P_i^{-1}(x_i - \bar{x}_i),$$

where we denote $H_i = \nabla_{x_i} h(\bar{x}_i) \in \mathbb{R}^{m \times n}$. On taking the derivative of J and setting it equal to zero, $\nabla_{x_i} J = 0$, we obtain,

$$-H_i^{\top} R^{-1}(y_i - h(\bar{x}_i) - H_i(x_i - \bar{x}_i)) + P_i^{-1}(x_i - \bar{x}_i) = 0,$$

which can be written in compact form as

$$(H_i^{\top} R^{-1} H_i + P_i^{-1})(x_i - \bar{x}_i) = H_i^{\top} R^{-1}(y_i - h(\bar{x}_i)),$$

or

$$\bar{x}_i^+ := x_i = \bar{x}_i + K_i(y_i - h(\bar{x}_i)), \tag{3.10}$$

where

$$K_i = (H_i^{\top} R^{-1} H_i + P_i^{-1}) H_i^{\top} R^{-1} = P_i H_i^{\top} (H_i P_i H_i^{\top} + R)^{-1},$$

using the Sherman–Morrison–Woodbury formula. This is nothing but the Kalman gain matrix for linear observation function h. In practice, we can use the prior ensemble of solutions to approximate the derivative of h and thus avoid taking an actual derivative on the observation operator. In particular, since the term $H_i X_i$ always occurs in the Kalman gain matrix (owing to (3.8)), we can employ a Taylor approximation on each column of $H_i X_i$,

$$[H_i X_i]_k = \nabla_{x_i} h(\bar{x}_i)(x_i^{k,-} - \bar{x}_i) \approx h(x_i^{k,-}) - h(\bar{x}_i) := [Y_i]_k, \tag{3.11}$$

where we denote by $[A]_k$ the kth column of the matrix A. We should note that, for general nonlinear observations, these ensemble perturbations are biased; that is, $Y_i \mathbf{1} \neq 0$, where $\mathbf{1}$ denotes a vector with every component equal to one. One can also replace $h(\bar{x}_i)$ with $\bar{y}_i = K^{-1} \sum_{k=1}^{K} h(x_i^{k,-})$ in (3.10) and (3.11) to remove the biases in the ensemble perturbations Y_i. In the remainder of this chapter, we will define Y_i as in (3.11).

With these definitions, we can write the Kalman gain in compact form as

$$K_i = \frac{X_i Y_i^{\top}}{K-1} \left(\frac{Y_i Y_i^{\top}}{K-1} + R \right)^{-1}. \tag{3.12}$$

Define the error of the posterior mean estimate, $\bar{x}_i^+$, as

$$\begin{aligned} e_i^+ &:= x_i - \bar{x}_i^+ = x_i - \bar{x}_i - K_i(y_i - h(\bar{x}_i)) \\ &= e_i - K_i(y_i - h(x_i) + h(x_i) - h(\bar{x}_i)) \\ &= e_i - K_i \zeta_i - K_i(h(x_i) - h(\bar{x}_i)), \end{aligned}$$

where we have also denoted by $e_i := x_i - \bar{x}_i$ the error of the prior mean estimate. Thus, we have

$$
\begin{aligned}
\mathbb{E}[e_i^+(e_i^+)^\top] = {} & \mathbb{E}[e_i e_i^\top] + K_i R K_i^\top - K_i \mathbb{E}[(h(x_i) - h(\bar{x}_i))e_i^\top] \\
& - \mathbb{E}[e_i((h(x_i) - h(\bar{x}_i)))^\top]K_i^\top \\
& + K_i \mathbb{E}[(h(x_i) - h(\bar{x}_i))(h(x_i) - h(\bar{x}_i))^\top]K_i^\top,
\end{aligned}
\tag{3.13}
$$

where the expectation is taken with respect to the distribution of x_i. Using the following ensemble-based approximations,

$$
\mathbb{E}[e_i e_i^\top] \approx P^i,
$$

$$
\mathbb{E}[(h(x_i) - h(\bar{x}_i))e_i^\top] \approx \frac{1}{K-1}Y_i X_i^\top,
$$

$$
\mathbb{E}[(h(x_i) - h(\bar{x}_i))(h(x_i) - h(\bar{x}_i))^\top] \approx \frac{1}{K-1}Y_i Y_i^\top,
$$

the statistical expression in (3.13) can be approximated as

$$
\begin{aligned}
\mathbb{E}[e_i^+(e_i^+)^\top] \approx {} & P_i^+ \\
= {} & P_i + K_i R K_i^\top - \frac{1}{K-1}(K_i Y_i X_i^\top - X_i Y_i^\top K_i^\top + K_i Y_i Y_i^\top K_i^\top) \\
= {} & P_i - K_i \frac{Y_i X_i^\top}{K-1},
\end{aligned}
\tag{3.14}
$$

where we have used the fact that

$$
K_i R K_i^\top + \frac{1}{K-1}(K_i Y_i Y_i^\top K_i^\top - X_i Y_i^\top K_i^\top) = 0,
$$

using (3.12).

To conclude, the ensemble Kalman filter posterior density is given by

$$
p(x_i|\mathcal{Y}_i) = \mathcal{N}(\bar{x}_i^+, P_i^+),
\tag{3.15}
$$

where $\bar{x}_i^+$ and P_i^+ are given by the posterior update formula in (3.10) and (3.14) with the Kalman gain in (3.12). To proceed, we need to sample from this posterior density in (3.15), $x_i^{k,+} \sim p(x_i|\mathcal{Y}_i)$. There are various ways to generate the sample posteriors. The original ensemble Kalman filter (Evensen 1994) samples the posterior as

$$
x_i^{k,+} = x_i^{k,-} + K_i(y_i + \chi_i^k - h(x_i^{k,-})), \quad \chi_i^k \sim \mathcal{N}(0, R),
\tag{3.16}
$$

where an additional perturbation χ_i^k is added for each ensemble member. One can check that the empirical mean and covariance from these samples consistently match those in (3.10) and (3.14). With this sampling method, one does not need to compute $\bar{x}_i^+$ and P_i^+. Basically, at each step, one computes the Kalman gain matrix in (3.12), draws an m-dimensional Gaussian random vector $\chi_i^k \sim \mathcal{N}(0, R)$, and updates the ensemble by applying the formula in (3.16).

Alternatively, there are variations of the ensemble square-root filter, such as those developed by Bishop *et al.* (2001), Anderson (2001), Tippett *et al.* (2003), which will give the same statistics. In the following section, we give one example of a square-root filter, namely the ensemble transform Kalman filter (ETKF), that will be used in the numerical simulations below.

3.1.1 The Ensemble Transform Kalman Filter

The basic idea of the ensemble transform Kalman filter (ETKF) (Bishop *et al.* 2001) is to construct the posterior sample as

$$x_i^{k,+} = \bar{x}_i^+ + \xi_i^k, \tag{3.17}$$

where $\xi_i^k \in \mathbb{R}^n$ is the kth column of the matrix $X_i^+ := X_i T$ and T is a transformation matrix that will be chosen such that

$$\frac{1}{K-1} X_i T T X_i^\top = \frac{1}{K-1} X_i^+ (X_i^+)^\top = P_i^+. \tag{3.18}$$

To derive T, notice that

$$Y_i^\top R^{-1}(Y_i Y_i^\top + R) = Y_i^\top R^{-1} Y_i Y_i^\top + Y_i^\top = (Y_i^\top R^{-1} Y_i + \mathcal{I})Y_i^\top,$$

which means that

$$Y_i^\top (Y_i Y_i^\top + R)^{-1} = (Y_i^\top R^{-1} Y_i + \mathcal{I})^{-1} Y_i^\top R^{-1}.$$

This identity allows us to rewrite the Kalman gain matrix in (3.12) as

$$K_i = X_i (Y_i^\top R^{-1} Y_i + (K-1)\mathcal{I})^{-1} Y_i^\top R^{-1},$$

such that

$$
\begin{aligned}
P_i^+ &= P_i - K_i \frac{Y_i X_i^\top}{K-1} \\
&= \frac{1}{K-1}(X_i X_i^\top - X_i(Y_i^\top R^{-1} Y_i + (K-1)\mathcal{I})^{-1} Y_i^\top R^{-1} Y_i X_i^\top) \\
&= \frac{1}{K-1} X_i(\mathcal{I} - (Y_i^\top R^{-1} Y_i + (K-1)\mathcal{I})^{-1} Y_i^\top R^{-1} Y_i) X_i^\top \\
&= X_i(Y_i^\top R^{-1} Y_i + (K-1)\mathcal{I})^{-1} X_i^\top.
\end{aligned}
$$

From this equality as well as the constraint in (3.18), we can specify T as

$$T = \sqrt{K-1} U S^{-1/2} U^\top, \tag{3.19}$$

where the columns of U and the diagonal components of S, respectively, are the eigenvectors and eigenvalues of

$$USU^\top = Y_i^\top R^{-1} Y_i + (K-1)\mathcal{I}. \tag{3.20}$$

Numerically, we construct the posterior mean of the ETKF using equation (3.10). Subsequently, we solve the $K \times K$ eigenvalue problem in (3.20) for U and S. Then we construct the transformation matrix T with (3.19). Finally, we form the matrix $X_i^+ = X_i T$ and add each column of X_i^+ to the posterior mean as in

(3.17). An efficient way to minimize the computational complexity of these steps was introduced by Hunt *et al.* (2007).

Example 3.1 Let's consider the following three-dimensional system of SDEs (Harlim *et al.* 2014):

$$dx = \left(Lx - Dx + B(x,x) \right) dt + \sigma \Gamma \, d\vec{W}, \qquad (3.21)$$

where $x = (u, v, w)^\top$, $B(x,x) = (0, auw, -auv)^\top$, $dW = (dW_1, dW_2)^\top$,

$$L = \begin{pmatrix} 0 & \omega & 0 \\ -2\omega & 0 & -\beta \\ 0 & \beta & 0 \end{pmatrix}, \qquad D = \begin{pmatrix} 0 & 0 & 0 \\ 0 & \gamma & 0 \\ 0 & 0 & \gamma \end{pmatrix}, \qquad \Gamma = \begin{pmatrix} 0 & 0 \\ 1 & 0 \\ 0 & 1 \end{pmatrix}. \quad (3.22)$$

Consider the inner product

$$\langle x_1, x_2 \rangle_* = u_1 u_2 + \frac{1}{2}(v_1 v_2 + w_1 w_2),$$

defined for any pair of three-dimensional vectors $x_1 = (u_1, v_1, w_1)$ and $x_2 = (u_2, v_2, w_2)$. Notice that L is skew-symmetric with respect to this inner product; that is, $\langle Lx, y \rangle_* = -\langle x, Ly \rangle_*$ for any $x, y \in \mathbb{R}^3$ and $\langle x, B(x,x) \rangle_* = 0$. Furthermore, if $\gamma > 0$ and $\omega \neq 0$, the system is *geometrically ergodic* with a unique invariant measure,

$$p_{\mathrm{eq}}(x) \propto \exp\left(-\frac{\gamma}{\sigma^2} \|x\|_*^2 \right). \qquad (3.23)$$

Geometrically ergodic means that the evolving density of the system converges to the invariant measure at an exponential rate as $t \to \infty$. To see this, notice that, when $\sigma = 0$, the deterministic dynamical system has a global Lyapunov function $V(x) = \langle x, x \rangle_*$, such that

$$\frac{dV}{dt} = 2u\frac{du}{dt} + v\frac{dv}{dt} + w\frac{dw}{dt} = -\gamma(v^2 + w^2) \leq 0.$$

Furthermore, one can check the controllability condition. That is, let $\mathcal{F}(x) = Lx - Dx + B(x,x)$ and $\mathcal{G}_1(x) = \Gamma_1$ and $\mathcal{G}_2(x) = \Gamma_2$ be the first and second columns of Γ, respectively. Define the Lie bracket

$$[\mathcal{F}, \mathcal{G}_i] = (D\mathcal{G}_i)\mathcal{F} - (D\mathcal{F})\mathcal{G}_i,$$

where $D\mathcal{F}$ denotes the Jacobian of $\mathcal{F}$. Then the controllability condition is satisfied when the matrix $M = (\mathcal{G}_1, \mathcal{G}_2, [\mathcal{F}, \mathcal{G}_1], [\mathcal{F}, \mathcal{G}_2])^\top$, which can be given explicitly as

$$M = \begin{pmatrix} 0 & 1 & 0 \\ 0 & 0 & 1 \\ -\omega & -\gamma & -au + \beta \\ 0 & au - \beta & -\gamma \end{pmatrix},$$

is of full rank (Harlim *et al.* 2014). Let M_j be a matrix M with deleted jth row. Then

$$\det(M_1) = -\omega(au - \beta); \quad \det(M_2) = -\gamma\omega; \quad \det(M_3) = 0; \quad \det(M_4) = -\omega.$$

Since ω is a common factor of the above determinants, the system is controllable. With global Lyapunov stability and controllability, the system is geometrically ergodic (Mattingly *et al.* 2002). One can verify that p_{eq} in (3.23) is the invariant measure of the system of SDEs in (3.21) by checking that $\mathcal{L}^* p_{\mathrm{eq}} = 0$, where $\mathcal{L}^*$ denotes the Fokker–Planck operator of (3.21).

Also, if ω in (3.22) is replaced by $-\omega$, then these two systems have the same temporal statistics for u in statistical equilibrium. This is a consequence of the fact that there is symmetry in the system; if (u, v, w) solves (3.21) with a given ω, then $(u, -v, -w)$ solves this system with $-\omega$ since $-\sigma \, dW \cong \sigma \, dW$ in probability law.

Suppose that the true solution is a single trajectory of (3.21) that is numerically realized with the Euler–Maruyama scheme,

$$x_{i+1} = x_i + \delta t(Lx_i - Dx_i + B(x_i, x_i)) + \sigma\sqrt{\delta t}\Gamma \, \Delta W_{i+1}, \qquad (3.24)$$

where $\Delta W_{i+1} \sim \mathcal{N}(0, \mathcal{I}_2)$. In compact form, this is an example of (3.1), where

$$f(x_i, \theta) = x_i + \delta t(Lx_i - Dx_i + B(x_i, x_i)), \quad Q = \sigma^2 \, \delta t \, \mathcal{I}_2,$$

with parameters $\theta = (\omega, \beta, \gamma, a)$. Here, $\mathcal{I}_2$ denotes a 2×2 identity matrix. In this numerical simulation, we set $\omega = 3/4, \beta = 1, \gamma = 1/2, a = 1, \sigma = 1/\sqrt{2}$, and $\delta t = 0.01$ and we assume that all of these parameters are known. In Section 3.2, we will assume that none of these parameters are known and they will be estimated from noisy observations,

$$y_i = Hx_i + \zeta_i, \quad \zeta_i \sim \mathcal{N}(0, R). \qquad (3.25)$$

Here, we will show results of the ETKF with full observations, $H = \mathcal{I}_3$. In this numerical experiment, we employ the ETKF with an ensemble of size $K = 10$ and observation time interval of $\Delta t = 0.1$. In our filtering simulation, we will integrate the filter model in (3.24) with time step $\Delta t = 0.1$ rather than with $\delta t = 0.01$. With this configuration, we found that the ETKF mean estimates track the true solutions accurately (see Figure 3.1). To quantify the filter accuracy, we compute the following two metrics, the RMSE and spread, defined respectively as

$$\mathrm{RMSE} = \sqrt{\frac{1}{nT} \sum_{i=1}^{T} \|x_i - \bar{x}_i^+\|^2},$$

$$\mathrm{Spread} = \sqrt{\frac{1}{nT} \sum_{i=1}^{T} \mathrm{Tr}(P_i^+)}.$$

Here the RMSE quantifies the actual error of using the posterior mean as an estimator for the true signal, whereas the spread quantifies the estimated error

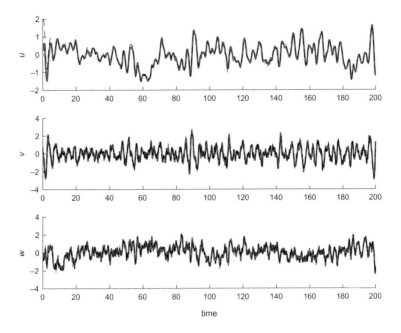

Figure 3.1 The ETKF filter mean estimates (gray) and the truth (dashes). In this simulation, RMSE $= 0.1941$ and spread $= 0.1534$.

(uncertainty) of the posterior mean estimates. Essentially the spread is a crude measure of the accuracy of the second-order posterior statistical estimates. In our simulation, we find that the RMSE $= 0.1941$ and the spread $= 0.1534$ on averaging over a total of $T = 2000$ assimilation cycles. In this case, notice that the estimated error is somewhat smaller than the actual error; that is, the spread is lower than the RMSE. This discrepancy is due to the finite ensemble size $K = 10$, which is a relatively small sample size for estimating the covariance statistics even though it is larger than the model state dimension $n = 3$. In the remaining examples in this chapter, we shall see that these two metrics become comparable when adaptive covariance estimations are used in tandem with the EnKF.

3.1.2   Remarks on the Practical Implementation and the Convergence

Since the EnKF involves various approximations for nonlinear and non-Gaussian problems, it is clear that the method won't be optimal for estimating the true filtering distribution. However, it is still interesting to check whether the method is consistent with its assumptions, namely, if one applies the EnKF on a linear and Gaussian problem, one expects to obtain the corresponding analytical Kalman filter solution in the limit of ensemble size $K \to \infty$. This convergence result (in L^p sense, where $1 \le p < \infty$) was reported for the EnKF in Mandel *et al.* (2011) and for ensemble square-root filters, including the ETKF, in Kwiatkowski & Mandel (2015).

For nonlinear problems, the successes of the EnKF in various applications are usually measured by the accuracy of the scheme as a state estimation method in tracking the underlying truth signal. Therefore, it is more relevant to understand why the EnKF can achieve this accuracy even with a finite ensemble size, $K < \infty$. In fact, the computational cost in high-dimensional applications prohibits the use of a large ensemble size. For example, in numerical weather prediction applications, the dimension of the state space, n, is on the order of $10^9 - 10^{12}$, but the computational resources allow implementation only with an ensemble size of order 100 or less. We should note that, in this configuration, $K \ll n$, the EnKF requires additional modifications to compensate for sampling errors, which manifest themselves as underestimated forecast error covariances, spurious long-range correlations, and ultimately filter divergence. The underestimation of forecast error covariances in the EnKF is usually compensated for with a covariance inflation (Anderson 2007), $P_i \leftarrow \alpha P_i + C$, where α denotes the multiplicative inflation factor and C denotes an additive inflation factor. In practice, one usually adopts just the multiplicative inflation since it is difficult to determine the appropriate additive inflation factor C. The problem of spurious correlations at long distances is usually addressed by the method of covariance localization (Houtekamer & Mitchell 1998, Hamill *et al.* 2001). The usual localization schemes use a parametric tapering or kernel functions such as the Gaspari–Cohn function (Gaspari & Cohn 1999) to reduce the unphysical correlations between observations and model state variables with distant locations. As an alternative to these parametric localization approaches, a nonparametric localization technique has been proposed by De La Chevrotière & Harlim (2017a, 2017b). This method uses ensemble archived data assimilation products to train nonparametric localization maps that transform the poorly estimated sample correlation into an improved correlation.

The convergence result with a finite ensemble size was first reported in González-Tokman and Hunt (2013) for hyperbolic systems with expanding and contracting subspaces, and a generic observation function that satisfies the hypothesis of the Takens embedding theorem. In this setup, they showed that, if the initial ensemble is close to the true trajectory with an error of $\mathcal{O}(\epsilon)$, the EnKF solutions with observation error covariance of $R = \epsilon^2 \mathcal{I}$ will stay close to or "shadow" the true trajectory with an error of order $\mathcal{O}(\epsilon)$. In Kelly *et al.* (2014), the well-posedness of the EnKF solutions is established for a nonlinear system of partial differential equations with quadratic terms that conserve the energy such that it has a global attractor. In particular, they showed that, for a nonlinear dynamical system of this type, the deviation of each ensemble member from the true signal (in L^2-norm) has an upper bound that grows exponentially as a function of the filtering temporal cycle when the system is fully observed with linear observation model h. Furthermore, they also proved the accuracy of the filter estimates for all times when a covariance inflation is implemented. In a separate work (Tong *et al.* 2016), an observable energy criterion was proposed as a sufficient condition for filter stability, which guarantees that the filter solutions remain bounded uniformly in time. In the same paper, Tong *et al.* also established the geometric ergodicity of the EnKF with appropriate conditions, which ensures that the filter has a unique invariant measure and errors in the initial ensemble will decay exponentially as a function of time. In Majda & Tong (2016), the accuracy of the EnKF with a finite ensemble size for high-dimensional linear filtering problems was reported.

3.2   Parameter Estimation Methods

The classical filtering technique to estimate parameters θ in (3.1) is to apply the Kalman filter on an augmented state-parameter filtering problem,

$$
\begin{aligned}
x_i &= f(x_{i-1}, \theta_{i-1}) + \Gamma \epsilon_i, \quad \epsilon_i \sim \mathcal{N}(0, Q), \\
\theta_i &= g(\theta_{i-1}, x_{i-1}), \\
y_i &= h(x_i) + \zeta_i, \quad \zeta_i \sim \mathcal{N}(0, R),
\end{aligned}
\tag{3.26}
$$

where the model g is typically chosen empirically (Friedland 1969, 1982). This approach can work only when the parameters are observable, which is a necessary condition to identify the parameters from the given set of observations when the noise vanishes, $Q, R = 0$ (Hwang & Seinfeld 1972). We should point out that the identifiability of the parameters does not guarantee an accurate parameter estimation, especially when the explicit dependence of the observations on the parameters is unknown. In our experience, this state-parameter augmentation technique is often sensitive to initial conditions.

When the true parameters θ are constant and identifiable, one usually applies the state-parameter augmentation strategy with a persistent model, $g = 0$ (Friedland 1969). When the parameters are time-dependent, choosing the appropriate parametric model, g, is a nontrivial task; classical choices often assumed g to be independent of x, and one usually needs to introduce new parameters to be determined in the empirically chosen parametric model for g. While this method is not completely reliable, it remains popular for correcting biases when the model is imperfect (Dee & da Silva 1998, Ménard 2010, Gershgorin *et al.* 2010, Majda & Harlim 2012, Reich & Cotter 2015).

Before we give numerical examples, we will now discuss methods for estimating the error covariance matrices, Q and R.

3.2.1   Adaptive Covariance Estimation Methods

The idea of estimating the covariance matrices Q and R within the linear Kalman filter framework was introduced in the early 1970s for stationary (Mehra 1970, 1972) and time-varying problems (Belanger 1974). It was only recently that these methods were adopted with the EnKF for estimating covariance matrices of nonlinear filtering problems (Berry & Sauer 2013, Harlim *et al.* 2014, Zhen & Harlim 2015). In this section, we will discuss the two techniques in those papers which have been used by the author on various estimation problems (Majda & Harlim 2013, Harlim *et al.* 2014, Berry & Harlim 2014, Zhen & Harlim 2015, Harlim & Li 2015, Berry & Harlim 2016c, Harlim 2017). We should note that there are many other covariance estimation methods, as discussed in the recent survey paper by Dunik *et al.* (2017) that we won't cover in this section.

The main idea of these adaptive covariance estimation methods (Mehra 1970, 1972, Belanger 1974) is to apply Bayes' theorem to sequentially estimate a posterior distribution of the state x_i and parameters Q_i, R_i at each time step t_i from the observations y_i as follows:

$$p(x_i, Q_i, R_i | \mathcal{Y}_i) \propto p(x_i, Q_i, R_i | \mathcal{Y}_{i-1}) p(y_i | x_i, Q_i, R_i). \tag{3.27}$$

Here, $p(y_i | x_i, Q_i, R_i)$ denotes the likelihood function of the augmented variables and $p(x_i, Q_i, R_i | \mathcal{Y}_{i-1})$ denotes the prior distribution of the augmented state and parameters at time t_i. Write the prior distribution as

$$p(x_i, Q_i, R_i | \mathcal{Y}_{i-1}) = p(Q_i, R_i) p(x_i | Q_i, R_i, \mathcal{Y}_{i-1}). \tag{3.28}$$

Upon inserting (3.28) into (3.27), we obtain

$$p(x_i, Q_i, R_i | \mathcal{Y}_i) \propto p(Q_i, R_i) p(x_i | Q_i, R_i, \mathcal{Y}_{i-1}) p(y_i | x_i, Q_i, R_i) \tag{3.29}$$

$$\propto p(Q_i, R_i) p(x_i | Q_i, R_i, \mathcal{Y}_i). \tag{3.30}$$

This formalism splits the task of estimating state x_i and parameters Q_i, R_i as follows. The first step in the Bayesian filtering algorithm is to estimate $p(x_i | Q_i, R_i, \mathcal{Y}_i)$ by applying Bayes' theorem to the last two components of (3.29). Subsequently, we apply a secondary filter in (3.30), using the updated density, $p(x_i | Q_i, R_i, \mathcal{Y}_i)$, to estimate $p(x_i, Q_i, R_i | \mathcal{Y}_i)$.

Numerically, the two-step Bayes' update in (3.29)–(3.30) can be approximated with the Kalman filter (Mehra 1970, 1972, Belanger 1974) or an extended Kalman filter for nonlinear systems (Dee *et al.* 1985). We should mention that this paper also provides an efficient implementation for the method in Belanger (1974). Recent extensions of these methods using ensemble Kalman filters were shown in Berry & Sauer (2013), Harlim *et al.* (2014), and Zhen & Harlim (2015). In this chapter, we will consider the ETKF as the primary filter to update the first two moments of $p(x_i | Q_i, R_i, \mathcal{Y}_i)$, which is assumed to be Gaussian. While $p(x_i | Q_i, R_i, \mathcal{Y}_i)$ is a density in terms of x_i, this likelihood function has a non-unique representation in terms of R_i and Q_i, as we shall see below. Now we will describe two different methods to realize the secondary Bayes update in (3.30).

The Berry–Sauer method

First, we derive an observation function to represent the likelihood function $p(x_i | Q_i, R_i, \mathcal{Y}_i)$. To simplify the discussion, assume that both the dynamical model and the observation function in (3.1)–(3.2) are linear, that is, $f(x_i) = F_i x_i$ and $h(x_i) = H_i x_i$. We define the innovation vector

$$d_i := y_i - H_i \bar{x}_i = H_i e_i + \zeta_i, \tag{3.31}$$

where we have used the notation $e_i := x_i - \bar{x}_i$ and $\zeta_i \sim \mathcal{N}(0, R)$.

With the innovation vector in (3.31), we can see that

$$\mathbb{E}[d_i d_i^\top] = \mathbb{E}[(H_i e_i + \zeta_i)(H_i e_i + \zeta_i)^\top] = H_i P_i H_i^\top + R, \qquad (3.32)$$

where the cross terms vanish since the ζ_i are independent. Also,

$$\begin{aligned} \mathbb{E}[d_{i+1} d_i^\top] &= \mathbb{E}[(H_{i+1} e_{i+1} + \zeta_{i+1})(H_i e_i + \zeta_i)^\top] \\ &= H_{i+1} \mathbb{E}[(F_i e_i^+ + \Gamma \epsilon_{i+1} + \zeta_{i+1})(H_i e_i + \zeta_i)^\top] \\ &= H_{i+1} \mathbb{E}[(F_i e_i + F_i K_i d_i + \Gamma \epsilon_{i+1} + \zeta_{i+1})(H_i e_i + \zeta_i)^\top] \\ &= H_{i+1} F_i P_i H_i^\top + H_{i+1} F_i K_i \mathbb{E}[d_i d_i^\top], \end{aligned} \qquad (3.33)$$

where we have used the identities

$$e_i = x_i - \bar{x}_i = F_{i-1} x_{i-1} + \Gamma \epsilon_i - F_{i-1} \bar{x}_i^+ = F_{i-1} e_{i-1}^+ + \Gamma \epsilon_i \qquad (3.34)$$

and

$$e_i^+ = x_i - \bar{x}_i^+ = e_i + K_i d_i, \qquad (3.35)$$

which form the recursive error formula of the Kalman update on linear problems. In (3.34), the noises $\epsilon_i \sim \mathcal{N}(0, Q)$. This implies that the prior covariance matrix, P_i, can be expressed explicitly in term of the posterior covariance matrix,

$$P_i = \mathbb{E}[e_i e_i^\top] = F_{i-1} P_{i-1}^+ F_{i-1}^\top + \Gamma Q \Gamma^\top.$$

By substituting this equation into (3.33), we obtain

$$\mathbb{E}[d_{i+1} d_i^\top] - H_{i+1} F_i K_i \mathbb{E}[d_i d_i^\top] = H_{i+1} F_i (F_{i-1} P_{i-1}^+ F_{i-1}^\top + \Gamma Q \Gamma^\top) H_i^\top. \quad (3.36)$$

Our goal here is to estimate Q and R, which are the second-order statistics of stationary processes, ϵ_i and ζ_i, respectively, from (3.32) and (3.33). Notice that this estimation problem involves approximations of non-stationary statistics, namely P_i, P_i^+, $\mathbb{E}[d_i d_i^\top]$, $\mathbb{E}[d_{i+1} d_i^\top]$, in general nonlinear filtering problems. Obviously, we have no access to the statistical quantities, $\mathbb{E}[d_i d_i^\top]$, $\mathbb{E}[d_{i+1} d_i^\top]$.

Berry and Sauer proposed approximating (3.32) and (3.33) as

$$d_i d_i^\top - H_i P_i H_i^\top = R_i + v_i,$$
$$d_{i+1} d_i^\top - H_{i+1} F_i K_i d_i d_i^\top - H_{i+1} F_i F_{i-1} P_{i-1}^+ F_{i-1}^\top H_i^\top = H_{i+1} F_i \Gamma Q_i \Gamma^\top H_i^\top + w_i, \qquad (3.37)$$

where v_i and w_i denote the errors in this approximation (Berry & Sauer 2013). We have also replaced Q and R with Q_i and R_i, respectively, to denote the estimates at time t_i. The two equations in (3.37) are examples of a pseudo-observation model corresponding to the likelihood function $p(x_i | Q_i, R_i, \mathcal{Y}_i)$. We call it the pseudo-observation model because it is a derived observation, namely the left-hand terms in (3.37) are indirectly observed given y_i. Numerically, the method in Berry & Sauer (2013) proceeds as follows. First, it minimizes the errors in (3.37) in the Frobenius matrix norm. Since the number of constraints is similar to the number of parameters in R_i for the first equation in (3.37), the solution of this minimization problem is given by

$$\hat{R}_i = d_i d_i^\top - H_i P_i H_i^\top.$$

For the second equation, when $Q \in \mathbb{R}^{q \times q}$ with $q > m$, where m is the number of observations, the minimization problem is under-determined. To avoid this issue, one usually parameterizes $Q_i = \sum_{s=1}^p \alpha_{s,i} Q^{(s)}$, where $p \leq m$ and $Q^{(s)}$ are chosen according to the underlying structure of Q if it is known or chosen arbitrarily otherwise. With this choice, we solve

$$\{\hat{\alpha}_{1,i}, \ldots, \hat{\alpha}_{p,i}\} = \arg\min_{\alpha_{s,i}, s=1,\ldots,p} \left\| d_{i+1} d_i^\top - H_{i+1} F_i K_i d_i d_i^\top \right.$$
$$- H_{i+1} F_i F_{i-1} P_{i-1}^+ F_{i-1}^\top H_i^\top$$
$$\left. - \sum_{s=1}^p \alpha_{s,i} H_{i+1} F_i \Gamma Q^{(s)} \Gamma^\top H_i^\top \right\|$$

and obtain $\hat{Q}_i = \sum_{s=1}^p \hat{\alpha}_{s,i} Q^{(s)}$. Once $\hat{Q}_i$ and $\hat{R}_i$ have been determined, a running average is proposed for the posterior estimate of Q and R,

$$\begin{aligned} Q_i^+ &= Q_{i-1}^+ + \frac{1}{\tau}(\hat{Q}_i - Q_{i-1}^+), \\ R_i^+ &= R_{i-1}^+ + \frac{1}{\tau}(\hat{R}_i - R_{i-1}^+), \end{aligned} \tag{3.38}$$

with a nuisance parameter τ. In principle, this running average is a filtering solution of a secondary Bayes update in (3.30), where the dynamical models for both Q_i and R_i are implicitly assumed to be constant in time. In particular, Q_{i-1}^+ and R_{i-1}^+, which are the posterior estimates at time t_{i-1}, are also the prior estimates at time t_i. The filtering update in (3.38) weights the newly estimated $\hat{Q}_i, \hat{R}_i$ by a parameter $1/\tau$ instead of using a Kalman weight. While this running average is numerically efficient, it is sensitive to the choice of τ, as we shall see in the example below, and it may suffer from some identifiability issue in a certain setting. Furthermore, it is also unclear whether the approximate $\hat{Q}_i, \hat{R}_i$ will induce biases in a long run.

In our implementation below, we will embed this secondary filter with the ETKF as the primary filter. To actually construct the equations (3.37) for nonlinear problems, we will use the ensemble of solutions obtained from the ETKF to approximate F_i and H_i. In particular, let $x_i^{k,d}$ denote the deterministic forecast from initial condition $x_{i-1}^{k,+}$, that is,

$$x_i^{k,d} = f(x_{i-1}^{k,+}, \theta).$$

Using our previous notation, we note that, $x_i^{k,-} = x_i^{k,d} + \Gamma \epsilon_i^k$, where $\epsilon_i^k \sim \mathcal{N}(0, \hat{Q}_i)$. Then we approximate

$$\begin{aligned} F_i &\approx X_{i+1}^d (X_i^+)^\dagger, \\ H_i &\approx Y_i X_i^\dagger, \end{aligned} \tag{3.39}$$

where † denotes the pseudo-inverse. Here, X_i^d is a matrix whose kth column is the deviation of the kth deterministic prior ensemble member, $x_i^{k,d}$, from its empirical mean, $\bar{x}_i^d$; X_i^+ is a matrix whose kth column is the deviation of the kth posterior ensemble member, $x_i^{k,+}$, from its empirical mean, $\bar{x}_i^+$; X_i is a matrix whose kth column is the deviation of the kth prior ensemble member, $x_i^{k,-}$, from its empirical mean, $\bar{x}_i$; and Y_i is a matrix whose kth column is the deviation of the kth predicted observation ensemble member, $y_i^{k,-} = h(x_i^{k,-})$, from its empirical mean, $h(\bar{x}_i)$, to be consistent with the notations and definitions in Section 3.1.

Example 3.2 Let us consider estimating Q and R together with the state x_i for the problem in Example 3.1. Consider observing the second component of the triad model, that is, $h(x) = (0, 1, 0)x = v$. In this numerical experiment, the true parameters to be estimated are $\sigma = 1/\sqrt{2}$ and $R = 0.05$. With this value of σ, the true parameter $Q = \sigma^2 \Delta t \mathcal{I}_2 = 0.05\mathcal{I}_2$, where $\Delta t = 0.1$ denotes the observation time interval. We use an ensemble size $K = 10$ and initial conditions $R_0^+ = 1, Q_0^+ = 1$. In Figure 3.2, we show the corresponding state estimates for $\tau = 100$ and $\tau = 500$. We find that the filter estimates with $\tau = 100$ have RMSE $= 0.3871$ and spread $= 0.3581$, whereas the estimates with $\tau = 500$ have RMSE $= 0.3878$ and spread $= 0.3885$. These quantitative measures are computed by averaging over 8000 assimilation cycles, ignoring the first 2000 cycles. Notice that the RMSE and spread are comparable, indicating that a relatively accurate second-order posterior statistical estimation has been achieved. In Figure 3.3, we show the corresponding estimates for σ and R. Notice that the estimates with the larger value of $\tau = 500$ are smoother and more accurate than those with the smaller value of $\tau = 100$. However, the estimates with larger τ converge slower than those with the smaller τ.

For this example, suppose that, if we observe only the first component of the triad model in (3.21), that is, $h(x) = Hx = [1, 0, 0]x = u$, then Q is not identifiable. This is because $\Gamma^\top H^\top = 0$ and the right-hand term in the second equation in (3.37) that involves Q vanishes. One way to overcome this issue is to infer from larger-time-lag innovation statistics, $\mathbb{E}[d_{i+\ell}d_i^\top]$ for $\ell > 1$, which will be discussed next.

Belanger's Method

For the discussion in this section, we will use the same notation as before. From (3.34) and (3.35), we have

$$
\begin{aligned}
e_i &= F_{i-1}e_{i-1}^+ + \Gamma\epsilon_i = F_{i-1}(x_{i-1} - \bar{x}_{i-1}^+) + \Gamma\epsilon_i \\
&= F_{i-1}(x_{i-1} - (\bar{x}_{i-1} + K_{i-1}(y_{i-1} - H_{i-1}\bar{x}_{i-1}))) + \Gamma\epsilon_i \\
&= F_{i-1}(x_{i-1} - \bar{x}_{i-1}) - F_{i-1}K_{i-1}(H_{i-1}x_{i-1} + \zeta_{i-1} - H_{i-1}\bar{x}_{i-1}) + \Gamma\epsilon_i \\
&= F_{i-1}(\mathcal{I} - K_{i-1}H_{i-1})e_{i-1} - F_{i-1}K_{i-1}\zeta_{i-1} + \Gamma\epsilon_i.
\end{aligned}
\tag{3.40}
$$

We can rewrite this equation as a function of e_0 as

$$
e_i = \Psi_{i,0}e_0 + \sum_{j=0}^{i-1} \Psi_{i,j+1}(\Gamma\epsilon_{j+1} - F_j K_j \zeta_j),
\tag{3.41}
$$

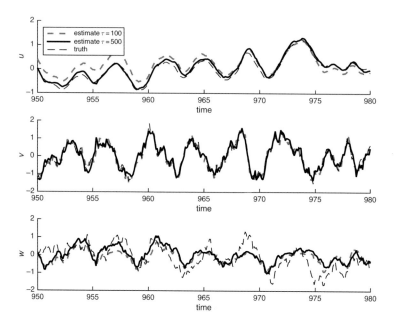

Figure 3.2 The ETKF with the Berry–Sauer estimation method: the primary filter mean estimates with $\tau = 100$ (gray, dashes), with $\tau = 500$ (black, solid), and the truth (black, dashes) at time interval $[950, 980]$. With $\tau = 100$, the filter estimates $\mathrm{RMSE} = 0.3871$ and spread $= 0.3581$ compared with those with $\tau = 500$ with $\mathrm{RMSE} = 0.3878$ and spread $= 0.3885$.

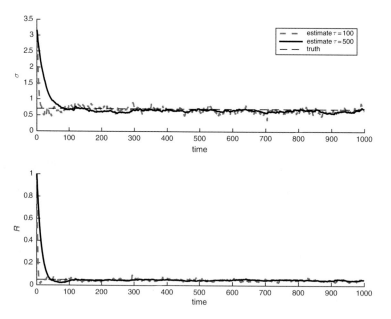

Figure 3.3 The ETKF with the Berry–Sauer estimation method: the secondary filter estimates for σ and R with $\tau = 100$ (gray, dashes), with $\tau = 500$ (black, solid), and the truth (black, dashes). The estimates with $\tau = 500$ are smoother and more accurate than those with smaller $\tau = 100$.

where we have defined

$$
\begin{aligned}
\Psi_{i,i} &= \mathcal{I}, \\
\Psi_{i,j} &= \Theta_{i-1}\Theta_{j-2}\cdots\Theta_j, \\
\Theta_i &= F_i(\mathcal{I} - K_{i-1}H_{i-1}).
\end{aligned}
\tag{3.42}
$$

From (3.41), we can deduce that, for $i \geq \ell \geq 0$,

$$
\mathbb{E}[e_i e_{i-\ell}^\top] = \Psi_{i,0}P_0\Psi_{i-\ell,0}^\top + \sum_{j=0}^{i-\ell-1}\Psi_{i,j+1}(\Gamma Q \Gamma^\top + F_j K_j R K_j^\top F_j^\top)\Psi_{i-\ell,j+1}^\top,
\tag{3.43}
$$

using the fact that $\mathbb{E}[e_0 e_0^\top] = P_0$, and ζ_j and ϵ_j are independent noises with covariance matrices $\mathbb{E}[\zeta_j \zeta_j^\top] = R$ and $\mathbb{E}[\epsilon_j \epsilon_j^\top] = Q$, respectively.

Now, consider the following parameterization model:

$$
Q = \sum_{s=1}^p \alpha_s Q^{(s)}, \qquad R = \sum_{s=1}^p \alpha_s R^{(s)},
\tag{3.44}
$$

such that p denotes the total number of parameters to be estimated in Q and R for some $Q^{(s)}, R^{(s)}$. With the parameterization model in (3.44), our goal is to estimate $\{\alpha_s\}_{s=1,\ldots,p}$. On substituting this parameterization model into (3.43), we can write

$$
\mathbb{E}[e_i e_{i-\ell}^\top] = A_{i,\ell} + \sum_{s=1}^p \alpha_s(B_{i,\ell,s} + C_{i,\ell,s}),
\tag{3.45}
$$

where

$$
A_{i,\ell} := \Psi_{i,0}P_0\Psi_{i-\ell,0}^\top = \Theta_{i-1}A_{i-1,0}\Theta_{i-\ell-1}^\top,
\tag{3.46}
$$

$$
\begin{aligned}
B_{i,\ell,s} &:= \sum_{j=0}^{i-\ell-1}\Psi_{i,j+1}\Gamma Q^{(s)}\Gamma^\top\Psi_{i-\ell,j+1}^\top \\
&= \Theta_{i-1}B_{i-1,\ell,s}\Theta_{i-\ell-1}^\top + \Psi_{i,i-\ell}\Gamma Q^{(s)}\Gamma^\top,
\end{aligned}
\tag{3.47}
$$

$$
\begin{aligned}
C_{i,\ell,s} &:= \sum_{j=0}^{i-\ell-1}\Psi_{i,j+1}F_j K_j R^{(s)} K_j^\top F_j^\top \Psi_{i-\ell,j+1}^\top \\
&= \Theta_{i-1}C_{i-1,\ell,s}\Theta_{i-\ell-1}^\top + \Psi_{i,i-\ell}F_{i-1}K_{i-1}R^{(s)}K_{i-1}^\top F_{i-1}^\top.
\end{aligned}
\tag{3.48}
$$

Here, we have written these three matrices in recursive form using the fact that $\Psi_{i,j} = \Theta_{i-1}\Psi_{i-1,j}$ from (3.42).

With these formulas, we can deduce that

$$
\begin{aligned}
\mathbb{E}[d_i d_i^\top] &= H_i P_i H_i^\top + R \\
&= H_i A_{i,0} H_i^\top + \sum_{s=1}^p \alpha_s \Big(H_i(B_{i,0,s} + C_{i,0,s})H_i^\top + R^{(s)}\Big).
\end{aligned}
\tag{3.49}
$$

Similarly, the expectation of the innovation at different lags can be expressed as

$$
\begin{aligned}
\mathbb{E}[d_i d_{i-\ell}^\top] &= H_i \mathbb{E}[e_i e_{i-\ell}^\top] H_{i-\ell}^\top + H_i \mathbb{E}[e_i \zeta_{i-\ell}^\top] \\
&= H_i \mathbb{E}[e_i e_{i-\ell}^\top] H_{i-\ell}^\top - H_i \Psi_{i-1,i-\ell+1} F_{i-\ell} K_{i-\ell} R \delta_{\ell,1} \\
&= \sum_{s=1}^{p} \alpha_s \Big(H_i (B_{i,\ell,s} + C_{i,\ell,s}) H_{i-\ell}^\top - H_i \Psi_{i-1,i-\ell+1} F_{i-\ell} K_{i-\ell} R^{(s)} \delta_{\ell,1} \Big) \\
&\quad + H_i A_{i,\ell} H_{i-\ell}^\top,
\end{aligned}
\tag{3.50}
$$

where we have used (3.41) and the notation $\delta_{\ell,1}$ for terms that occur only at lag $L = 1$. Since we don't have access to the statistics $\mathbb{E}[d_i d_i^\top]$ and $\mathbb{E}[d_i d_{i-\ell}^\top]$, as in the Berry–Sauer method, we approximate (3.49) and (3.50) as

$$
d_i d_i^\top = H_i A_{i,0} H_i^\top + \sum_{s=1}^{p} \alpha_{s,i} \Big(H_i (B_{i,0,s} + C_{i,0,s}) H_i^\top + R^{(s)} \Big) + v_{i,0},
$$

$$
\begin{aligned}
d_i d_{i-\ell}^\top = H_i A_{i,\ell} H_{i-\ell}^\top + \sum_{s=1}^{p} \alpha_{s,i} \Big(& H_i (B_{i,\ell,s} + C_{i,\ell,s}) H_{i-\ell}^\top \\
& - H_i \Psi_{i-1,i-\ell+1} F_{i-\ell} K_{i-\ell} R^{(s)} \delta_{\ell,1} \Big) + v_{i,\ell}.
\end{aligned}
\tag{3.51}
$$

Here, we have replaced α_s by $\alpha_{s,i}$ to denote the estimate at time t_i. We added $v_{i,0}$ and $v_{i,\ell}$ to denote the errors in this approximation. The two equations in (3.51) represent another pseudo-observation model (an alternative to (3.37)) corresponding to the likelihood function $p(x_i | Q_i, R_i, \mathcal{Y}_i)$.

In compact form, we can write the pseudo-observation model in (3.51) as

$$
\sigma_{i,\ell} = \bar{\mathcal{H}}_{i,\ell} + \mathcal{H}_{i,\ell} \alpha_i + \eta_{i,\ell},
\tag{3.52}
$$

where

$$
\begin{aligned}
\sigma_{i,\ell} &:= \mathrm{vec}(d_i d_{i-\ell}^\top) \\
\alpha_i &= (\alpha_{1,i}, \ldots, \alpha_{p,i})^\top, \\
\bar{\mathcal{H}}_{i,\ell} &= \mathrm{vec}\Big(H_i A_{i,\ell} H_{i-\ell}^\top \Big), \\
\eta_{i,\ell} &= \mathrm{vec}(v_{i,\ell}),
\end{aligned}
$$

and the matrix $\mathcal{H}_{i,\ell}$, whose sth column is

$$
\begin{aligned}
&[\mathcal{H}_{i,\ell}]_s \\
&= \mathrm{vec}\Big(H_i (B_{i,\ell,s} + C_{i,\ell,s}) H_{i-\ell}^\top + R^{(s)} \delta_{\ell,0} - H_i \Psi_{i-1,i-\ell+1} F_{i-\ell} K_{i-\ell} R^{(s)} \delta_{\ell,1} \Big).
\end{aligned}
$$

Here, we have defined an ordering map, $\mathrm{vec} \colon \mathbb{R}^{m \times m} \to \mathbb{R}^{m^2}$, as

$$
\mathrm{vec}(A) = \Big(a_{11}, a_{21}, \ldots, a_{m1}, a_{12}, a_{22}, \ldots, a_{m2}, \ldots, a_{1m}, a_{2m}, \ldots, a_{mm} \Big)^\top \in \mathbb{R}^{m^2},
$$

for any $A \in \mathbb{R}^{m \times m}$.

The noise estimation method proposed by Belanger (1974) assumes that $\eta_{i,\ell} \sim \mathcal{N}(0, W_{i,\ell})$ are independent Gaussian noises such that,

$$W_{i,\ell} = \mathbb{E}[d_i d_i^\top]\mathbb{E}[d_{i-\ell} d_{i-\ell}^\top] + \mathbb{E}[d_i d_{i-\ell}^\top]^2 \delta_{\ell,0}, \qquad (3.53)$$

where $\delta_{\ell,0}$ is added to satisfy the independence requirement. In each time step, we will use the right-hand terms of (3.49) evaluated at the current estimate $\alpha_{s,i}^+$ to approximate,

$$\mathbb{E}[d_i d_i^\top] \approx H_i A_{i,0} H_i^\top + \sum_{s=1}^{p} \alpha_{s,i}^+ \Big(H_i(B_{i,0,s} + C_{i,0,s})H_i^\top + R^{(s)} \Big). \quad (3.54)$$

Having constructed the pseudo-observation model in (3.52), we apply Kalman filtering with a persistent dynamical model for the parameters $\alpha_i = \alpha_{i-1}$. In particular, let the observation model in (3.52) be defined over $\ell = 0, 1, \ldots, L$. Suppose that α_i^+ and S_i are, respectively, the mean and covariance estimates for α at time t_i, then we apply the Kalman filter in a sequential fashion for $\ell = 0, 1, \ldots, L$,

$$\begin{aligned} a_{\ell+1} &= a_\ell + C_{\ell+1}\mathcal{H}_{i,\ell}^\top W_{i,\ell}^{-1}(\sigma_{i,\ell} - \bar{\mathcal{H}}_{i,\ell} - \mathcal{H}_{i,\ell}a_\ell), \\ C_{\ell+1} &= C_\ell - C_\ell \mathcal{H}_{i,\ell}^\top (W_{i,\ell} + \mathcal{H}_{i,\ell} C_\ell \mathcal{H}_{i,\ell})^{-1} \mathcal{H}_{i,\ell} C_{i,\ell}, \end{aligned} \qquad (3.55)$$

starting from

$$\begin{aligned} a_0 &= \alpha_i^+, \\ C_0 &= S_i. \end{aligned}$$

At the end of the Lth filtering step, we set the new Kalman estimate for α as

$$\begin{aligned} \alpha_{i+1}^+ &= a_{L+1}, \\ S_{i+1} &= C_{L+1}. \end{aligned}$$

This concludes the secondary Bayesian update in (3.30).

To summarize, at each filtering time step t_i, a primary filter is implemented to estimate the state variable x_i, using the estimate α_i^+. In our numerical simulation below, we will use the ETKF as the primary filter. To update the parameters α, first construct the components of (3.52). Numerically, this requires a construction of Θ_{i-1} and $\Theta_{i-\ell-1}$ as defined in (3.42), which will be used to update (3.46)–(3.48). Subsequently, we compute $\sigma_{i,\ell}$, $\bar{\mathcal{H}}_{i,\ell}$, $\mathcal{H}_{i,\ell}$, and $W_{i,\ell}$. Then, we apply the Kalman filter starting from (α_i^+, S_i) in (3.55) to obtain a new statistical estimate $(\alpha_{i+1}^+, S_{i+1})$. For nonlinear problems, we use the ensemble of solutions from the primary filter to approximate F_i and H_i as in (3.39).

We should point out that the secondary filter in (3.55) is numerically quite demanding if m is large, since it involves inverting a matrix of size $m^2 \times m^2$. To avoid this expensive inversion, one can adopt the same strategy as in the Berry–Sauer method. That is, apply a running average over some least-squares solutions of the observation model in (3.52); this is indeed the approach proposed in Zhen & Harlim (2015). We should also remark that, with the pseudo-observation model in (3.52), it is possible to estimate only one of the noise covariances, either Q or R; all we have to do is insert the true value of α_s corresponding to the covariance matrix that is not estimated.

Now let's close this section with two numerical examples. The first one repeats the numerical experiment in Example 3.2 with Belanger's secondary Kalman filter. The second example is on a configuration in which the parameters associated with Q are not identifiable with the Berry–Sauer pseudo-observation model in (3.37).

Example 3.3   Recall that, in Example 3.2, we consider estimating $R = 0.05$, which is a scalar quantity, and $Q = \sigma^2 \Delta t\, \mathcal{I}_2 = 0.05\mathcal{I}_2$, where $\sigma = 1/\sqrt{2}$ and $\Delta t = 0.1$. In this case, there are $p = 2$ parameters to be estimated, $\alpha_1 = 0.05$ and $\alpha_2 = 0.05$, where we use the parameterization model in (3.44) with $Q^{(1)} = \mathcal{I}_2$, $Q^{(2)} = 0$, and $R^{(1)} = 0, R^{(2)} = 1$. We start the secondary filter with an arbitrary initial condition, $\alpha_0^+ = (1, 1)$ and $S_0 = \mathcal{I}_{m^2}$. Recall that the observations are the second component, v, of the triad model in (3.21) and the primary filter uses the ETKF with $K = 10$ ensemble members and a maximum lag parameter $L = 1$. With this noise estimation method, the filter estimates are slightly better, with RMSE = 0.3775 and spread = 0.3639, than the estimates obtained with the Berry–Sauer method in Example 3.2. Note that both the RMSE and the spread are computed by averaging over 8000 assimilation cycles, ignoring the first 2000 cycles. Again, in this case the RMSE and the spread are comparable, indicating that a relatively accurate second-order posterior statistical estimation has been obtained. In Figures 3.4 and 3.5, we show the qualitative estimates of the state variables and both of the parameters Q and σ.

Example 3.4   Recall that, with the Berry–Sauer method, the parameter σ is not identifiable if one observes the first component, u, of the triad model in (3.21). With the pseudo-observation model in (3.52), notice that the coefficients corresponding to $Q^{(s)}$, which are $HB_{i,\ell,s}H^\top$, are not always zero, even when $L = 1$. Now, let's conduct the parameter estimation with the observation model $H = (1, 0, 0)$,

$$y_i = Hx_i + \zeta_i = u_i + \zeta_i, \quad \zeta_i \sim \mathcal{N}(0, R),$$

where $R = 0.05$. First, let us consider the experiment where all of the deterministic parameters, $\theta = (\omega, \beta, \gamma, a)$, are known. We set $K = 10$ and lag $L = 1$ as before. In Figure 3.6, we show the qualitative estimates of the parameters Q and σ. For this numerical experiment, the state estimates are less accurate than the estimates that assimilate the second component, v, of the triad model in (3.21), with RMSE = 0.4365 and spread = 0.4612.

As a second experiment, we will simultaneously estimate θ together with σ and R. In this numerical experiment, the primary filter is the ETKF for the state-parameter augmented system as in (3.26), where we assume a persistent model, $\theta_{i+1} = g(\theta_i) = \theta_i$, for the parameters. For this experiment, we set $L = 4$ and use the same configuration as before. In Figures 3.7–3.9, we show the trajectories

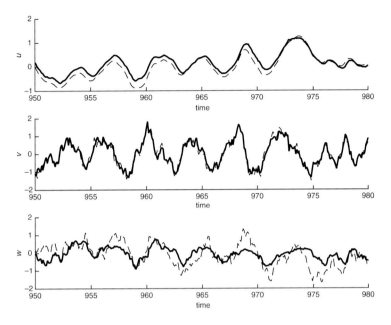

Figure 3.4 The ETKF with Belanger's estimation method: the primary filter mean estimates with $L = 1$ (solid), and the truth (dashes) at time interval $[950, 980]$. The filter estimates RMSE $= 0.3775$ and spread $= 0.3639$.

of the filter estimates. When the observations are only the first component of the triad model, the state and parameter estimation has RMSE $= 0.4245$ and spread $= 0.4623$. Notice that some of the parameters are not estimated accurately (see the black curves in Figures 3.7–3.9) since the state-parameter augmented approach in (3.26) is sensitive to initial conditions. For a fully observed system, $x = (u, v, w)$, the accuracy of both state and parameter estimation improves significantly, except for the parameter γ (see the gray curves in Figures 3.7–3.9), with RMSE $= 0.1146$ and spread $= 0.1165$.

We should note that more extensive comparisons between the two methods above and another scheme that merges these two, for various linear and nonlinear problems, were reported in Zhen & Harlim (2015).

3.3 Parameter Estimation of Reduced-Order Dynamics

One of the long-standing issues in modeling dynamical systems is how to construct a set of effective equations to capture the evolution of the quantity of interest. The main difficulty in this problem is that the variables of interest are typically low-dimensional components (or functions) of high-dimensional complex dynamical systems which are not fully understood. In almost all scientific disciplines, the key approach to representing the missing dynamics is with appropriate parameterization procedures. This is a nontrivial task in general. To

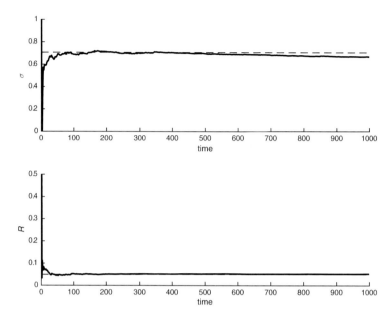

Figure 3.5 The ETKF with Belanger's estimation method: the secondary filter estimates for σ and R with $L = 1$ (solid), and the truth (dashes).

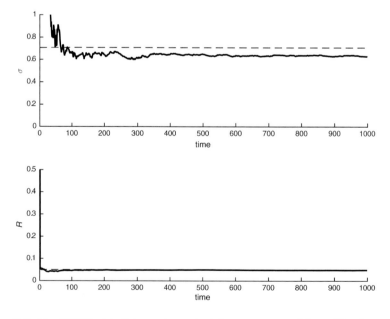

Figure 3.6 The ETKF with Belanger's method for estimation of (x, σ, R), observing the first component, u, of the triad model in (3.21). For this observation network, the parameter σ is not identifiable with the Berry–Sauer estimation method. In this illustration, we show the secondary filter estimates for σ and R with $L = 1$ (solid), and the truth (dashes).

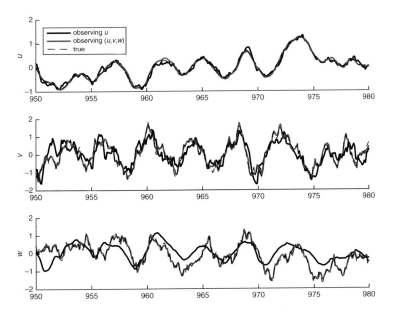

Figure 3.7 The ETKF with Belanger's method for estimation of (x, θ, σ, R). In this illustration, we show the primary filter estimates for x with $L = 4$ observing only u (black, solid) and observing the full components, $x = (u, v, w)$ (gray, solid). The true states are shown as dashes.

the best of the author's knowledge, there is no general way to construct reduced-order models. All existing methods are applicable only on a case-by-case basis. When the appropriate model is available, robust parameter estimation methods to achieve accurate statistical prediction are highly desirable. In this section, we illustrate the Mori–Zwanzig formalism (Mori 1965, Zwanzig 1973, 1961) as an idealistic concept to elucidate the difficulty in this problem. Subsequently, we will discuss a Markovian approximation for the generalized Langevin equation (GLE) derived from the Mori–Zwanzig formalism. Our main goal is to demonstrate the potential of the ETKF, implemented with Belanger's estimation scheme, as a parameter estimation method that produces statistically accurate reduced-order Markovian dynamics.

A general framework for constructing reduced-order models of complex dynamical systems is the Mori–Zwanzig projection formalism that was originally developed to model non-equilibrium processes in statistical mechanics. In a nutshell, this approach uses a projection operator, $\mathcal{P}$, to separate the quantities of interest from the remaining terms. In particular, consider a system with an initial value problem of the form

$$\dot{x} = f(x), \quad x(0) = z, \tag{3.56}$$

and an arbitrary observable $\varphi(z, t)$ that solves

$$\frac{\partial}{\partial t}\varphi(z, t) = \mathcal{L}\varphi(z, t), \tag{3.57}$$

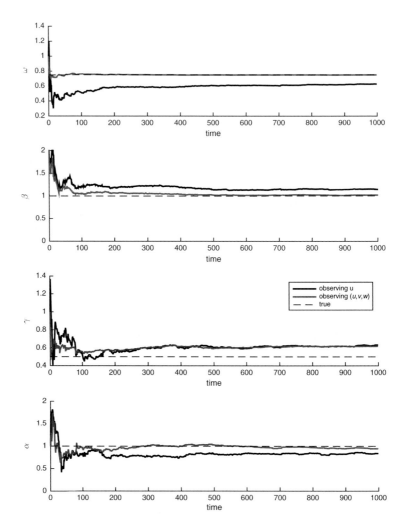

Figure 3.8 The ETKF with Belanger's method for estimation of (x, θ, σ, R). In this illustration, we show the primary filter estimates for $\theta = (\omega, \beta, \gamma, \alpha)$ with $L = 4$ observing only u (black, solid) and observing the full components, $x = (u, v, w)$ (gray, solid). The true parameters are shown as dashes.

where $\mathcal{L} = f(z) \cdot \nabla_z$. Formally, equation (3.57) is equivalent to $\varphi(z, t) = e^{t\mathcal{L}}\varphi(z, 0)$. We can rewrite (3.57) as

$$\frac{\partial}{\partial t}\varphi(z, t) = e^{t\mathcal{L}}\mathcal{L}\varphi(z, 0)$$
$$= e^{t\mathcal{L}}\mathcal{P}\mathcal{L}\varphi(z, 0) + e^{t\mathcal{L}}\mathcal{Q}\mathcal{L}\varphi(z, 0), \qquad (3.58)$$

where we have used the fact that $\mathcal{L}e^{t\mathcal{L}} = e^{t\mathcal{L}}\mathcal{L}$ and $\mathcal{Q} := \mathcal{I} - \mathcal{P}$. Let $w(z, t) = e^{t\mathcal{Q}\mathcal{L}}w(z, 0)$, then

$$\frac{\partial}{\partial t}w(z, t) = \mathcal{Q}\mathcal{L}w(z, t) = \mathcal{L}w(z, t) - \mathcal{P}\mathcal{L}w(z, t).$$

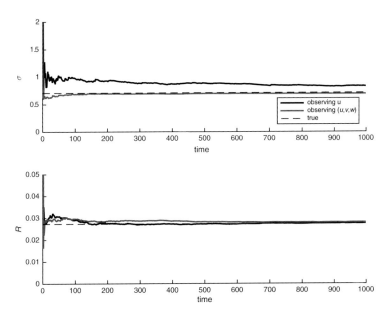

Figure 3.9 The ETKF with Belanger's method for estimation of (x, θ, σ, R). In this illustration, we show the secondary filter estimates for σ and R with $L = 4$ observing only u (black, solid) and observing the full components $x = (u, v, w)$ (gray, solid). The true parameters are shown as dashes.

Formally, this is equivalent to

$$e^{t\mathcal{Q}\mathcal{L}}w(z, 0) = e^{t\mathcal{L}}w(z, 0) - \int_0^t e^{(t-s)\mathcal{L}}\mathcal{P}\mathcal{L}e^{t\mathcal{Q}\mathcal{L}}w(z, 0)ds,$$

which is Dyson's formula (Morriss & Evans 1990),

$$e^{t\mathcal{L}} = \int_0^t e^{(t-s)\mathcal{L}}\mathcal{P}\mathcal{L}e^{t\mathcal{Q}\mathcal{L}}\, ds + e^{t\mathcal{Q}\mathcal{L}}.$$

Now let's apply this equation to $\mathcal{Q}\mathcal{L}\varphi(z, 0)$ and substitute it into (3.58), then we obtain a *generalized Langevin equation* (GLE),

$$\frac{\partial}{\partial t}\varphi(z, t) = e^{t\mathcal{L}}\mathcal{P}\mathcal{L}\varphi(z, 0) + \int_0^t e^{(t-s)\mathcal{L}}K(z, s)ds + \xi(z, t), \qquad (3.59)$$

where we have defined

$$\xi(z, t) = e^{t\mathcal{Q}\mathcal{L}}\mathcal{Q}\mathcal{L}\varphi(z, 0), \qquad (3.60)$$

$$K(z, t) = \mathcal{P}\mathcal{L}\xi(z, t). \qquad (3.61)$$

The first term in (3.59) is the Markovian term. The second term depends on φ at all times between 0 and t, so it incorporates the *memory effect* as a result of coarse-graining, The last term in (3.59) is referred to as the *orthogonal dynamics* and, if the initial condition z is random, then $\xi(t)$ is a stochastic forcing. We should point out that the GLE for the ODE in (3.56) is non-unique since there are different choices of the projection operator $\mathcal{P}$ (Mori 1965, Zwanzig 1973, Chorin et al. 2002). Note that the GLE in (3.59) is an exact representation of (3.57) since there is no approximation in any of these algebraic manipulations.

While solving the GLE in (3.59) directly is not much simpler than solving the full system in (3.56), since one has to estimate the orthogonal dynamics in (3.60) and the memory kernel function in (3.61), the GLE representation is conceptually useful for model reduction. As a concrete example, let's consider the model reduction for the nonlinear Schrödinger equation (NLS), which was considered in Chorin et al. (2000) and Harlim & Li (2015),

$$iu_t = -u_{xx} + |u|^2 u, \tag{3.62}$$

on a one-dimensional periodic domain $x \in [0, 2\pi]$. Here, the solutions of (3.62) can be described by the Fourier series

$$u(x, t) = \sum_{k \in \mathbb{Z}} u_k(t) e^{ikx}.$$

This turns the PDE into a set of ODEs for the Fourier modes $k \in \mathbb{Z}$,

$$\frac{d}{dt} u_k = -i \frac{\partial E}{\partial u_k^*}, \tag{3.63}$$

where

$$E = E_0 + E_1 = \sum_{k \in \mathbb{Z}} k^2 |u_k|^2 + \frac{1}{2} \sum_{k_1 \in \mathbb{Z}} \sum_{k_2 \in \mathbb{Z}} \sum_{k_3 \in \mathbb{Z}} u_{k_1} u_{k_2} u_{k_3}^* u_{k_1+k_2-k_3}^*.$$

Numerically, we can simulate the solutions of (3.63) with a pseudo-spectral method (Bao et al. 2003) on a finite wave number $|k| \leq N$.

Suppose we consider the zeroth Fourier component as an observable, that is, $u_0 = \varphi(\vec{u})$, where $\vec{u} = (u_k)_{k \in \mathbb{Z}}$. Our goal is to rewrite (3.63) in terms of u_0 with the projection operator $\mathcal{P} = \mathbb{E}[\cdot | u_0]$, where the expectation is defined with respect to the canonical Gibbs distribution $p_{eq}(\vec{u}) \propto e^{-\beta E(\vec{u})}$. Here the parameter β is a constant that is inversely proportional to the temperature. For low temperature, that is, when $\beta \gg 1$, this canonical distribution is approximately Gaussian, $p_{eq}(\vec{u}) \propto e^{-\beta E_0(\vec{u})}$, and we can apply the projection with respect to this density as suggested in Chorin et al. (2002). In this case, given initial condition $u_0(0) = z_0$, the Markovian term of the GLE in (3.59) becomes

$$e^{t\mathcal{L}} \mathcal{P} \mathcal{L} z_0 = \mathbb{E}\left[\frac{\partial E}{\partial u_0^*}(t) | u_0(t) \right] = -icu_0 - i|u_0|^2 u_0,$$

where c is a positive constant. One can also deduce the memory terms and the orthogonal dynamics such that

$$\frac{du_0}{dt} = -icu_0 - i|u_0|^2 u_0 + \int_0^t \kappa_0(t-\tau) u_0(\tau) d\tau$$

$$+ i \int_0^t \phi_0(t-\tau)|u_0(\tau)|^2 u_0(\tau) d\tau + \xi(t), \tag{3.64}$$

where κ_0 and ϕ_0 are complex-valued kernel functions with complicated expressions that are not important in our discussion here (see Chorin *et al.* (2000) for the complete derivation and a general model reduction with an arbitrary number of Fourier modes).

Again, we should point out that (3.64) is just a different representation of the zeroth mode of (3.63) with the projection operator $\mathcal{P}$ defined with respect to the conditional Gaussian density; in other words, (3.64) is not a reduced-order model of (3.63). With the representation in (3.64), it becomes clear that the important ingredient for achieving an accurate reduced-order model for the variable u_0 depends on how well we can approximate the memory and noise terms. In the following example, we review one systematic simple approach to approximate the memory and noise terms using a rational approximation.

Example 3.5   Here, we consider the following approximation (Harlim & Li 2015) on the first integral term in (3.64):

$$bf := \int_0^t \kappa_0(t - \tau)u_0(\tau)d\tau, \tag{3.65}$$

where $b \in \mathbb{C}$ is a parameter to be determined. First, taking the Laplace transform on (3.65), we arrive at

$$b\widetilde{f}(s) = \tilde{\kappa}_0(s)\tilde{u}_0(s), \tag{3.66}$$

where we denote by $\widetilde{h}$ the Laplace coefficient (defined in the frequency domain) of any function h that is locally integrable on $\mathbb{R}^+$.

Consider the following rational approximation on the kernel function:

$$\widetilde{\kappa}_0(s) \approx \frac{-|b|^2}{s - a}, \tag{3.67}$$

where $a \in \mathbb{C}$ is the second parameter to be determined. This particular form of the rational function is chosen to ensure the stability of the resulting parametric model, as we will explain below. In principle, these two coefficients, a and b, can be determined with Padé approximations (or more general rational approximations) of the exact kernel. Here, we will use the ETKF to determine those parameters. On converting (3.66) and (3.67) back to the time domain (via the inverse Laplace transform), we find that f satisfies a differential equation,

$$\dot{f} = af - b^*u_0(t), \quad f(0) = 0. \tag{3.68}$$

For the low-temperature case, one can neglect the second memory term in (3.64) that involves ψ_0, since this higher-order term is negligible.

With these approximations, we arrive at the following Markovian reduced-order model:

$$\begin{cases} \dot{x} = -icx - id|x|^2x + bf, \\ \dot{f} = af - b^*x + \sigma\dot{W}_f, \end{cases} \tag{3.69}$$

where we have replaced u_0 with x. This change of notation is to distinguish u_0, which is the solution of the truncated NLS in (3.63), from x, which is the solution of the reduced-order model in (3.69). In (3.69) we have also introduced two additional non-negative parameters c and d. In principle, these parameters can be determined from the Mori–Zwanzig reduction procedure as we saw above. However, since the derivation in Chorin *et al.* (2000) is with respect to the (conditional) Gaussian distribution, the resulting values for c and d may not be optimal. Therefore, we keep the form of the equations suggested by the Mori–Zwanzig formalism, but leave c and d as additional parameters, which will be determined using a filtering procedure. Also, we have introduced a white noise $\dot{W}_f$. When the second equation in (3.69) is analytically solved and subsequently substituted into the first equation, this white noise will become a colored-noise approximation to the random process $\xi(t)$. We should point out that the resulting reduced-order model is a Markovian system in the form of the physics-constrained regression model proposed in Majda & Harlim (2013); one can show that this Markovian model is geometrically ergodic when $\mathrm{Re}\{a\} < 0$.

Now let's estimate the parameters $\theta = \{a, b, c, d\}$, σ, and R, using the ETKF with Belanger's scheme discussed in Section 3.2, from noisy observations of the zeroth Fourier mode of the NLS in (3.63),

$$y_i = (u_0)_i + \zeta_i, \quad \zeta_i \sim \mathcal{N}(0, R),$$

where the true value of R is chosen to be 0.01. Here, the underlying truth is numerically solved with a pseudo-spectral method (Bao *et al.* 2003) with Strang's splitting method in time on a finite wave number $|k| \leq N$, where $N = 32$. We consider an observation time interval of $\Delta t = t_i - t_{i-1} = 0.02$. Once the parameters have been estimated, we compare the statistics of x of the reduced-order model in (3.69) and of u_0 which solves the truncated NLS model in (3.63). In Table 3.1, we compare the first four moments for the low-temperature case, $\beta = 10^4$; notice that the errors are on the order of 10^{-2}. Notice also the agreement of the estimates and the truth in terms of the marginal density and the autocorrelation function (see Figure 3.10). See Harlim & Li (2015) for a more comprehensive comparison for high-temperature cases, multidimensional rational approximation, and reduced-order models for multidimensional observables.

Note that many other methods by which to estimate the memory and noise terms in (3.59), have been proposed see, e.g., Chorin & Hald (2013) and the

Table 3.1 Comparison of the equilibrium statistics of $\mathrm{Re}(u_0)$

Statistics	Truth	Estimate
Mean	−0.0037	−0.0717
Variance	2.4018	2.4570
Skewness	0.0840	0.0658
Kurtosis	1.5071	1.5123

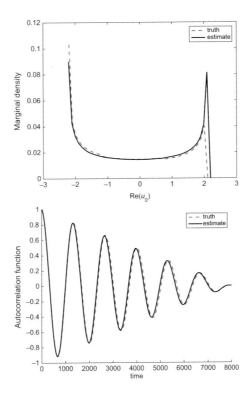

Figure 3.10 The marginal distribution (left) and the time correlation function (right) predicted by the reduced-order model in (3.69) for low temperature, $\beta = 10^4$, compared with the corresponding true statistics.

references therein. Alternatively, there are many other methods that were not directly designed to estimate the right-hand terms in (3.59), but do implicitly simulate these terms. For example, see O'Kane & Frederiksen (2010), Majda & Grooms (2014), Sapsis & Majda (2013), Gottwald *et al.* (2017), Majda & Qi (2016*a*, 2016*b*), and Lu *et al.* (2017), to name just a few.

4   Stochastic Spectral Methods

In this chapter, we discuss the spectral methods for representing stochastic processes; in particular, the so-called polynomial chaos expansion. The main goal of this introductory chapter is to discuss an elegant mathematical concept, namely representing random variables with basis functions of a weighted Hilbert space. This representation idea will serve as a foundation for the data-driven nonparametric modeling approach discussed in Chapter 6.

We begin by giving a brief review on orthogonal polynomials and making the connection to the polynomial chaos expansion. Subsequently, we discuss the weak polynomial chaos expansion. This is a method for representing general random variables with orthogonal polynomials corresponding to other basic random variables, assuming that the relationship between the two random variables is not known. Given the polynomial expansions for random variables, we discuss Galerkin, collocation, and spectral projection methods for approximating random fields associated with dynamical systems with random parameters. Since this approximation involves multidimensional integrals, we briefly review a sparse grid quadrature rule to facilitate efficient integration.

4.1   A Quick Review on Orthogonal Polynomials

Consider a weighted Hilbert space,

$$L^2(\mathcal{M}, p) = \left\{ f(x) : \int_{\mathcal{M}} |f(x)|^2 p(x) dx < \infty \right\},$$

that is, a complete normed vector space equipped with the induced norm $\|f\|_p = \sqrt{\langle f, f \rangle_p}$ defined with the inner product

$$\langle f, g \rangle_p = \int_{\mathcal{M}} f(x) g(x) p(x) dx. \tag{4.1}$$

Here, $p(x)$ is a non-negative weight function.

Definition 4.1   Let $\varphi_n(x) \in L^2(\mathcal{M}, p)$ be a polynomial of degree n, where $n \in \mathcal{N}$. Polynomials of the set $\{\varphi_n(x)\}_{n \in \mathcal{N}}$, where $\mathcal{N} = \{0, 1, 2, \ldots\}$ or $\mathcal{N} = \{0, 1, 2, \ldots, N\}$, are mutually orthogonal with respect to a weight function $p(x)$ if $\langle \varphi_n, \varphi_m \rangle_p = \|\varphi_n\|_p^2 \delta_{mn}$ for any $m, n \in \mathcal{N}$. Here δ_{mn} is the Kronecker delta function, which equals one when $m = n$ and zero otherwise.

It is not difficult to show that the orthogonal polynomials of the set $\{\varphi_n(x)\}_{n \in \mathcal{N}}$ are linearly independent.

Example 4.2 The Hermite polynomials are defined through the following recursive formula:

$$\varphi_0(x) = 1, \quad \varphi_1(x) = x,$$
$$\varphi_{n+1}(x) = x\varphi_n(x) - n\varphi_{n-1}(x), \quad n > 1.$$

One can show that the φ_n are orthogonal under the weighted inner product in (4.1), with weighting function $p(x) = (1/\sqrt{2\pi})e^{-x^2/2}$ defined on $\mathcal{M} = \mathbb{R}$ with the normalization constant $\langle \varphi_n, \varphi_n \rangle_p = n!$.

Example 4.3 The Legendre polynomials are defined through the following recursive formula:

$$\varphi_0(x) = 1, \quad \varphi_1(x) = x,$$
$$\varphi_{n+1}(x) = \frac{2n+1}{n+1}x\varphi_n(x) - \frac{n}{n+1}\varphi_{n-1}(x).$$

One can verify that the φ_n are orthogonal with respect to $p(x) = 1/2$ defined on $\mathcal{M} = [-1, 1]$ with the normalization constant $\langle \varphi_n, \varphi_n \rangle_p = 1/(2n+1)$.

In the two examples above, notice that, for the Hermite polynomials, the weighting function $p(x)$ is the density of the standard Gaussian distribution $\mathcal{N}(0, 1)$, whereas for the Legendre polynomials, the weighting function is the density of the uniform distribution $\mathcal{U}[-1, 1]$. From this observation, one can define a continuous random variable $X: \Omega \to \mathcal{M}$ with density function $p(x)$ (such that $p(x) > 0$ and $\int_{\mathcal{M}} p(x)dx = 1$), and denote the inner product in (4.1) as an expectation under density p,

$$\mathbb{E}[fg] = \langle f, g \rangle_p.$$

This notation also implies that $\mathbb{E}[f^2] = \|f\|_p^2$, so any function $f \in L^2(\mathcal{M}, p)$ has a finite second-order moment. Beyond the two examples above, we list in Table 4.1 other random variables whose orthogonal polynomials are known (see Xiu (2010) for details).

4.2 Polynomial Chaos Expansion

Polynomial chaos expansion, which is also known as the Wiener–Hermite expansion, was introduced by Norbert Wiener (1938) to approximate Gaussian random variables. Subsequently, Cameron & Martin (1947) proved the convergence of this expansion in the L^2 sense for any stochastic process with a finite second-order moment. Dongbin Xiu (2010), in his thesis work, generalized this idea to various continuous and discrete random variables using polynomials from the Askey scheme of hypergeometric orthogonal polynomials (listed in Table 4.1), and called it the *generalized polynomial chaos expansion*.

Table 4.1 A class of random variables with the corresponding orthogonal polynomials

Distribution	Polynomial	$\mathcal{M}$
Gaussian	Hermite	$\mathbb{R}$
Gamma	Laguerre	$[0, \infty)$
Beta	Jacobi	$[a, b]$
Uniform	Legendre	$[a, b]$
Poisson	Charlier	$\{0, 1, 2, \ldots\}$
Binomial	Krawtchouk	$\{0, 1, 2, \ldots, N\}$
Negative binomial	Meixner	$\{0, 1, 2, \ldots\}$
Hypergeometric	Hahn	$\{0, 1, 2, \ldots, N\}$

In practice, the key idea of polynomial chaos expansion is to represent any function $f(x) \in L^2(\mathcal{M}, p)$ as a linear combination of a finite number of orthogonal polynomial basis functions,

$$f_N(x) = \sum_{k=0}^{N} \hat{f}_k \varphi_k(x), \tag{4.2}$$

where the expansion coefficients

$$\hat{f}_k = \frac{\langle f, \varphi_k \rangle_p}{\langle \varphi_k, \varphi_k \rangle_p} \tag{4.3}$$

are the representation of $f(x)$ on the coordinate $\varphi_k(x)$. We should note that the coefficients $\hat{f}_k$ are obtained in the least-square sense, that is,

$$f_N = \arg \min_{g \in \mathcal{P}_N(\mathcal{M})} \|f - g\|_{L^2(\mathcal{M}, p)},$$

where $\mathcal{P}_N(\mathcal{M}) = \text{span}\{\varphi_0, \ldots, \varphi_N\}$. Here, the convergence of the polynomial expansion in (4.2) is in the mean-square sense, $\|f_N - f\|_{L^2(\mathcal{M}, p)} \to 0$ as $N \to \infty$, following the standard result from approximation theory.

For uncertainty quantification (UQ) applications, one is interested in computing the following statistics:

$$\mathbb{E}[f] = \int_{\mathcal{M}} f(x) p(x) dx, \tag{4.4}$$

$$\mathbb{E}[(f - \mathbb{E}[f])^2] = \int_{\mathcal{M}} (f(x) - \mathbb{E}[f])^2 p(x) dx. \tag{4.5}$$

Given the polynomial expansion in (4.2), a straightforward approximation to the mean statistic is given as follows:

$$\mathbb{E}[f] \approx \mathbb{E}[f_N] = \int_E f_N(x)p(x)dx$$

$$= \sum_{k=0}^{N} \hat{f}_k \int_{\mathcal{M}} \varphi_k(x)p(x)dx$$

$$= \sum_{k=0}^{N} \hat{f}_k \langle \varphi_k, 1 \rangle_p = \hat{f}_0, \tag{4.6}$$

using the fact that φ_k are orthogonal to $\varphi_0(x) = 1$ for $k > 0$. Similarly, by virtue of the orthogonality, one can approximate the second-order moment as

$$\mathbb{E}[f^2] \approx \mathbb{E}[f_N^2] = \sum_{i,j=0}^{N} \hat{f}_i \hat{f}_j \, \mathbb{E}[\varphi_i \varphi_j] = \sum_{i,j=0}^{N} \hat{f}_i \hat{f}_j \langle \varphi_i, \varphi_j \rangle_p = \sum_{i=0}^{N} \hat{f}_i^2 \|\varphi_i\|_p^2,$$

such that the variance can be approximated as

$$\mathbb{E}[(f - \mathbb{E}[f])^2] \approx \mathbb{E}[f_N^2] - \hat{f}_0^2 = \sum_{i=1}^{N} \hat{f}_i^2 \|\varphi_i\|_p^2. \tag{4.7}$$

Example 4.4   The uniform random variable Y on an arbitrary domain $[a, b]$ can be represented exactly as a linear combination of Legendre polynomials up to degree one that are defined on $[-1, 1]$. To see this, let $Y = \hat{u}_0 + \hat{u}_1 X$, Since $\mathbb{E}[Y] = (a+b)/2$ and $\text{Var}[Y] = (b-a)^2/12$, one can use the mean and variance formulas in (4.6) and (4.7) to show that $\hat{u}_0 = (a+b)/2$ and $\hat{u}_1 = (b-a)/2$.

4.2.1   Multidimensional Random Variables

Let $X = (X_1, \ldots, X_d)$ be a random vector with mutually independent components and distribution $F_X(x) = \prod_{i=1}^{d} F_{X_i}(x_i)$. Let $\{\varphi_k(X_i)\}_{k=0}^{N}$ be the set of univariate polynomial basis functions of X_i up to degree N. Define polynomial functions from a product of univariate basis functions

$$\Phi_{\mathbf{k}}(X) = \prod_{i=1}^{d} \varphi_{k_i}(X_i), \tag{4.8}$$

where the multi-index is defined as components of

$$\mathcal{J}_N = \left\{ \mathbf{k} = (k_1, \ldots, k_d) | k_i \in \{0, 1, 2, \ldots\}, |\mathbf{k}| = \sum k_i \leq N \right\}. \tag{4.9}$$

One can show that $\Phi_{\mathbf{k}}(X)$ forms an orthogonal basis of $L^2(\mathcal{M}^d, p_X)$, where $p_X(x_1, \ldots, x_d) = \prod_{i=1}^{d} p_{X_i}(x_i)$ denotes the joint density of X.

Then, for $f(x_1, \ldots, x_d) \in L^2(\mathcal{M}^d, p_X)$, we have

$$f_N(X) = \sum_{\mathbf{k} \in \mathcal{J}_N} \frac{\langle f, \Phi_{\mathbf{k}} \rangle_{p_X}}{\langle \Phi_{\mathbf{k}}, \Phi_{\mathbf{k}} \rangle_{p_X}} \Phi_{\mathbf{k}}(X),$$

which forms a set of polynomials $\mathcal{P}_N^d = \{f_N(X)\}$ whose dimension is $(N+d)!/$ $(N!d!)$. From the standard approximation theory, it is easy to verify that $f_N \overset{\text{m.s.}}{\to} f$ and $f_N = \arg\min_{g \in \mathcal{P}_N^d} \|f - g\|_{L^2(\mathcal{M}^d, p_X)}$.

4.2.2   Representing General Random Variables

In many applications, one may be interested in representing random variables other than those listed in Table 4.1 for which the corresponding polynomials are unknown. For example, the distributions of the solutions of nonlinear dynamical systems are almost always non-Gaussian (and will be different from those listed in Table 4.1). Therefore, a fair question is to what extent one can represent random variables $Y = f(X)$ in terms of the orthogonal polynomials corresponding to the random variable X. In the following simple example, we show a special case where the functional relation f that maps X to Y is known. In the next section, we will consider the case where the functional relation is unknown.

Example 4.5 Suppose $Y = f(Z) = e^Z$, where $Z \sim \mathcal{N}(\mu, \sigma^2)$ is a Gaussian random variable. The distribution of Y is lognormal with a support on the nonnegative axis. Let $X \sim \mathcal{N}(0, 1)$ be the standard Gaussian random variable. Since $Z = \mu + \sigma X$, one can write $Y = e^Z = e^{\mu + \sigma X}$. Let's represent Y in terms of Hermite polynomials $\varphi_k(x) \in L^2(\mathbb{R}, p_X)$. Note that, since

$$\hat{f}_0 = \int_{\mathbb{R}} e^{\mu + \sigma x} \frac{e^{-x^2/2}}{\sqrt{2\pi}} \, dx = e^{\mu + \frac{\sigma^2}{2}},$$

$$\hat{f}_1 = \int_{\mathbb{R}} e^{\mu + \sigma x} x \frac{e^{-x^2/2}}{\sqrt{2\pi}} \, dx = \sigma e^{\mu + \frac{\sigma^2}{2}},$$

$$\vdots$$

$$\hat{f}_k = \frac{1}{k!} \int_{\mathbb{R}} e^{\mu + \sigma x} \varphi_k(x) \frac{e^{-x^2/2}}{\sqrt{2\pi}} \, dx = \frac{\sigma^k}{k!} e^{\mu + \frac{\sigma^2}{2}},$$

we have

$$Y_N(X) = e^{\mu + \frac{\sigma^2}{2}} \sum_{k=0}^{N} \frac{\sigma^k}{k!} \varphi_k(X)$$

as an approximation to Y.

Figure 4.1 shows the numerical approximations of the density of the lognormal distribution Y with $\mu = 1$ and $\sigma = 0.2$ for various N. Notice the significant improvement on going from $N = 1$ to $N = 2$ and negligible improvement beyond the quadratic approximations, Y_2. Here, the plots of the density estimates are smoothed using a kernel density estimation.

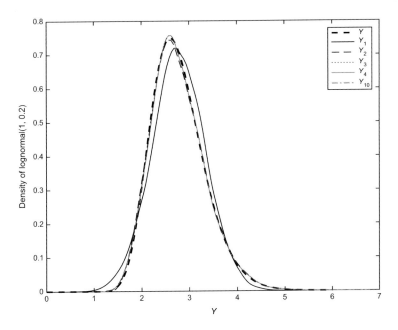

Figure 4.1 Approximation of the density of Y, for a lognormal distribution, with Hermite polynomials of degree N, Y_N. The plots of these densities are smoothed using a kernel density estimation.

4.3   The Weak Polynomial Chaos Approximation

In the previous example, notice that one needs to know f to determine the coefficients

$$\hat{f}_k = \frac{\langle f, \varphi_k \rangle_p}{\langle \varphi_k, \varphi_k \rangle_p}.$$

In this section we consider representing a random variable $Y = f(X)$ in terms of the orthogonal polynomial expansion of a random variable X without knowing f. One way to circumvent this issue is to use the (cumulative) distribution functions. The key idea exploits the fact that the cumulative distribution function of Y,

$$F_Y(y) = \int_{-\infty}^{y} p_Y(s)ds,$$

maps Y to U, a uniformly distributed random variable on $[0, 1]$. The inverse function, F_Y^{-1}, which is defined as $F_Y^{-1}(u) = \inf\{y|F_Y(y) \geq u, u \in [0, 1]\}$ since F_Y is not strictly increasing, maps the uniform random variable U to Y. To clarify these assertions, let $U = F_Y(Y)$, then the distribution of U is given as

$$F_U(u) = \mathbb{P}(U \leq u) = \mathbb{P}(F_Y(Y) \leq u) = \mathbb{P}(Y \leq F_Y^{-1}(u))$$

$$= F_Y(F_Y^{-1}(u)) = u = \int_0^u ds,$$

which confirms that U is uniform on $[0,1]$ since $p_U(u) = 1$. Conversely, if U is a uniform distribution on $[0,1]$, then the distribution of the following random variable $F_Y^{-1}(U)$ is the distribution of Y:

$$F_{F_Y^{-1}(U)}(y) = \mathbb{P}(F_Y^{-1}(U) \leq y) = \mathbb{P}(U \leq F_Y(y)) = \int_0^{F_Y(y)} ds = F_Y(y).$$

This identity is fundamental to the inverse sampling theory.

In our application below, we use these facts and approximate $y = f(x)$ with $y = F_Y^{-1}(u) = F_Y^{-1}(F_X(x))$ such that the coefficients of the representation of $y = f(x)$ in terms of the polynomials of X are given as follows:

$$\hat{f}_k = \frac{1}{\gamma_k} \int_{\mathcal{M}} f(x)\varphi_k(x)p_X(x)dx$$

$$\approx \frac{1}{\gamma_k} \int_{\mathcal{M}} F_Y^{-1}(F_X(x))\varphi_k(x)p_X(x)dx, \qquad (4.10)$$

where $\gamma_k = \langle \varphi_k, \varphi_k \rangle_{p_X} = \int_{\mathcal{M}} \varphi_k(x)^2 p_X(x)dx$. With this approximation, the polynomial expansion converges only in a weak sense, as in the following theorem.

Theorem 4.6 *Let X and Y be random variables with distribution functions $F_X(x)$ and $F_Y(y)$, respectively. Assume that $Y \in L^2(\mathcal{Y}, p_Y)$ and $X \in L^2(\mathcal{M}, p_X)$. Also, let $\{\varphi_n(x)\}_{n \in \mathcal{N}}$ be the PC basis functions of $L^2(\mathcal{M}, p_X)$. Let*

$$Y_N(X) = \sum_{k=0}^N \hat{f}_k \varphi_k(X), \qquad (4.11)$$

where the coefficients $\hat{f}_k$ are given by (4.10). Then $Y_N \xrightarrow{\mathrm{d}} Y$ as $N \to \infty$.

Proof   Let $\tilde{Y} := G(X) = F_Y^{-1}(F_X(X))$. First, notice that the distribution of $\tilde{Y}$ and that of Y are the same, that is,

$$F_{\tilde{Y}}(y) = \mathbb{P}(\tilde{Y} \leq y) = \mathbb{P}(F_Y^{-1}(U) \leq y) = \mathbb{P}(U \leq F_Y(y)) = \int_0^{F_Y(y)} du = F_Y(y),$$

and we denote this fact as $Y \stackrel{\mathrm{d}}{=} \tilde{Y}$. Furthermore,

$$\mathbb{E}[\tilde{Y}^2] = \int_{\mathcal{Y}} y^2 p_Y(y)dy$$

$$= \int_0^1 (F_Y^{-1}(u))^2 \, du$$

$$= \int_{\mathcal{M}} (F_Y^{-1}(F_X(x)))^2 p_X(x)dx$$

$$= \int_{\mathcal{M}} G(x)^2 p_X(x)dx < \infty,$$

where the second equality is due to the transformation $u = F_Y(y)$ which maps Y to the uniform distribution $U[0,1]$; here, we denote $du = dF_Y(y) = p_Y(y)dy$. The third equality is due to the transformation $u = F_X(x)$, and the bounded integral follows from the fact that $Y \in L^2(\mathcal{Y}, p_Y)$. So far, what we have shown is that $\tilde{Y} = G(X) \in L^2(\mathcal{M}, p_X)$. From approximation theory, we have that $Y_N \overset{\text{m.s.}}{\to} \tilde{Y}$. By the Chebyshev inequality, we have $Y_N \overset{\text{p}}{\to} \tilde{Y}$, which also implies that $Y_N \overset{\text{d}}{\to} \tilde{Y}$ (see Theorem A.26 in Appendix A). Since $Y \overset{\text{d}}{=} \tilde{Y}$, the proof is complete. □

Since the polynomial expansion Y_N in (4.11) converges only in a weak sense to Y as $N \to \infty$, we refer to this expansion as weak generalized polynomial chaos (Xiu 2010). In the following example, we consider approximating a beta distribution Y in terms of Hermite polynomials of random variables X.

Example 4.7   Let $Y \sim B(\alpha, \beta)$ be a beta distribution with density

$$p_Y(y) \propto (1 - y)^\alpha (1 + y)^\beta.$$

We will consider approximating Y in terms of Hermite polynomials of $X \sim \mathcal{N}(0, 1)$. Numerically, we use the standard Gauss–Kronrod quadrature MATLAB function `quadgk.m` to approximate these coefficients:

$$\hat{f}_k \approx \frac{1}{\gamma_k} \int_{\mathcal{M}} F_Y^{-1}(F_X(x)) \varphi_k(X) p_X(x) dx = \frac{1}{\gamma_k} \int_0^1 F_Y^{-1}(u) \varphi_k(F_X^{-1}(u)) du.$$

In our numerical example, we also use the standard MATLAB library for an inverse of cumulative distribution functions, `icdf.m`. In Figure 4.2, we show the numerical approximation of the beta distribution with $\alpha = 0$ and $\beta = 2$ by Hermite polynomials of degree $N = 1, 2, 3, 10$. Notice that the approximation improves as N increases.

To conclude this section, we give a representation for $Y = f(X)$, where the components of $X = (X_1, \ldots, X_d)$ are independent random variables $X_i \colon \Omega \to \mathcal{M}$. Let $\Phi_{\mathbf{k}}(X)$ be the orthogonal polynomials as defined in (4.8). In this case, notice that, both in strong and in weak polynomial expansions, we represent the random variable Y as

$$Y = f(X) = \sum_{\mathbf{k}} \hat{f}_{\mathbf{k}} \Phi_{\mathbf{k}}(X), \tag{4.12}$$

where the only difference is that the coefficients $\hat{f}_{\mathbf{k}}$ are defined as in (4.3) for strong expansion and as in (4.10) for weak expansion. So, when f is unknown or when the orthogonal polynomials corresponding to Y are not known, we have freedom in choosing X (or $\Phi_{\mathbf{k}}(X)$). In applications, we typically will choose X to be random variables with known orthogonal polynomials such as those listed in Table 4.1. In the remainder of this chapter, we will adopt the notation in (4.12) for representing random fields.

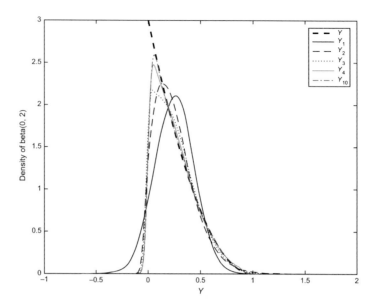

Figure 4.2 Approximation of the density of Y, beta distribution with $\alpha = 0$ and $\beta = 2$, with Hermite polynomials of degree N, Y_N. The plots of these densities are smoothed using a kernel density estimation.

4.4   The Stochastic Galerkin Method

Let $x \in \mathcal{X}$ and $t \geq 0$ denote the spatial and temporal variables, respectively. Let Z be a multivariate random variable. Consider a random field $u(x, t, Z)$ that solves the following dynamical system:

$$\partial_t u(x, t, Z) = \mathcal{L}[u(x, t, Z), Z], \tag{4.13}$$

$$\mathcal{B}u(y, t, Z) = g(t, Z), \qquad y \in \partial\mathcal{X}, \tag{4.14}$$

$$u(x, 0, Z) = u_0(x, Z). \tag{4.15}$$

Here, $\mathcal{L}$ denotes a random nonlinear differential operator of arbitrary order with respect to x. The randomness is due to its dependence on Z. Essentially, equation (4.13) is a time-dependent PDE with random parameters. If u and $\mathcal{L}$ do not depend on x, then (4.13) reduces to an ODE with random parameters. Here, we also allow for uncertainties in the boundary and initial conditions by having g and u_0, respectively, be random fields. In (4.14), $\mathcal{B}$ denotes a linear differential operator.

Consider approximating a random field $u(x, t, Z)$ with a finite number of orthogonal polynomials $\{\Phi_{\mathbf{k}}(Y)\}_{\mathbf{k} \in \mathcal{J}_N}$ corresponding to an independent multivariate random variable $Y = (Y_1, \ldots, Y_d)$, where the function $Z(Y)$ may or may not be known. As we discussed before, if $Z(Y)$ is known, then one can apply the strong polynomial expansion. Otherwise, one can use the weak polynomial expansion. In particular,

$$u(x, t, Z(Y)) \approx u_N(x, t, Y) = \sum_{\mathbf{k} \in \mathcal{J}_N} \hat{u}_{\mathbf{k}}(x, t) \Phi_{\mathbf{k}}(Y). \qquad (4.16)$$

Here, the multi-index $\mathbf{k} \in \mathcal{J}_N$ means that the highest order of $\Phi_{\mathbf{k}}$ is N, as defined in (4.9). To simplify the notation, we also denote $\gamma_{\mathbf{k}} = \langle \Phi_{\mathbf{k}}, \Phi_{\mathbf{k}} \rangle_{p_Y}$.

The essence of the Galerkin method is to specify the coefficients $\hat{u}_{\mathbf{k}}(x, t)$ such that the residual in approximating the solution of (4.13) with (4.16) is orthogonal to the basis function $\Phi_{\mathbf{k}}(Y)$ under the inner product defined for $L^2(\mathcal{M}^d, p_Y)$, that is,

$$\langle \partial_t u_N(x, t, \cdot) - \mathcal{L}[u_N(x, t, \cdot), \cdot], \Phi_{\mathbf{k}} \rangle_{p_Y} = 0,$$

which yields a system of coupled PDEs for the coefficients $\hat{u}_{\mathbf{k}}$,

$$\partial_t \hat{u}_{\mathbf{k}}(x, t) = \frac{1}{\gamma_{\mathbf{k}}} \left\langle \mathcal{L}[\sum_{\mathbf{j} \in \mathcal{J}_N} \hat{u}_{\mathbf{j}}(x, t) \Phi_{\mathbf{j}}, \cdot], \Phi_{\mathbf{k}} \right\rangle_{p_Y}, \qquad (4.17)$$

where the stochastic terms are averaged by the inner product operation and we have simplified the time derivative term using the linearity of ∂_t and the orthogonality of $\Phi_{\mathbf{k}}(Y)$. We also impose the orthogonality condition on the boundary and initial conditions (4.14), (4.15), respectively,

$$\left\langle \mathcal{B}[\sum_{\mathbf{j} \in \mathcal{J}_N} \hat{u}_{\mathbf{j}}(y, t) \Phi_{\mathbf{j}}], \Phi_{\mathbf{k}} \right\rangle_{p_Y} = \langle g(t, \cdot), \Phi_{\mathbf{k}} \rangle_{p_Y}, \quad y \in \partial \mathcal{X},$$

$$\left\langle \sum_{\mathbf{j} \in \mathcal{J}_N} \hat{u}_{\mathbf{j}}(x, 0) \Phi_{\mathbf{j}}, \Phi_{\mathbf{k}} \right\rangle_{p_Y} = \langle u_0(x, \cdot), \Phi_{\mathbf{k}} \rangle_{p_Y},$$

which can be simplified to

$$\mathcal{B}\hat{u}_{\mathbf{k}}(y, t) = \frac{1}{\gamma_{\mathbf{k}}} \langle g(t, \cdot), \Phi_{\mathbf{k}} \rangle_{p_Y}, \qquad y \in \partial \mathcal{X}, \qquad (4.18)$$

$$\hat{u}_{\mathbf{k}}(x, 0) = \frac{1}{\gamma_{\mathbf{k}}} \langle u_0(x, \cdot), \Phi_{\mathbf{k}} \rangle_{p_Y}, \qquad (4.19)$$

using the linearity of $\mathcal{B}$ and the orthogonality of $\Phi_{\mathbf{k}}$. Thus, one can solve the system of coupled PDEs in (4.17) with the boundary and initial conditions in (4.18) and (4.19), respectively, with appropriate PDE solvers. In most applications, one needs to approximate the inner products in (4.17), (4.18), or (4.19) with an appropriate numerical integration method such as the quadrature rule.

Below, we will give two examples. The first is a scalar PDE with a random coefficient, and the second is a system of ODEs with two random coefficients.

Example 4.8 Consider a one-dimensional heat equation on an isolated one-dimensional domain $[0, 1]$ with a scalar stochastic coefficient,

$$u_t = Z u_{xx},$$
$$u(0, t, Z) = u(1, t, Z) = 0,$$
$$u(x, 0, Z) = \sin^2(2\pi x),$$

where Z is a uniformly distributed random variable on $\mathcal{M} = [0.1, 1.9]$. First, let $Z(Y) = 1 + 0.9Y$, where Y is a uniform distribution on $[-1, 1]$. Now, let's approximate the solutions

$$u(x, t, Z(Y)) \approx u_N(x, t, Y) = \sum_{j=0}^{N} \hat{u}_j(x, t)\varphi_j(Y),$$

where we used the single-index notation since the random variable Y is one-dimensional, $d = 1$. Applying the Galerkin projection, we obtain

$$\partial_t \hat{u}_i = \frac{1}{\gamma_i} \sum_{j=0}^{N} \langle (1 + 0.9Y)\varphi_j, \varphi_i \rangle_{p_Y} \, \partial_{xx} \hat{u}_j,$$

$$= \frac{1}{\gamma_i} \sum_{j=0}^{N} (\gamma_i \delta_{i,j} + 0.9 \langle \varphi_1 \varphi_j, \varphi_i \rangle_{p_Y}) \partial_{xx} \hat{u}_j,$$

where we have used the orthogonality condition, $\langle \varphi_j, \varphi_i \rangle_{p_Y} = \gamma_i \delta_{i,j}$, and represented the random variable Y by a Legendre polynomial of degree one, φ_1.

In compact form, we can write this system of $(N + 1)$-dimensional PDEs as

$$\partial_t \vec{u} = A\vec{u}_{xx},$$

where $\vec{u} = (\hat{u}_0, \ldots, \hat{u}_N)^\top \in \mathbb{R}^{N+1}$ and $A_{ij} = \delta_{i,j} + (0.9/\gamma_i)\langle \varphi_1 \varphi_j, \varphi_i \rangle_{p_Y}$. On projecting both the boundary conditions and the initial conditions, we obtain

$$\hat{u}_i(0, t) = \hat{u}_i(1, t) = 0,$$
$$\hat{u}_i(x, 0) = \sin^2(2\pi x)\delta_{i,0},$$

for all $i = 0, \ldots, N$.

Consider a numerical approximation with the backward time difference and the spatial Crank–Nicolson schemes. In particular, let $\vec{w}_{m,n} \approx \vec{u}(x_m, t_n)$, where $x_m = m \, \Delta x$, with $m = 0, 1, \ldots, M = 1/\Delta x$, and $t_n = n \, \Delta t$,

$$\frac{\vec{w}_{m,n} - \vec{w}_{m,n-1}}{\Delta t} = \frac{1}{2} A \frac{\vec{w}_{m+1,n} - 2\vec{w}_{m,n} + \vec{w}_{m-1,n}}{\Delta x^2}$$
$$+ \frac{1}{2} A \frac{\vec{w}_{m+1,n-1} - 2\vec{w}_{m,n-1} + \vec{w}_{m-1,n-1}}{\Delta x^2},$$

or

$$-\tilde{A}\vec{w}_{m+1,n} + 2(\mathcal{I} + \tilde{A})\vec{w}_{m,n} - \tilde{A}\vec{w}_{m-1,n} = \tilde{A}\vec{w}_{m+1,n-1} + 2(\mathcal{I} - \tilde{A})\vec{w}_{m,n-1}$$
$$+ \tilde{A}\vec{w}_{m-1,n-1}, \qquad (4.20)$$

where $\tilde{A} = (\Delta t/\Delta x^2)A$. Let $\vec{v}_n = (\vec{w}_{1,n}^\top, \ldots, \vec{w}_{M-1,n}^\top)^\top \in \mathbb{R}^{(M-1)(N+1)}$ be a column vector and $\vec{b}_n = ((\tilde{A}\vec{w}_{0,n})^\top, 0, \ldots, 0, (\tilde{A}\vec{w}_{M,n})^\top)^\top \in \mathbb{R}^{(M-1)(N+1)}$, then (4.20) can be rewritten as

$$\vec{v}_n = B^{-1}(C\vec{v}_{n-1} + \vec{b}_n + \vec{b}_{n-1}),$$

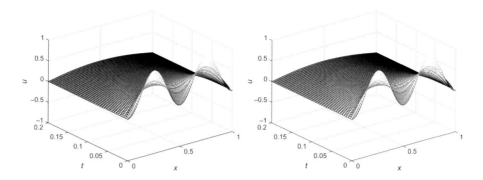

Figure 4.3 Mean of the solutions from the Galerkin approximation (left) and the Monte Carlo estimate (right).

where

$$B = \begin{pmatrix} 2(\mathcal{I} + \tilde{A}) & -\tilde{A} & & \\ -\tilde{A} & 2(\mathcal{I} + \tilde{A}) & -\tilde{A} & \\ & -\tilde{A} & 2(\mathcal{I} + \tilde{A}) & -\tilde{A} \\ & & \ddots & \ddots & \ddots \end{pmatrix},$$

$$C = \begin{pmatrix} 2(\mathcal{I} - \tilde{A}) & \tilde{A} & & \\ \tilde{A} & 2(\mathcal{I} - \tilde{A}) & \tilde{A} & \\ & \tilde{A} & 2(\mathcal{I} - \tilde{A}) & \tilde{A} \\ & & \ddots & \ddots & \ddots \end{pmatrix}.$$

In Figure 4.3, we show the mean estimates from the Monte Carlo simulations and the Galerkin approximation. Here, the Monte Carlo average is taken over 10,000 random samples. On the other hand, the Galerkin solutions are implemented with $N = 20$ and the coefficients in A are computed using the Clenshaw–Curtis quadrature rule with $R = 2^{10} + 1$ nodes to ensure its accuracy (see Section 4.5.1 for a detailed discussion of the quadrature rule). Numerically, we apply the Crank–Nicolson scheme in (4.20) with $\Delta x = 0.01$ and $\Delta t = 0.005$. In Figure 4.4, we show the evolution of the mean and a standard deviation error of the solutions at spatial location $x = 1/4$, $u(1/4, t)$. Notice that the Galerkin estimates agree with the Monte Carlo estimates.

Example 4.9 Consider a system of the J-dimensional Lorenz-96 model (Lorenz 1996) with two random parameters,

$$\frac{du_j}{dt} = u_{j-1}(u_{j+1} - u_{j-2}) - Z_1 u_j + Z_2, \qquad j = 1, \ldots, J,$$

$$u_j(0) = u_{j,0} \tag{4.21}$$

on a periodic domain, that is, $u_{j+J} = u_j$, and set $J = 40$. Here, the two independent random parameters are $Z_1 \sim U[0.8, 1.2]$ and $Z_2 \sim U[7, 9]$. First, let's represent these random variables in terms of the uniformly distributed random

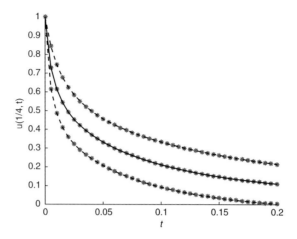

Figure 4.4 The mean plus/minus one standard deviation of $u(1/4, t)$. Galerkin (asterisks); Monte Carlo (black dashes).

variables Y_i on $[-1, 1]$, that is,

$$(Z_1, Z_2) = Z(Y) = (1 + 0.2Y_1, 8 + Y_2).$$

We will consider solutions of the following form:

$$u_j(t, Z(Y)) = \sum_{\mathbf{k}} \hat{u}_{j,\mathbf{k}}(t) \Phi_{\mathbf{k}}(Y),$$

where $\Phi_{\mathbf{k}}(Y) = \varphi_{k_1}(Y_1)\varphi_{k_2}(Y_2)$ is the product of two univariate Legendre polynomials, φ_{k_j}. Here, $\mathbf{k} = (k_1, k_2)$ is a multi-index for the two-dimensional problem, and the summation is defined over the set $\mathcal{J}_N = \{(k_1, k_2) | k_i \in \{0\} \cup \mathbb{Z}^+, k_1 + k_2 \leq N\}$. Let the number of basis functions be denoted by $P = \text{Card}(\mathcal{J}_N) = (N + 2)!/(N!2!)$. To simplify the notation below, we define,

$$e_{ijk} = \langle \varphi_i, \varphi_j \varphi_k \rangle_{p_Y},$$

which will occur quite often.

The Galerkin projection of each term on the right-hand side of (4.21) is

$$\langle \Phi_{\mathbf{j}}, \sum_{\mathbf{i},\mathbf{k}} \hat{u}_{j-1,\mathbf{i}} \hat{u}_{j+1,\mathbf{k}} \Phi_{\mathbf{i}} \Phi_{\mathbf{k}} \rangle_{p_Y} = \sum_{\mathbf{i},\mathbf{k}} e_{i_1 j_1 k_1} e_{i_2 j_2 k_2} \hat{u}_{j-1,\mathbf{i}} \hat{u}_{j+1,\mathbf{k}},$$

$$\langle \Phi_{\mathbf{j}}, -\sum_{\mathbf{i},\mathbf{k}} \hat{u}_{j-1,\mathbf{i}} \hat{u}_{j-2,\mathbf{k}} \Phi_{\mathbf{i}} \Phi_{\mathbf{k}} \rangle_{p_Y} = -\sum_{\mathbf{i},\mathbf{k}} e_{i_1 j_1 k_1} e_{i_2 j_2 k_2} \hat{u}_{j-1,\mathbf{i}} \hat{u}_{j-2,\mathbf{k}},$$

$$\langle \Phi_{\mathbf{j}}, -(1 + .2Y_1) \sum_{\mathbf{k}} \hat{u}_{j,\mathbf{k}} \Phi_{\mathbf{k}} \rangle_{p_Y} = -\sum_{\mathbf{k}} (\gamma_{\mathbf{j}} \delta_{\mathbf{j},\mathbf{k}} + .2 e_{1 j_1 k_1} \gamma_{j_2} \delta_{j_2, k_2}) \hat{u}_{j,\mathbf{k}},$$

$$\langle \Phi_{\mathbf{j}}, 8 + Y_2 \rangle_{p_Y} = 8 \delta_{\mathbf{j},\mathbf{0}} + \gamma_1 \delta_{j_1,0} \delta_{j_2,1}.$$

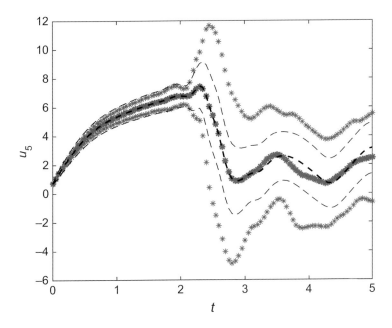

Figure 4.5 The Mean plus/minus one standard deviation of $u_5(t)$. Galerkin (asterisks); Monte Carlo (black dashes).

By collecting all these terms, we obtain a deterministic system of coupled $J \times P$ ODEs,

$$\frac{d}{dt}\hat{u}_{j,\mathbf{j}} = \frac{1}{\gamma_{\mathbf{j}}} \sum_{\mathbf{i},\mathbf{k}} e_{i_1 j_1 k_1} e_{i_2 j_2 k_2} \hat{u}_{j-1,\mathbf{i}}(\hat{u}_{j+1,\mathbf{k}} - \hat{u}_{j-2,\mathbf{k}})$$

$$- \sum_{\mathbf{k}} \left(\delta_{\mathbf{j},\mathbf{k}} + \frac{e_{1 j_1 k_1}}{5 \gamma_{j_1}} \delta_{j_2,k_2} \right) \hat{u}_{j,\mathbf{k}} + \frac{8}{\gamma_{\mathbf{j}}} \delta_{\mathbf{j},\mathbf{0}} + \frac{\gamma_1}{\gamma_{\mathbf{j}}} \delta_{j_1,0} \delta_{j_2,1}, \quad (4.22)$$

with initial conditions

$$\hat{u}_{j,\mathbf{j}} = \frac{u_{j,0}}{\gamma_{\mathbf{j}}} \delta_{\mathbf{j},\mathbf{0}}$$

for $j = 1, \ldots, J$ and $\mathbf{j} \in \mathcal{J}_N$.

In Figure 4.5, we compare the mean and a one standard deviation error for the fifth component, u_5, obtained from the Monte Carlo simulation and from solving the system of ODEs in (4.22). The Monte Carlo average is over 10,000 samples while the Galerkin approximation is solved with expansion up to order $N = 15$. In this case, the full system is already large, $J \times P = 40 \times 136 = 5440$. Here, the mean estimates agree up to time $t = 3$, while the variance estimates agree only up to time $t = 2$. For longer times, the Galerkin estimates for the variance statistic are larger than the Monte Carlo estimates.

We have seen that the Galerkin method transforms a system of random differential equations into a system of deterministic differential equations for the coefficients $\hat{u}_{\mathbf{k}}$. The resulting deterministic system, however, is P times larger than the original system, where P denotes the total number of basis functions in the Galerkin expansion, and has more complicated expressions. Although Galerkin expansion ensures that the errors are orthogonal to the space spanned by the orthogonal polynomials, this approach may not be easily implemented in large-scale applications and can be quite expensive when higher-order expansions are used for accurate estimations. This *intrusive* nature, which requires one to derive a new system of differential equations, is not appealing in practical applications.

4.5   The Stochastic Collocation Method

In this section, we discuss a *non-intrusive* method, which does not formulate a new system of differential equations. To simplify the discussion, let's illustrate the collocation method by solving the following random dynamical system:

$$\frac{d}{dt}u(t,Z) = f(u(t,Z),Z),$$
$$u(0,Z) = u_0(Z).$$

Assume that the solutions of this dynamical system can be approximated as

$$u(t,Z(Y)) \approx u_N(t,Y) = \sum_{\mathbf{k}\in\mathcal{J}_N} \hat{u}_{\mathbf{k}}(t)\Phi_{\mathbf{k}}(Y), \tag{4.23}$$

where $Y \in \mathcal{M}^d$ has independent components. Here, one uses the strong expansion if the transformation $Z(Y)$ is known or the weak expansion otherwise. Of course, one can also choose different polynomial expansions. Subsequently, prescribe a fixed set of nodes $\{y^i\}_{i=1}^M$ on $\mathcal{M}^d$ such that $z^i := Z(y^i)$ and solve an ensemble of deterministic ODEs,

$$\frac{d}{dt}u(t,z^i) = f(u(t,z^i),z^i),$$
$$u(0,z^i) = u_0(z^i).$$

Let's denote the solutions as $u^i(t) := u(t,z^i)$, for $i = 1,\ldots,M$. The basic idea of the collocation method is to specify the coefficients $\hat{u}_{\mathbf{k}}$ such that $u_N(t,z^i) = u^i(t)$. That is, we solve

$$u^i(t) = \sum_{\mathbf{k}\in\mathcal{J}_N} \hat{u}_{\mathbf{k}}(t)\Phi_{\mathbf{k}}(y^i), \qquad i = 1,\ldots,M \tag{4.24}$$

for $\hat{u}_{\mathbf{k}}$. Let's denote the total number of basis functions as $P = \mathrm{Card}(\mathcal{J}_N) = (N+d)!/(N!d!)$. Then, for any fixed time t, we can write (4.24) in a compact form as a linear problem $Ax = b$, where

$$A_{ij} = \Phi_j(y^i), \qquad x_j = \hat{u}_j, \qquad b_i = u^i, \qquad i = 1,\ldots,M, \quad j = 1,\ldots,P,$$

Table 4.2 Graded lexicographical ordering for $d = 3$

$|\mathbf{k}|$	Multi-index $\mathbf{k}$	Single index j
0	(0,0,0)	1
1	(1,0,0)	2
	(0,1,0)	3
	(0,0,1)	4
2	(2,0,0)	5
	(1,1,0)	6
	(1,0,1)	7
	(0,2,0)	8
	$\dots$	$\dots$

where we have denoted the multi-index $\mathbf{k}$ with a single-index j notation to simplify the discussion below. For example, one could use the graded lexicographic ordering to map the multi-index to a single-index ordering (see Table 4.2).

If the total number of collocation nodes is equal to the number of basis functions in the expansion, $M = P$, then matrix A is a polynomial-Vandermonde matrix and it is invertible when $y^i \neq y^{i'}$, for any pair of $i \neq i'$ (Bella *et al.* 2010). With appropriate choices of y^i such that the condition number of A is reasonably small, we can solve this linear problem by direct inversion. In this case, the collocation method is interpolating the solutions u^i.

If the total number of collocation nodes is larger than the number of basis functions in the expansion, $M > P$, then the linear problem in (4.24) is over-determined. This linear least-square problem can be solved directly as $x = (A^\top A)^{-1} A^\top b$, whose components are

$$\hat{u}_j = \sum_{k=1}^{P} B_{jk} \left(\sum_i \Phi_k(y^i) u^i \right), \tag{4.25}$$

where

$$B_{jk} = \left(\sum_{i=1}^{M} \Phi_j(y^i) \Phi_k(y^i) \right)^{-1}_{jk}.$$

If the nodes $y^i \sim \mathcal{M}^d$ are chosen such that the matrix B is diagonal, then (4.25) reduces to

$$\hat{u}_j = \frac{\sum_{i=}^{M} \Phi_j(y^i) u^i}{\sum_{s=1}^{M} \Phi_j^2(y^s)}. \tag{4.26}$$

In fact, (4.26) is a Monte Carlo approximation for the least-square solutions to (4.23) provided that $y^i \in \mathcal{M}^d$ are i.i.d. samples of Y. To see this, consider the least-square solution to (4.23), that is,

$$\hat{u}_j(t) = \arg\min_{\hat{w}_j} \left\| u_N(t, Y) - \sum_{j=1}^{P} \hat{w}_j(t)\Phi_j(Y) \right\|_{p_Y}^2,$$

where we have replaced the multi-index α with a single-index ordering j for consistency with the previous discussion. By orthogonality, it is easy to verify that

$$\hat{u}_j(t) = \frac{\langle \Phi_j, u_N(t, \cdot) \rangle_{p_Y}}{\|\Phi_j\|_{p_Y}^2} \tag{4.27}$$

are the expansion coefficients (that are equivalent to (4.3)). If y^i are i.i.d. samples of a random variable Y, then we can approximate the inner products in (4.27) with Monte Carlo integrations,

$$\langle \Phi_j, u_N(t, \cdot) \rangle_{p_Y} \approx \frac{1}{M} \sum_{i=1}^{M} \Phi_j(y^i)u^i,$$

$$\|\Phi_j\|_{p_Y}^2 \approx \frac{1}{M} \sum_{i=1}^{M} \Phi_j^2(y^i).$$

Thus it is clear that, if the collocation nodes y^i are i.i.d. samples of Y, then the least-square solution in (4.26) is a Monte Carlo approximation of the expansion coefficients in (4.27).

Alternatively, one can just directly approximate the expansion coefficients in (4.27) with a quadrature rule on the collocation nodes. This method is known as the *discrete projection* or *pseudo-spectral* approach (Xiu 2010, Smith 2013) or *non-intrusive spectral projection* (NISP). In particular, one approximates the numerator of (4.27) by

$$\langle \Phi_j, u_N(t, \cdot) \rangle_{p_Y} = \int_{\mathcal{M}^d} \Phi_j(y)u_N(t, y)p_Y(y)dy \approx \sum_{i=1}^{M} w^i \Phi_j(y^i)u_N(t, y^i),$$

where the w^i denote the corresponding quadrature weights, and uses the analytical solution for the normalization factor (or the denominator in (4.27)). An interesting feature with this approach is that one can compute each coefficient separately, as shown in (4.27). In contrast, the Galerkin method requires solving the fully coupled system in (4.17) for all of the coefficients.

While implementing the collocation or NISP is rather straightforward even for complex systems, it introduces errors from the interpolation and/or the quadrature approximation to the solutions. Of course, one can always reduce these errors by employing more collocation nodes, but this might not be feasible in high-dimensional complex applications. In practice, it is important to have a computationally scalable NISP with a small number of collocation nodes yet producing accurate approximations. A popular approach to address this computational issue is by using an appropriate sparse-grid quadrature rule. This is our next topic.

4.5.1   Sparse-Grid Quadrature Rules

In the standard one-dimensional numerical quadrature, one approximates $I^{(1)}f = \int_{\mathcal{M}} f(z)dz$ with a quadrature rule,

$$Q_\ell^{(1)}f = \sum_{z_j^\ell \in \mathcal{Z}_\ell} f(z_j^\ell)w_j^\ell,$$

which is a weighted sum of the function f evaluated on a set of nodes $\mathcal{Z}_\ell = \{z_1^\ell, \ldots, z_{R_\ell}^\ell\}$ such that the polynomial degree of exactness increases with ℓ. For example, a Gaussian quadrature rule with $R_\ell+1$ points integrates g exactly when it is a polynomial of order $2R_\ell+1$ or less, but it takes of order R_ℓ^2 operations to compute the nodes and weights (Golub & Welsch 1969). For multidimensional integration problems, we will consider quadrature rules with nested nodes, that is, the set of nodes satisfies $\mathcal{Z}_m \subset \mathcal{Z}_\ell$ for $m < \ell$. With such nested points, we shall see below that the sparse-grid construction won't introduce new nodes on each coordinate.

Among the nested quadrature rules, one of the most widely used is the Clenshaw–Curtis quadrature rule, with a total number of nodes specified as

$$R_\ell = \begin{cases} 2^{\ell-1} + 1, & \text{when } \ell > 1, \\ 1, & \text{when } \ell = 1. \end{cases} \tag{4.28}$$

This quadrature rule integrates f exactly when it is a polynomial of order R_ℓ, and it takes $\mathcal{O}(R_\ell \log R_\ell)$ operations (with the fast Fourier transform) to compute the nodes and weights. A detailed comparison between Gaussian quadrature rules and the Clenshaw–Curtis quadrature rule was reported in Trefethen (2008). Also, we refer interested readers to Le Maître & Knio (2010) for the detailed computation of the nodes and weights for the Clenshaw–Curtis quadrature rule. We should also mention that other nested quadrature rules have also been considered, such as the Kronrod–Patterson Scheme (Heiss & Winschel 2008).

To simplify the discussion, let's consider Z to be a d-dimensional uniform random variable on $\mathcal{M} = [0,1]^d$. For other random variables, one can use the cumulative distribution function to map to Z (as discussed in Section 4.3). Suppose that, for each direction $j = 1, \ldots, d$, we consider the quadrature rule Q_{ℓ_j} with R_{ℓ_j} nodes from the following set $\mathcal{Z}_{\ell_j} = \{z_1^{\ell_j}, \ldots, z_{R_{\ell_j}}^{\ell_j}\}$, then the tensor product integration rule is defined as

$$\left(Q_{\ell_1}^{(1)} \otimes \cdots \otimes Q_{\ell_d}^{(1)}\right)f = \sum_{j_1=1}^{R_{\ell_1}} \cdots \sum_{j_d=1}^{R_{\ell_d}} f(z_{j_1}^{\ell_1}, \ldots, z_{j_d}^{\ell_d})w_{j_1}^{\ell_1} \cdots w_{j_d}^{\ell_d},$$

where the total number of nodes is $R = \prod_{j=1}^d R_{\ell_j}$. This means that if, for each direction, we consider a quadrature rule with exactly the same number of nodes, $R_\ell = R_{\ell_j}$, then the total number of nodes grows exponentially as the dimension increases, $R = R_\ell^d$. This curse of dimensionality motivates the construction of a sparse grid, which was originally proposed by Smolyak (1969).

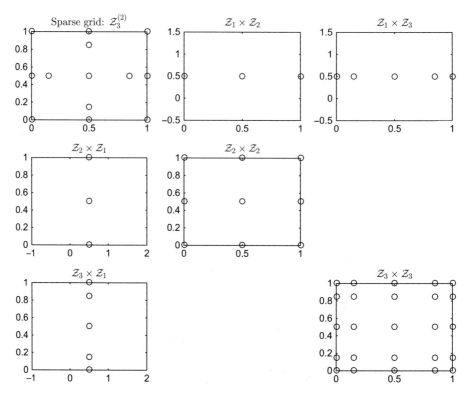

Figure 4.6 The sparse grid $\mathcal{Z}_3^{(2)}$ based on the one-dimensional Clenshaw–Curtis quadrature rule of level $\ell = 3$ (upper left) based on summing the sets $\{\mathcal{Z}_i \times \mathcal{Z}_j\}_{3 \leq |i+j| \leq 4}$. Here the total number of nodes in the sparse grid is 13, compared with 25 from the tensor product grid $\mathcal{Z}_3 \times \mathcal{Z}_3$ (bottom right).

The sparse-grid quadrature is given by

$$Q_\ell^{(d)} f = \sum_{\ell-d+1 \leq |\mathbf{l}| \leq \ell} (-1)^{\ell-|\mathbf{l}|} \binom{d-1}{\ell-|\mathbf{l}|} \left(Q_{\ell_1}^{(1)} \otimes \cdots \otimes Q_{\ell_d}^{(1)} \right) f,$$

where $\mathbf{l} = (\ell_1, \ldots, \ell_d)$ is the multi-index which satisfies $|\mathbf{l}| = \sum_{j=1}^{d} \ell_j$. The set of sparse nodes is given by

$$\mathcal{Z}_\ell^{(d)} = \bigcup_{\ell-d+1 \leq |\mathbf{l}| \leq \ell} \mathcal{Z}_{\ell_1} \times \cdots \times \mathcal{Z}_{\ell_d}. \tag{4.29}$$

To understand this cumbersome notation, in Figure 4.6 we show an example of the sparse-grid construction with the Clenshaw–Curtis quadrature rule on a two-dimensional domain $d = 2$ with level $\ell_1 = \ell_2 = \ell = 3$. Here, the one-dimensional Clenshaw–Curtis quadrature in each direction is implemented with R_ℓ specified as in (4.28) to ensure that the nodes are nested, $\mathcal{Z}_1 \subset \mathcal{Z}_2 \subset \mathcal{Z}_3$. In this figure, we show the components of (4.29) and the set $\mathcal{Z}_3^{(2)}$ compared with the tensor product $\mathcal{Z}_3 \times \mathcal{Z}_3$.

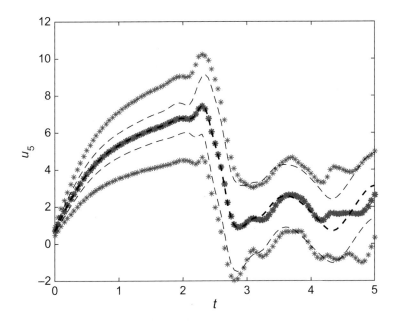

Figure 4.7 The mean plus/minus one standard deviation of $u_5(t)$. Non-intrusive spectral projection (asterisks); Monte Carlo (black dashes).

In general, there is no analytical formula for specifying the total number of nodes in the sparse grid in terms of d and ℓ. In high-dimensional cases, $d \gg 1$, the total number of nodes $\tilde{R} \sim (2d)^\ell/\ell!$ is much smaller than the total number of nodes obtained by taking the tensor product, $R = R_\ell^d$. The error of integrating $f \in \mathcal{C}^\alpha([0,1]^d)$ with the sparse quadrature rule (Novak & Ritter 1996) is

$$\left| \left(Q_\ell^{(d)} - I^{(d)} \right) f \right| = \mathcal{O}(\tilde{R}^{-\alpha} \log \tilde{R}^{(\alpha+1)(d-1)}).$$

We should point out that a sparse-grid construction can also be carried for high-dimensional interpolation problems using a similar idea, which we will not discuss here. Interested readers should consult Barthelmann *et al.* (2000). To conclude this chapter, we present a numerical example, implementing the sparse-grid Clenshaw–Curtis quadrature for quantifying uncertainties with the collocation and the spectral projection methods.

Example 4.10   Consider the Lorenz-96 model from Example 4.9 and let's compute the evolution of the first two moments. In Figure 4.7, we show the mean and the one-standard-deviation error of $u_5(t)$ obtained from the non-intrusive spectral projection (NISP) and the Monte Carlo simulations. In the NISP experiment, we consider a sparse grid of level $L = 8$, which yields a total of $M = 705$ nodes. This is a significant computational saving compared with the Monte Carlo estimates which use 10,000 samples. For the NISP, we compute the statistics with polynomials up to degree $N = 100$, which yields a total of $P = 5151$ polynomial functions. While the mean is relatively accurate, notice that the second-order statistics are overestimated for $t \le 2$.

5   Karhunen–Loève Expansion

In Chapter 4, we saw that the strong polynomial chaos expansion requires assumptions on the underlying distribution of the random variables that are to be represented. This tacit requirement may not be desirable if the underlying distribution is different from those that are listed in Table 4.1. While the weak polynomial expansion can be used to handle such situations, it still assumes that the random variable of interest can be represented by some chosen orthogonal polynomials. Furthermore, inverting cumulative distribution functions as formulated in the weak polynomial expansion is nontrivial for multivariate random variables.

Ultimately, our goal is to construct a set of basis functions corresponding to the random variables defined on the non-Euclidean domain, generalizing the idea of polynomial basis functions. To realize this goal in a data-driven fashion, we would like to construct the basis functions using samples of the underlying random variables. Since this goal is ultimately related to a nonlinear manifold learning method with kernels (which is the topic of Chapter 6), in this chapter we discuss Karhunen–Loève (KL) expansion, whose applications include the well-known linear manifold learning method known as proper orthogonal decomposition (POD).

While a general exposition of KL expansion can be formulated for any autocovariance function defined under an appropriate inner product, in our discussion we will formulate KL expansion for correlated random processes. First, we briefly review Mercer's theorem, which serves as the backbone of KL expansion. We will also mention the relevant numerical methods to realize the expansion when the analytical solutions are not available, and provide an example of the application of uncertainty quantification. We conclude this chapter with a discussion on the proper orthogonal decomposition, a linear manifold learning algorithm that is popular for dimensional reduction. This is nothing other than an application of KL expansion with empirical autocovariance functions.

5.1   Mercer's Theorem

Karhunen–Loève expansion is an important application of the spectral theory on functions of a Hilbert space. To understand this in detail, we review a few facts from functional analysis.

Definition 5.1 Let $T \subset \mathbb{R}$ be a bounded domain. The function $k \colon T \times T \to \mathbb{R}$ is a Hilbert–Schmidt kernel if $k \in L^2(T \times T)$, that is, it satisfies

$$\int_{T \times T} |k(t,s)|^2 \, dt \, ds < \infty.$$

The associated Hilbert–Schmidt integral operator is defined as

$$(Ku)(t) = \int_T k(t,s)u(s)ds, \quad \text{for all } u \in L^2(T). \tag{5.1}$$

From this definition, it is clear that

$$
\begin{aligned}
\int_T |(Ku)(t)|^2 \, dt &= \int_T \left| \int_T k(t,s)u(s)ds \right|^2 dt \\
&\leq \int_T \left(\int_T |k(t,s)|^2 \, ds \right) \left(\int_T |u(s)|^2 \, ds \right) dt \\
&= \|k\|_{L^2(T \times T)}^2 \|u\|_{L^2(T)}^2 < \infty,
\end{aligned}
$$

which means that $Ku \in L^2(T)$ or $K \colon L^2(T) \to L^2(T)$.

Definition 5.2 Let H be a Hilbert space. A linear operator $K \colon H \to H$ is self-adjoint if $\langle Ku, v \rangle = \langle u, Kv \rangle$, for all $u, v, \in H$. The operator K is positive if $\langle Ku, u \rangle \geq 0$, for all $u \in H$, which implies that $\lambda := \langle Ku, u \rangle / \langle u, u \rangle \geq 0$.

It is easy to check that the Hilbert–Schmidt operator defined in (5.1) is self-adjoint if and only if $k(x, y) = k(y, x)$, for all $x, y, \in T$. The main result that we need for understanding KL expansion is summarized as follows.

Theorem 5.3 (Mercer's theorem) *Let $k \colon T \times T \to \mathbb{R}$ be a continuous function on $T \times T$, where $T \subset \mathbb{R}$ is a compact interval. Also, let k be a symmetric Hilbert–Schmidt kernel and let its corresponding Hilbert–Schmidt operator K be positive. Then there exist non-negative λ_j and functions $\varphi_j(t) \in L^2(T)$ that satisfy $(K\varphi_j)(t) = \lambda_j \varphi_j(t)$ such that*

$$k(t,s) = \sum_j \lambda_j \varphi_j(t) \varphi_j(s)$$

uniformly on $T \times T$. Indeed, $\varphi_j(t)$ forms an orthonormal basis of $L^2(T)$, which means that any function $f \in L^2(T)$ can be described as an infinite sum of these basis functions.

In the next section, we shall see that KL expansion is nothing other than an application of Mercer's theorem for a specific choice of kernel function, namely the autocovariance function of stationary stochastic processes.

5.2 KL Expansion of Random Processes

Let $T \subset \mathbb{R}$ be a bounded interval. Let $X \colon \Omega \times T \to \mathbb{R}$ be a centered m.s.-continuous stochastic process and let $X \in L^2(\Omega \times T)$. Define an integral operator

$$K \colon L^2(T) \to L^2(T),$$

$$[Ku](t) = \int_T k(t,s)u(s)ds, \quad k(t,s) = R_X(t,s), \tag{5.2}$$

where $R_X(t,s)$ is the autocovariance function of X (see Appendix B for the definition). Requiring X to be m.s.-continuous means that $R_X(t,s)$ is continuous on $T \times T$ (see Theorem B.8 in Appendix B). Since $X \in L^2(\Omega \times T)$, it is clear that $\int_T \mathbb{E}[X_t^2]dt < \infty$, and since $\mathbb{E}[X_t X_s]^2 \le \mathbb{E}[X_t^2]\mathbb{E}[X_s^2]$, it is clear that

$$\int_T \int_T |k(t,s)|^2\, dt\, ds = \int_T \int_T |\mathbb{E}[X_t X_s]|^2\, dt\, ds \le \int_T \mathbb{E}[X_t^2]dt \int_T \mathbb{E}[X_s^2]ds < \infty,$$

which means that $k(t,s)$ is a Hilbert–Schmidt kernel. Furthermore, it is clear that, since R_X is symmetric, for all $u, v \in L^2(T)$,

$$\langle Ku, v \rangle = \int_T (Ku)(t)v(t)ds = \int_T \left(\int_T k(t,s)u(s)ds \right) v(t)dt$$

$$= \int_T \left(\int_T k(s,t)v(t)dt \right) u(s)ds = \langle u, Kv \rangle,$$

which means that K is self-adjoint. Note also that, for all $u \in L^2(T)$,

$$\langle Ku, u \rangle = \int_T (Ku)(t)u(t)dt = \int_T \left(\int_T k(t,s)u(s)ds \right) u(t)dt$$

$$= \int_T \left(\int_T R_X(t,s)u(s)ds \right) u(t)dt$$

$$= \int_T \left(\int_T \mathbb{E}[X_t X_s]u(s)ds \right) u(t)dt$$

$$= \mathbb{E}\left[\int_T \left(\int_T X_t X_s u(s)ds \right) u(t)dt \right]$$

$$= \mathbb{E}\left[\left(\int_T X_t u(t)dt \right) \left(\int_T X_s u(s)ds \right) \right]$$

$$= \mathbb{E}\left[\left(\int_T X_t u(t)dt \right)^2 \right] \ge 0,$$

which means that the corresponding Hilbert–Schmidt operator K is also positive. Therefore the integral operator K defined with a kernel that is an autocovariance function of an m.s.-continuous process as in (5.2) satisfies the hypothesis of Theorem 5.3. As a consequence, K has eigenfunctions $\varphi_j(t)$ with real and non-negative eigenvalues λ_j that form an orthonormal basis of $L^2(T)$; that is,

$$(K\varphi_j)(t) = \int_T R_X(t,s)\varphi_j(s)ds = \lambda_j \varphi_j(t), \tag{5.3}$$

such that $\langle \varphi_i, \varphi_j \rangle = \delta_{i,j}$. Since $X \in L^2(\Omega \times T)$, we can write

$$X(\omega, t) = \sum_{j=1}^{\infty} x_j(\omega)\varphi_j(t), \tag{5.4}$$

with expansion coefficients

$$x_j(\omega) = \langle X(\omega, \cdot), \varphi_j \rangle = \int_T X(\omega, s)\varphi_j(s)ds. \tag{5.5}$$

In particular, the expansion in (5.4) and (5.5) is understood in the following sense.

Theorem 5.4 (KL expansion) *Let $X: \Omega \times T \to \mathbb{R}$ be a centered m.s.-continuous stochastic process and $X \in L^2(\Omega \times T)$. Then there exists an orthonormal basis $\varphi_j(x) \in L^2(T)$ such that the expansion in (5.4) and (5.5) holds in the sense of $L^2(\Omega)$ and uniformly in T. Furthermore, the coefficients are of mean zero and uncorrelated, that is,*

$$\mathbb{E}[x_j] = 0, \quad \mathbb{E}[x_j x_k] = \lambda_j \delta_{jk}, \quad \mathrm{Var}[x_j^2] = \lambda_j. \tag{5.6}$$

Proof First, let us show (5.6):

$$\mathbb{E}[x_j] = \mathbb{E}\left[\int_T X_s \varphi_j(s)ds\right] = \int_T \mathbb{E}[X_s]\varphi_j(s)ds = \int_T \mu_X(s)\varphi_j(s)ds = 0,$$

since X is a centered stochastic process and we have used the notation $X_s = X(\cdot, s)$. Furthermore,

$$\begin{aligned}
\mathbb{E}[x_j x_k] &= \mathbb{E}\left[\int_T \int_T X_t \varphi_j(t) X_s \varphi_k(s)ds\,dt\right] \\
&= \int_T \int_T \mathbb{E}[X_t X_s]\varphi_j(t)\varphi_k(s)ds\,dt \\
&= \int_T \int_T k(s,t)\varphi_j(t)\varphi_k(s)ds\,dt \\
&= \int_T (K\varphi_j)(s)\varphi_k(s)ds \\
&= \lambda_j \int_T \varphi_j(s)\varphi_k(s)ds = \lambda_j \delta_{ij},
\end{aligned}$$

since the basis functions φ_j are orthonormal in $L^2(T)$. Consequently, we have $\mathrm{Var}[x_j^2] = \mathbb{E}[x_j^2] = \lambda_j$.

To prove the convergence of the expansion in (5.4), we define

$$E_N(t) = \mathbb{E}\left[\left(X_t - \sum_{j=1}^N x_j \varphi_j(t)\right)^2\right],$$

and we will show that, as $N \to \infty$, $E_N(t) \to 0$ for all t. Notice that

$$E_N(t) = \mathbb{E}[X_t^2] - 2\mathbb{E}\left[X_t \sum_{j=1}^N x_j \varphi_j(t)\right] + \mathbb{E}\left[\sum_{i,j}^N x_i \varphi_i(t) x_j \varphi_j(t)\right]. \tag{5.7}$$

By definition, $\mathbb{E}[X_t^2] = R_X(t,t) = k(t,t)$. The second term is

$$\mathbb{E}\left[X_t \sum_{j=1}^N x_j \varphi_j(t)\right] = \mathbb{E}\left[X_t \sum_{j=1}^N \left(\int_T X_s \varphi_j(s)ds\right) \varphi_j(t)\right]$$

$$= \sum_{j=1}^N \left(\int_T \mathbb{E}[X_t X_s]\varphi_j(s)ds\right) \varphi_j(t)$$

$$= \sum_{j=1}^N \left(\int_T k(t,s)\varphi_j(s)ds\right) \varphi_j(t)$$

$$= \sum_{j=1}^N \lambda_j \varphi_j(t)^2.$$

With similar arguments, we can show that the third term in (5.7) is

$$\mathbb{E}\left[\sum_{i,j}^N x_i \varphi_i(t) x_j \varphi_j(t)\right] = \sum_{j=1}^N \lambda_j \varphi_j(t)^2.$$

Therefore, we deduce that $E_N(t) = k(t,t) - \sum_{j=1}^N \lambda_j \varphi_j(t)^2$, and, by Theorem 5.3, it is clear that $\lim_{N\to\infty} E_N(t) = 0$ for all t, and the proof is complete. $\square$

Notice that, if $\lambda_k = 0$, then $\mathrm{Var}[x_k] = 0$, which means that x_k has no uncertainty and, since $\mathbb{E}[x_k] = 0$, the coefficient $x_k = 0$. This implies that the coefficients x_j that appears in the KL expansion in (5.4) must correspond to eigenfunctions φ_j with nonzero eigenvalues. With this in mind, let us consider the rescaling

$$\xi_j(\omega) = \frac{x_j(\omega)}{\sqrt{\lambda_j}},$$

such that

$$\mathbb{E}[\xi_j] = 0, \quad \mathbb{E}[\xi_j \xi_k] = \delta_{jk}, \quad \mathrm{Var}[\xi_j^2] = 1.$$

Then we can rewrite the expansion in (5.4) as

$$X(\omega,t) = \sum_{j=1}^\infty \sqrt{\lambda_j}\xi_j(\omega)\varphi_j(t), \quad \xi_j(\omega) = \frac{1}{\sqrt{\lambda_j}}\int_T X(\omega,s)\varphi_j(s)ds. \quad (5.8)$$

Notice that the expansion is with respect to the eigenfunctions of a Hilbert–Schmidt operator corresponding to the autocovariance function of X and the resulting coefficients are random. In general applications, when the stochastic process is not centered, that is, $\mu_X \neq 0$, KL expansion is defined with respect to the centered process, $\mu_X(t) = \mathbb{E}[X(\cdot,t)]$, such that

$$X(\omega,t) = \mu_X(t) + \sum_{j=1}^\infty \sqrt{\lambda_j}\xi_j(\omega)\varphi_j(t),$$

where (λ_j, φ_j) solve the continuous eigenvalue problem in (5.3). In practice, of course, we will use the truncated expansion such that the error of the truncated sum is in the L^2 sense, as shown in the proof of Theorem 5.4 above.

Example 5.5 Consider a mean-zero m.s.-continuous stochastic process with autocovariance function $R_X(t, s) = e^{-\gamma|t-s|}$ on $t, s \in T = [0, 1]$, where $\gamma > 0$ is constant. One can verify that this is the autocovariance function of the Ornstein–Uhlenbeck process X, which solves

$$dX = -\gamma X\, dt + \sqrt{2\gamma}\, dW_t,$$

where W_t denotes the Wiener process.

Let $\lambda_k, \varphi_k(t)$ be the eigenpairs of the Hilbert–Schmidt integral operator associated with the kernel function, $k(t, s) = R_X(t, s)$,

$$\int_0^1 e^{-\gamma|t-s|}\varphi_k(s)ds = \lambda_k\varphi_k(t). \tag{5.9}$$

This is equivalent to

$$\int_0^t e^{-\gamma(t-s)}\varphi_k(s)ds + \int_t^1 e^{-\gamma(s-t)}\varphi_k(s)ds = \lambda_k\varphi_k(t).$$

By the Leibniz rule, it is clear that the derivative with respect to t is given by

$$-\gamma\int_0^t e^{-\gamma(t-s)}\varphi_k(s)ds + \gamma\int_t^1 e^{-\gamma(s-t)}\varphi_k(s)ds = \lambda_k\frac{d}{dt}\varphi_k(t). \tag{5.10}$$

On taking another derivative with respect to t, we obtain

$$-2\gamma\varphi_k(t) + \gamma^2\int_0^1 e^{-\gamma|t-s|}\varphi_k(s)ds = \lambda_k\frac{d^2}{dt^2}\varphi_k(t),$$

which can be rewritten as

$$\frac{d^2}{dt^2}\varphi_k(t) + \omega_k^2\varphi_k(t) = 0,$$

where $\omega_k^2 = (2\gamma - \gamma^2\lambda_k)/\lambda_k$. This harmonic oscillator has solutions of the form

$$\varphi_k(t) = A\cos(\omega_k t) + B\sin(\omega_k t), \tag{5.11}$$

where A and B can be determined as follows. First, the frequency ω_k can be found by enforcing the following boundary conditions, which are obtained by setting $t = 0$ and $t = 1$ in (5.10), respectively:

$$\frac{d}{dt}\varphi_k(0) - \gamma\varphi_k(0) = 0,$$

$$\frac{d}{dt}\varphi_k(1) + \gamma\varphi_k(1) = 0.$$

Upon inserting the ansatz in (5.11) into these boundary conditions, we find that

$$\begin{pmatrix} \gamma & -\omega_k \\ \gamma - \omega_k\tan\omega_k & \gamma\tan\omega_k + \omega_k \end{pmatrix}\begin{pmatrix} A \\ B \end{pmatrix} = \begin{pmatrix} 0 \\ 0 \end{pmatrix}, \tag{5.12}$$

whose nontrivial solution exists only when

$$\det \begin{pmatrix} \gamma & -\omega_k \\ \gamma - \omega_k \tan\omega_k & \gamma\tan\omega_k + \omega_k \end{pmatrix} = 0,$$

or, equivalently, when

$$\tan\omega_k = \frac{2\gamma\omega_k}{w_k^2 - \gamma^2}. \tag{5.13}$$

From the first component in (5.12), we have $B = (\gamma/\omega_k)A$. Then, by requiring the eigenfunctions to be normalized to one, $\int_0^1 \varphi_k(t)^2\, dt = 1$, we obtain

$$A^2 \int_0^1 \left(\sin(\omega_k t) + \frac{\gamma}{\omega_k}\cos(\omega_k t) \right)^2 dt = 1,$$

and, using the equality in (5.13), we find that

$$A = \sqrt{\frac{2\omega_k^2}{2\gamma + \gamma^2 + \omega_k^2}}$$

and thus

$$B = \frac{\gamma}{\omega_k}A = \sqrt{\frac{2\gamma^2}{2\gamma + \gamma^2 + \omega_k^2}}.$$

Therefore, the eigenvalues can be found by solving the nonlinear equation in (5.13) for ω_k and using the formula

$$\lambda_k = \frac{2\gamma}{\omega_k^2 + \gamma^2}.$$

The corresponding eigenfunctions are given by

$$\varphi_k(t) = \sqrt{\frac{2\omega_k^2}{2\gamma + \gamma^2 + \omega_k^2}}\cos(\omega_k t) + \sqrt{\frac{2\gamma^2}{2\gamma + \gamma^2 + \omega_k^2}}\sin(\omega_k t).$$

While the explicit expression for the eigenvalues and eigenfunctions for this problem is found in terms of γ and ω_k, notice that the solutions are not explicit, since they require solution of the nonlinear equation in (5.13) for ω_k. In general, one will not be able to solve the continuous eigenvalue problem in (5.3) explicitly. Next, we will provide a short discussion on several numerical methods to approximate the solutions of this eigenvalue problem.

5.2.1   Numerical Approximation

A direct method to approximate the continuous eigenvalue problem in (5.3) is to discretize the integral operator on nodes $s_i \in T$; that is,

$$\int_T k(t,s)\varphi_j(s)ds \approx \sum_i k(t,s_i)\varphi_j(s_i)w_i, \tag{5.14}$$

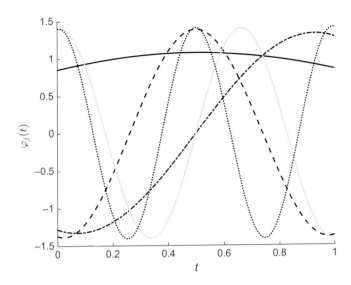

Figure 5.1 The first five Mercer eigenfunctions of the Hilbert–Schmidt operator corresponding to the exponential kernel $R_X(t, s) = e^{-|t-s|}$.

where w_i denotes the quadrature weights, such that the orthogonality condition is satisfied; that is,

$$\int_T \varphi_i(s)\varphi_j(s)ds \approx \sum_k \varphi_i(s_k)\varphi_j(s_k)w_k = \delta_{ij}.$$

With this approximation, the continuous eigenvalue problem can be approximated by $\hat{K}W\vec{\varphi}_j = \lambda_j\vec{\varphi}_j$, where $\hat{K}_{ij} = k(s_i, s_j)$, $W_{ij} = w_i\delta_{ij}$, and $[\vec{\varphi}_j]_i = \varphi_j(s_i)$.

For the simple case of Example 5.5, Toby Driscoll wrote a MATLAB script[1] that approximates the eigenfunctions. He basically used an adaptive quadrature scheme to approximate the integral operator in (5.14). Using his code, we show the first five eigenfunctions of the corresponding Hilbert–Schmidt operator in Figure 5.1. In Figure 5.2, we verify Mercer's theorem with a finite summation using only $N = 50$ modes.

In Figure 5.3, we show 20 realizations of X_t on $t \in [0, 1]$, simulated with the KL expansion in (5.8), where $\xi_j \sim \mathcal{N}(0, 1)$ for each realization. Here, the mean (solid line) is estimated by averaging 20,000 realizations. In the same figure, we also plot the histogram of X_t at $t = 0.7$ and compare it with the density of the standard Gaussian distribution.

An alternative approach for solving the continuous eigenvalue problem in (5.3) is to apply a Galerkin expansion (Ghanem & Spanos 2003). That is, one chooses orthonormal basis functions $v_k(t) \in L^2(T)$ and assumes that the eigenfunctions

---

[1] This code can be downloaded at
www.chebfun.org/examples/stats/MercerKarhunenLoeve.html.

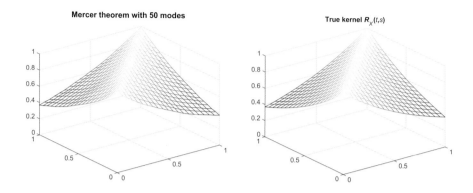

Figure 5.2 Reconstruction of the kernel with Mercer's theorem using $N = 50$ (left) compared with the true kernel, $R_X(t,s) = e^{-|t-s|}$ (right). The error of the estimate is 0.0076 in the ℓ_2-norm.

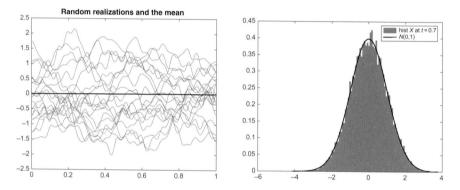

Figure 5.3 Twenty realizations of X_t for $t \in [0, 1]$, simulated using KL expansion with $N = 50$ (left). Histogram of X_t at $t = 0.7$ compared with the standard Gaussian distribution (right).

φ_j of (5.3) are in the form

$$\varphi_i(t) = \sum_{k=1}^{M} c_{ik} v_k(t).$$

By substituting this ansatz into the continuous eigenvalue problem in (5.3), we obtain

$$\sum_{k=1}^{M} c_{ik} \int_T k(t,s) v_k(s) ds = \lambda_j \sum_{k=1}^{M} c_{ik} v_k(s).$$

As in the usual Galerkin approximation, the coefficients c_{ik} are specified by requiring the residuals to be orthogonal to $\text{span}\{v_0, \ldots, v_M\}$, which yields

$$\left\langle v_j, \int_T \sum_{k=1}^{M} k(t,s) c_{ik} v_k(s) ds \right\rangle = \lambda_i \left\langle v_j, \sum_{k=1}^{M} c_{ik} v_k \right\rangle,$$

or

$$\sum_{k=1}^{M} c_{ik} \int_T \int_T k(t,s) v_k(s) v_j(t) ds\, dt = \lambda_i c_{ij},$$

which can be written in compact form as $CA = \Lambda C$, where

$$A_{ij} = \int_T \int_T k(t,s) v_i(s) v_j(t) ds\, dt,$$
$$\Lambda_{ij} = \lambda_j \delta_{ij}.$$

Thus, we have discretized the eigenvalue problem on the space spanned by v_i. With this approach, the accuracy of the estimates depends on the choice of basis functions v_i (see Ghanem & Spanos (2003) for a detailed discussion).

5.2.2 An Uncertainty Quantification Application

To apply the strong PC expansion, we assume that the distribution of the random parameters is known. In practical applications, however, the distribution of these parameters is typically unknown and it is often difficult to estimate (which is the topic of Chapter 2). Often we know only its first-order statistics and it is a luxury to even know its second-order statistics such as the autocovariance function. But, supposing we do know these statistics, we can approximate the underlying random variable with KL expansion. Below, we give an example of uncertainty quantification with such random parameters.

Example 5.6 Consider solving the heat equation

$$u_t = (a(x,\omega) u_x)_x,$$
$$u(0,t,\omega) = u(1,t,\omega) = 0,$$
$$u(x,0,\omega) = \sin^2(2\pi x),$$

where $a(x,\omega)$ is a random parameter with mean $\bar{a}(x) = 4$ and autocovariance function $R_X(x,y) = e^{-|x-y|}$, on the domain $[0,1]$. In this case, we consider the finite KL expansion

$$a(x,\omega) = \bar{a}(x) + \sum_{i=1}^{d} \sqrt{\lambda_i} \xi_i(\omega) \varphi_i(x),$$

where the ξ_i are i.i.d. uniform random variables on $[-\sqrt{3}, \sqrt{3}]$ such that $\mathbb{E}[\xi_i] = 0$ and $\mathbb{E}[\xi_i^2] = 1$. With this expansion, the PDE becomes

$$u_t = \left(\left(\bar{a}(x) + \sum_{i=1}^{d} \sqrt{\lambda_i} \xi_i(\omega) \varphi_i(x) \right) u_x \right)_x. \tag{5.15}$$

Below we will compare the Monte Carlo method and the NISP (discussed in Section 4.5), which requires integrating the deterministic PDE with fixed ξ_i. We integrate the PDE with the backward time difference and the spatial Crank–Nicolson schemes. In particular, let $w_{k,j} \approx u(x_k, t_j)$ and discretize the spatial domain at $x_k = k\,\Delta x$, where $k = 0, 1, \ldots, n = 1/\Delta x$, and the time $t_j = j\,\Delta t$. With this discretization, we have

$$
w_{k,j} - w_{k,j-1} = \frac{1}{2}\Big(\sigma_{k+1}w_{k+1,j} - (\sigma_{k+1} + \sigma_k)w_{k,j} + \sigma_k w_{k-1,j}\Big)
$$
$$
+ \frac{1}{2}\Big(\sigma_{k+1}w_{k+1,j-1} - (\sigma_{k+1} + \sigma_k)w_{k,j-1} + \sigma_k w_{k-1,j-1}\Big),
$$

where $\sigma_k = (\Delta t/\Delta x^2)(\bar{a} + \sum_{i=1}^{d} \sqrt{\lambda_i}\xi_i(\omega)\varphi_i(x_k))$. In compact form, we can rewrite this finite discretization as

$$
\vec{w}_k = A^{-1}B\vec{w}_{k-1},
$$

where

$$
A = \begin{pmatrix}
2 + \sigma_1 + \sigma_2 & -\sigma_2 & & & \\
-\sigma_2 & 2 + \sigma_2 + \sigma_3 & -\sigma_3 & & \\
& -\sigma_3 & 2 + \sigma_3 + \sigma_4 & -\sigma_4 & \\
& & \ddots & \ddots & \ddots \\
& & & -\sigma_{n-1} & 2 + \sigma_{n-1} + \sigma_n
\end{pmatrix},
$$

$$
B = \begin{pmatrix}
2 - \sigma_1 - \sigma_2 & \sigma_2 & & & \\
\sigma_2 & 2 - \sigma_2 - \sigma_3 & \sigma_3 & & \\
& \sigma_3 & 2 - \sigma_3 - \sigma_4 & \sigma_4 & \\
& & \ddots & \ddots & \ddots \\
& & & \sigma_{n-1} & 2 - \sigma_{n-1} - \sigma_n
\end{pmatrix}.
$$

Numerically, we will set $\Delta x = 0.01$ and $\Delta t = 0.005$, and we solve the eigenpairs $\lambda_i, \varphi_i(x_k)$ as in the previous example.

For the Monte Carlo estimates, we simply draw 10,000 independent samples of $\xi_i \sim U[-\sqrt{3}, \sqrt{3}]$ and average the solutions over these estimates. On the other hand, for the NISP, we will write $\xi_i = \sqrt{3}u_i$, where $u_i \sim U[-1, 1]$, and apply the spectral projection on a tensor product of the Legendre polynomials, $\Phi_{\mathbf{k}}(u) = \prod_{k_i=1}^{d} \varphi_{k_i}(u_i)$. In this numerical test, we use the Smolyak sparse grid of level $L = 6$, which yields a total of $M = 2433$ nodes. So, computationally this is about four times less expensive than the Monte Carlo simulations. In the NISP implementation, we approximate only the solutions using polynomials of up to degree 10, which yields a total of $P = 3003$ modes. Figure 5.4 shows the mean and mean plus/minus one standard deviation. Notice that the number of modes is already so large even with just a five-dimensional KL expansion and polynomials of degree up to 10. Yet the variance is still underestimated.

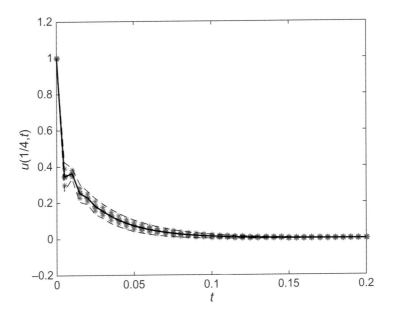

Figure 5.4 Mean plus/minus one standard deviation of $u_5(t)$. Non-intrusive spectral projection (asterisks); Monte Carlo (black dashes).

5.3   Connection to POD

In this section, we will connect KL expansion to a popular linear manifold learning method for analyzing data, the so-called proper orthogonal decomposition (POD), which is sometimes also known as principal component analysis (PCA), depending on the field of application. Essentially, POD is an application of KL expansion that uses the empirically estimated autocovariance functions derived from the given data.

Consider observations $\{u_i(x) = u(x, t_i) \in L^2(\mathcal{M})\}_{i=1}^N$ on a compact domain $\mathcal{M}$; e.g., u can be solutions of a PDE at times t_i. Without lost of generality, assume that this data set has zero temporal mean, $\bar{u}(x) = (1/N) \sum_{i=1}^N u_i(x) = 0$. The main idea of POD is to express the data in terms of the coordinates for which the data have the largest mean-square statistics. To be more precise, the problem is to find

$$\phi(x) = \sum_{i=1}^N v_i u_i(x), \tag{5.16}$$

where the v_i are to be chosen such that

$$\max_\phi \sum_{i=1}^N |\langle u_i, \phi \rangle|^2, \quad \text{subject to } \|\phi\|^2 = 1. \tag{5.17}$$

Choosing an empirical kernel function,

$$k(x,y) = \sum_{i=1}^{N} u_i(x)u_i(y),\tag{5.18}$$

we can write

$$\sum_{i=1}^{N} |\langle u_i, \phi \rangle|^2 = \sum_{i=1}^{N} \int_{\mathcal{M}} u_i(x)\phi(x)dx \int_{\mathcal{M}} u_i(y)\phi(y)dy$$

$$= \int_{\mathcal{M}} \int_{\mathcal{M}} \sum_{i=1}^{N} u_i(x)u_i(y)\phi(y)dy\, \phi(x)dx$$

$$= \int_{\mathcal{M}} \int_{\mathcal{M}} k(x,y)\phi(y)dy\, \phi(x)dx$$

$$= \langle K\phi, \phi \rangle,$$

where K denotes the Hilbert–Schmidt integral operator corresponding to the kernel function k, assuming that $k(x,y) \in L^2(\mathcal{M} \times \mathcal{M})$. From the construction above, it is clear that K is a self-adjoint and positive operator. Hence solving the constrained optimization problem $\max_\phi \langle K\phi, \phi \rangle$ subject to $\|\phi\|^2 = 1$ is equivalent to finding the eigenfunctions of K corresponding to the largest eigenvalue. To see this, one can define a Lagrangian function

$$\mathcal{L}(\phi, \lambda) = \langle K\phi, \phi \rangle + \lambda(1 - \|\phi\|^2),$$

where λ denotes the Lagrange multiplier. On taking the derivatives with respect to ϕ and λ and setting them equal to zero, we obtain

$$K\phi = \lambda\phi \quad \text{and} \quad \|\phi\|^2 = 1.\tag{5.19}$$

From the spectral theory (see, e.g., Brezis (2010)), the eigenfunctions φ_j of a self-adjoint compact operator K form an orthonormal basis of $L^2(\mathcal{M})$ with eigenvalues $\lambda_1 \geq \lambda_2 \geq \ldots > 0$. Thus, for $\|\phi\|^2 = 1$,

$$\max_\phi \langle K\phi, \phi \rangle = \max_\phi \langle \lambda\phi, \phi \rangle = \max_\phi \lambda\|\phi\|^2 = \lambda_1,$$

and thus $\varphi_1 = \arg\max_\phi \langle K\phi, \phi \rangle$. Indeed, this result is a consequence of the Courant–Rayleigh minimax principle (see, e.g., Lax (2007)) for a self-adjoint compact operator K. That is,

$$\lambda_k = \min_{H_{k-1}} \max_{\substack{\|\phi\|=1 \\ \phi \in H_{k-1}^\perp}} \langle K\phi, \phi \rangle,$$

where $H_{k-1} \subset L^2(\mathcal{M})$ denotes a $(K-1)$-dimensional subspace and $H_{k-1}^\perp$ denotes the orthogonal complement of H_{k-1}.

Therefore, the direction corresponding to the jth-largest mean-square projection is

$$\varphi_j(x) = \sum_{i=1}^{N} v_i^{(j)} u_i(x),\tag{5.20}$$

where the coefficients $v_i^{(j)}$ are determined in such a way as to satisfy

$$K\varphi_j = \lambda_j \varphi_j. \tag{5.21}$$

On substituting (5.20) and (5.18) into (5.21), for each j, we obtain

$$\int_{\mathcal{M}} \sum_{i=1}^{N} u_i(x) u_i(y) \sum_{k=1}^{N} v_k^{(j)} u_k(y) dy = \lambda_j \sum_{i=1}^{N} v_i^{(j)} u_i(x),$$

$$\sum_{i=1}^{N} \sum_{k=1}^{N} \left(\int_{\mathcal{M}} u_i(y) u_k(y) dy \right) v_k^{(j)} u_i(x) = \lambda_j \sum_{i=1}^{N} v_i^{(j)} u_i(x).$$

Since $u_i(x)$ is arbitrary, we have

$$\sum_{k=1}^{N} \left(\int_{\mathcal{M}} u_i(y) u_k(y) dy \right) v_k^{(j)} = \lambda_j v_i^{(j)}, \tag{5.22}$$

which is an N-dimensional eigenvalue problem. In compact form, we can write (5.22) as $A\vec{v}_j = \lambda_j \vec{v}_j$, where

$$A_{ik} = \int_{\mathcal{M}} u_i(y) u_k(y) dy, \quad \text{and} \quad \vec{v}_j = (v_1^{(j)}, \dots, v_N^{(j)})^\top. \tag{5.23}$$

Since A is a symmetric and positive matrix, it has eigenvectors $\vec{v}_1, \dots, \vec{v}_N$ that are orthonormal with eigenvalues $\lambda_1 \geq \lambda_2 \geq \dots \geq \lambda_N \geq 0$. Hence the jth mode is given by

$$\varphi_j(x) = \frac{1}{\sqrt{\lambda_j}} \sum_{i=1}^{N} v_i^{(j)} u_i(x), \tag{5.24}$$

where $v_i^{(j)}$ is the ith component of $\vec{v}_j$, the eigenvector of A corresponding to eigenvalue λ_j. The functions $\{\varphi_j(x)\}_{j=1,\dots,N}$ are called the POD modes (or bases) of rank N. Given a finite number of modes, we have

$$u_i(x) = \sum_{k=1}^{N} \langle u_i, \varphi_k \rangle \varphi_k(x)$$

$$= \sum_{k=1}^{N} \left\langle u_i, \frac{1}{\sqrt{\lambda_k}} \sum_{j=1}^{N} v_j^{(k)} u_j \right\rangle \varphi_k(x)$$

$$= \sum_{k=1}^{N} \frac{1}{\sqrt{\lambda_k}} \sum_{j=1}^{N} A_{ij} v_j^{(k)} \varphi_k(x)$$

$$= \sum_{k=1}^{N} \sqrt{\lambda_k} v_i^{(k)} \varphi_k(x), \tag{5.25}$$

which now looks like the KL expansion in (5.8), except that $\xi_j(\omega)$ are replaced by $\vec{v}_j$. The representation in (5.25) has diverse names in various fields: proper orthogonal decomposition (POD), the empirical orthogonal function (EOF), principal component analysis (PCA), the hotelling transform, the Kosambi–Karhunen–Loève transform (KKLT), and perhaps many more.

5.3.1   Discrete Data

For discrete data $\{\vec{u}_i \in \mathbb{R}^M\}_{i=1}^N$, where $\bar{u} = (1/N)\sum_{i=1}^N \vec{u}_i = \vec{0}$, we define the matrix $U = [\vec{u}_1, \ldots, \vec{u}_N] \in \mathbb{R}^{M \times N}$. Here, the inner product in the previous discussion (of $L^2(\mathcal{M})$) becomes the standard dot product of $\mathbb{R}^M$. In this case, the matrix $A \in \mathbb{R}^{N \times N}$ defined in (5.23) becomes $A = U^\top U$. Define $A = V\Lambda V^\top$, where $V = [\vec{v}_1, \ldots, \vec{v}_N] \in \mathbb{R}^{N \times N}$ is an orthonormal matrix (since A is symmetric positive definite). In this eigenvalue decomposition, we also define an $N \times N$ diagonal matrix $\Lambda_{ij} = \lambda_j \delta_{ij}$. Then, the jth POD mode in (5.24) becomes

$$\vec{\varphi}_j = \frac{1}{\sqrt{\lambda_j}} U\vec{v}_j, \quad j = 1, \ldots, N,$$

or, in compact form,

$$\Phi = UV\Lambda^{-1/2}, \tag{5.26}$$

where $\Phi = [\vec{\varphi}_1, \ldots \vec{\varphi}_N] \in \mathbb{R}^{M \times N}$. This means that the POD modes are the left singular vectors of matrix U. In fact, equation (5.25) is nothing more than the singular value decomposition for matrix U,

$$U = \Phi\Lambda^{1/2}V^\top,$$

where the columns of the orthogonal matrix Φ and V are the left and right singular vectors, respectively, and the diagonal components of $\Lambda^{1/2} \in \mathbb{R}^{N \times N}$ are the corresponding singular values.

When the amount of data is less than the dimensionality of the observed data, $N < M$, then one can compute the POD modes by solving the N-dimensional eigenvalue problem, $U^\top U = A = V\Lambda V^\top$, and using the relationship in (5.26). When $N > M$, then one may just solve the M-dimensional eigenvalue problem $UU^\top = \Phi\Lambda\Phi^\top$ directly.

A popular application of POD is for representing data (or manifold learning). In this application, one can consider a dimensionality reduction with a reduced-rank decomposition, $U \approx \Phi_R \Lambda_R^{1/2} V_R^\top$, using only the first R POD modes, $\Phi_R = [\vec{\varphi}_1, \ldots, \vec{\varphi}_R] \in \mathbb{R}^{M \times R}$, where $R < \min(M, N)$. In this reduced-rank decomposition, we also define $\Lambda_R^{1/2} \in \mathbb{R}^{R \times R}$ and $V_R = [\vec{v}_1, \ldots, \vec{v}_R] \in \mathbb{R}^{N \times R}$. The *principal components* of U (or the representation of data U in coordinates Φ_R) are defined to be the row vectors of

$$Y := \Phi_R^\top U = \Lambda_R^{1/2} V_R^\top \in \mathbb{R}^{R \times N}, \tag{5.27}$$

which are nothing other than the coefficients in the POD decomposition in (5.25). Intuitively, Φ_R rotates the data to align with the coordinate axes $\{\vec{\varphi}_j\}_{j=1,\ldots,R}$ and λ_j denotes the variance along these coordinates.

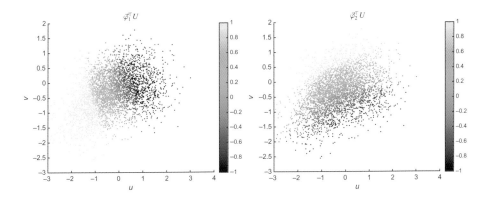

Figure 5.5 Principal components for the Gaussian data in Example 5.7.

In Example 1.3, we showed that the principal components of the uniformly distributed data on the unit circle are the embedding coordinates. Geometrically, these coordinates are also the principal axes of the unit circle. To close this chapter, we give another example for which the data do not lie on an ellipsoid but the principal components obtained from the POD are the principal axes of an ellipsoid that is fitted to the data.

Example 5.7 Consider the two-dimensional system of SDEs

$$
\begin{aligned}
\frac{du}{dt} &= \frac{1}{2}uv - d\Lambda_{11}u + (1 - d\Lambda_{12})v + S_{11}\dot{W}_1 + S_{12}\dot{W}_2, \\
\frac{dv}{dt} &= -\frac{1}{2}u^2 + (-1 - d\Lambda_{12})u - d\Lambda_{22}v + S_{12}\dot{W}_1 + S_{22}\dot{W}_2,
\end{aligned}
\tag{5.28}
$$

where the nonlinear terms conserve energy and W_i denotes white noise. This model is a special case of the canonical model for turbulence introduced in Sapsis & Majda (2013). In our numerical simulation we will set $d = 1/2$, $S = \Lambda^{1/2}$ with

$$
\Lambda = \begin{pmatrix} 1 & 1/4 \\ 1/4 & 1 \end{pmatrix}.
$$

We simulate the solutions of this model with the Euler–Maruyama scheme with time discretization $\tau = 0.01$. From the solutions at $N = 40{,}000$ instances, we construct the matrix $U \in \mathbb{R}^{M \times N}$, with $M = 2$ as defined above, where each column consists of the deviation of the solutions from its temporal mean.

In Figure 5.5, we show the two principal components computed from the POD. Here, we plot the principal components as functions of the data. Notice that the first principal component identifies the data along a linear direction corresponding to the largest variance. The second principal component is orthogonal to the first one. Geometrically, these two components correspond to the principal axes (with length $\sqrt{\lambda_j}$) of an ellipsoid that is fitted to the data by this manifold learning algorithm. In the next chapter, we will revisit this example using a nonlinear manifold learning technique called the diffusion maps algorithm.

6 Diffusion Forecast

In Chapters 2 and 3, we discussed how to leverage data to estimate parameters in dynamical models. The basic assumptions of this class of approaches are that a parametric model for the dynamical system is given and the hidden parameters of interest are identifiable from the given observations. We saw in Chapter 3 that this inverse problem is nontrivial when the underlying dynamical model is not completely known due to modeling errors. In this chapter, we discuss how to use data to learn the entire dynamical model without assuming any parametric form. This is an extension of the statistical notion of nonparametric modeling to dynamical systems.

The particular nonparametric modeling that we will discuss is called the "diffusion forecast." Intuitively, this method follows the idea of representing random variables with basis functions of a weighted Hilbert space, such as the polynomial basis discussed in Chapter 4. In particular, the key idea of the diffusion forecast is to represent the time-dependent probability density functions of the underlying dynamical systems with data-adapted basis functions, assuming that the probability densities are solutions of the corresponding Fokker–Planck equation. So, the diffusion forecast is nothing but a spectral Galerkin representation of the solution operator of the Fokker–Planck equation corresponding to the underlying dynamics on data-adapted basis functions.

The next question is that of how to construct the basis functions from the given data. While our discussion in Chapter 4 suggests that each random variable in Table 4.1 determines a set of orthogonal polynomial basis functions, one can also deduce these polynomial functions as solutions of an appropriate Dirichlet eigenvalue problem (or the Sturm–Liouville eigenvalue problem in the one-dimensional case with "symmetric" boundary conditions). This is an eigenvalue problem of a self-adjoint second-order differential operator (Andrews & Askey 1985). With this intuition, our aim is to approximate a self-adjoint second-order differential operator on the manifold where the data lie and solve the corresponding eigenvalue problem to obtain a set of eigenbases. The diffusion maps algorithm (Coifman & Lafon 2006) is a method designed to perform this task on nonlinear data manifolds. This method is a kernel-based algorithm which approximates a weighted Laplacian operator on the data manifold with an integral operator. In some sense, the diffusion maps algorithm is the reverse of the technique shown in Example 5.5 of Chapter 5 which turns an eigenvalue problem of an integral operator into an eigenvalue problem of a second-order linear differential operator.

To implement the nonparametric probabilistic modeling in real applications, one needs to specify the initial density given a new observed datum that is not one of the data used to train the model. If the new observed datum is noise-free, then one can use the Nyström extension idea to generate initial conditions (Harlim & Yang 2017). On the other hand, when the data are noisy, one can use nonparametric Bayesian filtering to generate initial conditions (Berry & Harlim 2016a). This nonparametric filtering method represents the prior and posterior densities of the state variables with smooth basis functions estimated from the data. This idea is quite different from MCMC, which represents the distributions with point measures defined on the samples that are generated by the Markov chain, and than the EnKF, which approximates the distributions with empirically estimated Gaussian measures.

To make the discussion concise, we first give a quick review of the diffusion maps algorithm. First, we review the basic theory behind the diffusion maps, which relies on an asymptotic expansion of an integral operator for a class of decaying kernel functions (Coifman & Lafon 2006). For completeness, we also provide a minimal background on basic differential geometry theory in Appendix C. Subsequently, we introduce the diffusion forecasting method which leverages the basis functions obtained from the diffusion maps algorithm for solving the Fokker–Planck equation when the explicit expression of this equation is unknown. The diffusion forecast method is provably consistent for Itô diffusion processes (Berry *et al.* 2015) on smooth manifolds embedded in Euclidean space. We close the chapter with the two methods used to specify the initial densities for the diffusion forecast.

6.1   Diffusion Maps

The diffusion maps algorithm (Belkin & Niyogi 2003, Coifman & Lafon 2006) is a data-driven method that approximates the eigenfunctions of a weighted Laplacian on d-dimensional compact Riemannian manifolds $\mathcal{M} \subset \mathbb{R}^n$. Essentially, given a set of training data points $x_i \in \mathcal{M}$, the method approximates the differential operator (Laplacian) with an integral operator, which can be realized numerically via Monte Carlo averages over the training data.

Fundamentally, the diffusion maps algorithm relies on the following asymptotic expansion (Coifman & Lafon 2006).

Theorem 6.1 *Let $f \in C^3(\mathcal{M})$ be a smooth real-valued function on a d-dimensional compact manifold $\mathcal{M}$ without a boundary (or assume that f satisfies the Neumann boundary condition) embedded in $\mathbb{R}^n$. Let $h \colon [0, \infty) \to [0, \infty)$*

be an exponentially decaying function. Then we have

$$G_\epsilon f(x) := \epsilon^{-d/2} \int_{\mathcal{M}} h\left(\frac{||x-y||^2}{\epsilon}\right) f(y) dV(y)$$
$$= m_0 f(x) + \epsilon m_2 (\omega(x) f(x) + \Delta f(x)) + \mathcal{O}(\epsilon^2),$$

where $m_0 = \int_{\mathbb{R}^d} h(||z||^2) dz$ and $m_2 = \frac{1}{2} \int_{\mathbb{R}^d} z_1^2 h(||z||^2) dz$ are constants determined by h, and ω depends on the induced geometry of $\mathcal{M}$.

Note that $dV(y)$ is the volume form inherited by $\mathcal{M}$ from the ambient space $\mathbb{R}^n$ and Δ denotes the (negative definite) Laplace–Beltrami operator on $\mathcal{M}$, and both of them are defined with respect to the Riemannian metric inherited from the ambient space as discussed in Appendix C. Before we prove this theorem, we first define the relevant basic tools from differential geometry.

Consider a d-dimensional Riemannian manifold $\mathcal{M}$ embedded in $\mathbb{R}^n$. Locally, since a manifold is diffeomorphic to a Euclidean space, the Riemannian metric inherited from the ambient space is simply the standard inner product in $T_x\mathcal{M} \cong \mathbb{R}^d$ considered as a linear subspace of the ambient space $\mathbb{R}^n$. This means that, for each $x \in \mathcal{M}$, the identity map $\iota \colon \mathcal{M} \hookrightarrow \mathbb{R}^n$ such that $\iota(\mathcal{M}) = \mathcal{M}$ is a local embedding. For any $u, v \in T_x\mathcal{M}$, the Riemannian metric inherited from the ambient space is given by

$$g_x(u, v) = u^\top D\iota(x)^\top D\iota(x) v = u^\top v = \langle u, v \rangle_{\mathbb{R}^d}.$$

Let $y \in \mathcal{M}$ be such that $||y - x|| = \mathcal{O}(\sqrt{\epsilon})$. Define γ to be a geodesic, connecting x and y. Loosely speaking, a geodesic curve can be understood as a curve where a particle can move without acceleration. Technically, this means that the acceleration, γ'', is orthogonal to the tangent space $T_x\mathcal{M}$ at every point of the curve γ. This condition will be used in deriving the asymptotic expansion of the lemma above. For convenience, we choose to parameterize the curve by the arc-length

$$s = \int_0^s ||\gamma'(t)|| dt,$$

where $\gamma(0) = x$, $\gamma(s) = y$. On taking the derivative with respect to s, we obtain a constant velocity, $1 = ||\gamma'(t)||$ for all $0 \le t \le s$. Let $\vec{s} = (s_1, \ldots, s_d)$ be the geodesic normal coordinates of y defined by an exponential map, $\exp_x \colon T_x\mathcal{M} \to \mathcal{M}$. That is, $\vec{s}$ satisfies

$$s\gamma'(0) = \vec{s} = \exp_x^{-1}(y),$$

where

$$s^2 = s^2 ||\gamma'(0)||^2 = ||\vec{s}||^2 = \sum_{i=1}^d s_i^2. \tag{6.1}$$

Consider the Taylor expansion of γ centered at 0,

$$\gamma(s) = \gamma(0) + s\gamma'(0) + \frac{s^2}{2}\gamma''(0) + \frac{s^3}{6}\gamma'''(0) + \mathcal{O}(s^4). \tag{6.2}$$

Since $y - x = \gamma(s) - \gamma(0)$, one can see that

$$\|y - x\|^2 = s^2 \|\gamma'(0)\|^2 + \frac{s^4}{4} \|\gamma''(0)\|^2 + \frac{s^4}{3} \langle \gamma'(0), \gamma'''(0) \rangle + \mathcal{O}(s^5), \quad (6.3)$$

using the fact that $\langle \gamma'(0), \gamma''(0) \rangle = 0$, since $\gamma''(0) \in T_x^\perp \mathcal{M}$ while $\gamma'(0) \in T_x \mathcal{M}$ (i.e., γ is a geodesic).

From (6.1), it is clear that

$$\|y - x\|^2 = \|\vec{s}\|^2 + P_{4,x}(\vec{s}) + P_{5,x}(\vec{s}) + \mathcal{O}(s^5),$$

where $P_{n,x}(\vec{s})$ denotes the polynomials of degree n in the components of $\vec{s}$ with coefficients depending on the base point x. Since we assume that $\|y - x\| = \mathcal{O}(\sqrt{\epsilon})$, we also have $s = \|\vec{s}\| = \mathcal{O}(\sqrt{\epsilon})$.

To derive the key asymptotic expansion of the integral operator

$$G_\epsilon f(x) = \epsilon^{-d/2} \int_{\mathcal{M}} h\left(\frac{\|x - y\|^2}{\epsilon} \right) f(y) dV(y), \quad (6.4)$$

where h has exponential decay, we need to change the coordinates in (6.4) to the geodesic normal coordinates $\vec{s}$. Notice that, from (6.3), we have

$$h\left(\frac{\|x - y\|^2}{\epsilon} \right) = h\left(\frac{\|\vec{s}\|^2}{\epsilon} \right) + h'\left(\frac{\|\vec{s}\|^2}{\epsilon} \right) \left(P_{4,x}(\vec{s}) + P_{5,x}(\vec{s}) \right) + \mathcal{O}(\epsilon^2). \quad (6.5)$$

Define $\tilde{f}(\vec{s}) = f(\exp_x(\vec{s})) = f(y)$, such that $\tilde{f}(\vec{0}) = f(x)$. Then,

$$f(y) = \tilde{f}(\vec{s}) = \tilde{f}(\vec{0}) + \sum_{i=1}^{d} s_i \frac{\partial}{\partial s_i} \tilde{f}(\vec{0}) + \frac{1}{2} \sum_{i=1,j=1}^{d} s_i s_j \frac{\partial^2}{\partial s_i \partial s_j} \tilde{f}(\vec{0})$$

$$+ P_{3,x}(\vec{s}) + \mathcal{O}(\epsilon^2). \quad (6.6)$$

Since the inherited Riemannian metric is locally represented by the identity matrix, the volume form becomes $dV(y) = \sqrt{|g|} dy = dy$ in the coordinate system of the ambient space. On writing the volume form with respect to the geodesic coordinates, we find that

$$dV(y) = dy = \sqrt{\det(d\exp_x(\vec{s})^\top d\exp_x(\vec{s}))} d\vec{s} = d\vec{s}, \quad (6.7)$$

where we have used the fact that $d\exp_x(\vec{s}) = \mathcal{I}_{d \times d}$.

Now, we are ready to prove Theorem 6.1. The proof is split into two parts summarized by the two lemmas below: the first one deals with the data that are ϵ^r away from the boundary, where $0 < r < 1/2$; and the second deals with the data close to the boundary (within $\epsilon^r, 0 < r < 1/2$, of $\partial \mathcal{M}$) if the manifold has a boundary.

Lemma 6.2 *Let $\mathcal{M}$ be a d-dimensional compact Riemannian manifold embedded in $\mathbb{R}^n$. For $f \in \mathcal{C}^3(\mathcal{M})$, with h having exponential decay and for any $0 < r < 1/2$, we have that, for all $x \in \mathcal{M}$ whose distance is larger than ϵ^r from the boundary $\partial \mathcal{M}$,*

$$G_\epsilon f(x) = m_0 f(x) + \epsilon m_2(\omega(x) f(x) + \Delta f(x)) + \mathcal{O}(\epsilon^2),$$

where

$$m_0 = \int_{\mathbb{R}^d} h(\|\vec{s}\|)d\vec{s}, \quad m_2 = \frac{1}{2}\int_{\mathbb{R}^d} s_1^2 h(\|\vec{s}\|)d\vec{s}, \tag{6.8}$$

and

$$\omega(x) = \frac{1}{m_2}\int_{\mathbb{R}^d} h'(\|\vec{t}\|^2)P_{4,x}(\vec{t})d\vec{t}. \tag{6.9}$$

Proof For each $x \in \mathcal{M}$, we define $\mathcal{M}_{\epsilon,x} = \{y \in \mathcal{M}, \|y - x\| < \epsilon^r\}$ as a set of points within ϵ^r away from x. Then

$$\left| \epsilon^{-d/2} \int_{\mathcal{M}\backslash\mathcal{M}_{\epsilon,x}} h\left(\frac{\|x-y\|^2}{\epsilon}\right) f(y)dy \right| \le \|f\|_\infty \epsilon^{-d/2} \int_{\mathcal{M}\backslash\mathcal{M}_\epsilon} \left| h\left(\frac{\|x-y\|^2}{\epsilon}\right) \right| dy$$

$$\le \|f\|_\infty \int_{y'\in\mathcal{M},\|y'\|\ge\epsilon^{r-1/2}} \left| h\left(\|y'\|^2\right) \right| dy'$$

$$\le C\|f\|_\infty \epsilon^{d(1/2-r)} e^{-\epsilon^{2r-1}}, \tag{6.10}$$

for some constant C. In the previous equation we applied the change of variables $y' = (x - y)/\sqrt{\epsilon}$ in the second line and we used the following bound on the Gaussian tails:

$$\int_{\|y\|\ge\sigma} e^{-\|y\|^2}\,dy \le \int_{|y_1|,\dots,|y_d|\ge\sigma/\sqrt{d}} e^{-\|y\|^2}\,dy = \left(\int_{|y_1|\ge\sigma/\sqrt{d}} e^{-y_1^2}\,dy_1\right)^d$$

$$\le \frac{2}{\sigma^d}\left(\int_{|y_1|\ge\sigma/\sqrt{d}} y_1 e^{-y_1^2}\,dy_1\right)^d = 2^{1-d}\sigma^{-d}e^{-\sigma^2},$$

where the first inequality follows from inscribing a d-dimensional cube of radius $\sigma/\sqrt{d}$ inside the ball $\|y\| > \sigma$. In (6.10), for any $0 < r < 1/2$, the upper bound $e^{-\epsilon^\alpha}$ will decay very fast as a function of ϵ, since $\alpha = 2r - 1 < 0$. This means the error is exponentially small, or $\mathcal{O}(\epsilon^k)$ for any k, and therefore we can write the integral operator in (6.4) as a local integral around x,

$$G_\epsilon f(x) = \epsilon^{-d/2}\int_{\mathcal{M}_{\epsilon,x}} h\left(\frac{\|x-y\|^2}{\epsilon}\right) f(y)dy + \mathcal{O}(\epsilon^2).$$

Using the expansions in (6.5), (6.6), and (6.7), we can write

$$G_\epsilon f(x) = \epsilon^{-d/2}\int_{\mathbb{R}^d} \left[h\left(\frac{\|\vec{s}\|^2}{\epsilon}\right) + h'\left(\frac{\|\vec{s}\|^2}{\epsilon}\right)(P_{4,x}(\vec{s}) + P_{5,x}(\vec{s})) \right]$$

$$\times \left(\tilde{f}(\vec{0}) + \sum_{i=1}^d s_i \frac{\partial}{\partial s_i}\tilde{f}(\vec{0}) + \frac{1}{2}\sum_{i,j=1}^d s_i s_j \frac{\partial^2}{\partial s_i \partial s_j}\tilde{f}(\vec{0}) + P_{3,x}(\vec{s}) \right) d\vec{s}$$

$$+ \mathcal{O}(s^4).$$

By symmetry, the odd-power terms vanish, and we obtain

$$G_\epsilon f(x) = \epsilon^{-d/2} \left(\tilde{f}(\vec{0}) \int_{\mathbb{R}^d} h\left(\frac{\|\vec{s}\|^2}{\epsilon}\right) d\vec{s} + \tilde{f}(\vec{0}) \int_{\mathbb{R}^d} h'\left(\frac{\|\vec{s}\|^2}{\epsilon}\right) P_{4,x}(\vec{s}) d\vec{s} \right.$$

$$\left. + \frac{1}{2} \sum_{i=1}^{d} \frac{\partial^2}{\partial s_i^2} \tilde{f}(\vec{0}) \int_{\mathbb{R}^d} s_i^2 h\left(\frac{\|\vec{s}\|^2}{\epsilon}\right) d\vec{s} \right) + \mathcal{O}(s^4),$$

$$= f(x) \int_{\mathbb{R}^d} h(\|\vec{t}\|^2) d\vec{t} + \epsilon f(x) \int_{\mathbb{R}^d} h'(\|\vec{t}\|^2) P_{4,x}(\vec{t}) d\vec{t}$$

$$+ \frac{\epsilon}{2} \sum_{i=1}^{d} \frac{\partial^2}{\partial s_i^2} f(x) \int_{\mathbb{R}^d} t_i^2 h(\|\vec{t}\|^2) d\vec{t} + \mathcal{O}(\epsilon^2),$$

where $\vec{t} = \vec{s}/\sqrt{\epsilon}$. Defining m_0, m_2 and ω as in (6.8) and (6.9) and $\Delta f(x) = \sum_{i=1}^{d} \partial^2 f(x)/\partial s_i^2$ to be the negative-definite Laplace–Beltrami operator, the proof is complete. □

Near the boundary, we have the following result.

Lemma 6.3 *For $f \in \mathcal{C}^3(\mathcal{M})$ and $0 < r \le 1/2$, we have that uniformly for all $x \in \mathcal{M}$ whose distance is at most ϵ^r from the boundary $\partial\mathcal{M}$,*

$$G_\epsilon f(x) = m_0^\epsilon f(x_0) + \sqrt{\epsilon} m_1^\epsilon \frac{\partial f}{\partial \nu}(x_0) + \mathcal{O}(\epsilon),$$

where x_0 is the closest point that belongs to the boundary and $m_0^\epsilon, m_1^\epsilon$ are bounded functions of x and ϵ. Here, ν is the direction normal to the boundary.

The proof of this fact is more technical (see the appendix of Coifman & Lafon (2006)). Notice that there is a term of order $\sqrt{\epsilon}$. This is because the integrals of the odd-power terms do not vanish in the direction normal to the boundary since the domain of integration is no longer symmetric. However, if we assume that f satisfies the Neumann boundary condition, $(\partial f/\partial \nu)(x_0) = 0$, or if $\mathcal{M}$ has no boundary, we recover the conclusion of Theorem 6.1.

6.1.1   Estimation of the Laplacian

Consider the data $x_i \in \mathcal{M}$, with sampling density $q(x)$ which is not necessarily uniform. Our goal is to perform several normalizations (algebraic manipulations) to extract the Laplacian term from the asymptotic expansion in Theorem 6.1. In particular, the construction is as follows. Define

$$G_{q,\epsilon} f(x) := G_\epsilon(fq)(x)$$
$$= m_0 f(x)q(x) + \epsilon m_2(\omega(x)f(x)q(x) + \Delta(f(x)q(x))) + \mathcal{O}(\epsilon^2)$$
$$= m_0 f(x)q(x)(1 + \epsilon m(\omega(x) + f^{-1}(x)q^{-1}(x)\Delta(f(x)q(x)))) + \mathcal{O}(\epsilon^2),$$

where we have introduced the constant $m = m_2/m_0$. Define also

$$q_\epsilon := G_{q,\epsilon} 1 = m_0 q(1 + \epsilon m(\omega + q^{-1}\Delta q) + \mathcal{O}(\epsilon^2)), \tag{6.11}$$

and introduce a parameter α so that

$$q_\epsilon^\alpha = m_0^\alpha q^\alpha (1 + \epsilon \alpha m(\omega + q^{-1}\Delta q) + \mathcal{O}(\epsilon^2)).$$

Take the integral

$$
\begin{aligned}
G_{q,\epsilon}\left(\frac{f}{q_\epsilon^\alpha}\right) &= m_0 \frac{fq}{q_\epsilon^\alpha}\left(1 + \epsilon m(\omega + \frac{q_\epsilon^\alpha}{fq}\Delta\left(\frac{fq}{q_\epsilon^\alpha}\right) + \mathcal{O}(\epsilon^2)\right) \\
&= m_0^{1-\alpha} fq^{1-\alpha}(1 - \epsilon\alpha m\omega - \epsilon\alpha m q^{-1}\Delta q + \mathcal{O}(\epsilon^2)) \\
&\quad \times (1 + \epsilon m\omega + \epsilon m f^{-1}q^{\alpha-1}\Delta(fq^{1-\alpha}) + \mathcal{O}(\epsilon^2)) \\
&= m_0^{1-\alpha} fq^{1-\alpha}\left(1 + \epsilon m\omega(1-\alpha) - \epsilon m\alpha\frac{\Delta q}{q} + \epsilon m\frac{\Delta(fq^{1-\alpha})}{fq^{1-\alpha}} + \mathcal{O}(\epsilon^2)\right).
\end{aligned}
$$

$$(6.12)$$

Subsequently, we compute

$$
\begin{aligned}
\hat{q}_\epsilon &:= G_{q,\epsilon}\left(\frac{1}{q_\epsilon^\alpha}\right) \\
&= m_0^{1-\alpha} q^{1-\alpha}\left(1 + \epsilon m\omega(1-\alpha) - \epsilon m\alpha\frac{\Delta q}{q} + \epsilon m\frac{\Delta(q^{1-\alpha})}{q^{1-\alpha}} + \mathcal{O}(\epsilon^2)\right),
\end{aligned}
$$

$$(6.13)$$

and define

$$
\begin{aligned}
S_\epsilon f &:= \frac{G_{q,\epsilon}(f/q_\epsilon^\alpha)}{\hat{q}_\epsilon} \\
&= f\left(1 - \epsilon m\omega(1-\alpha) + \epsilon m\alpha\frac{\Delta q}{q} - \epsilon m\frac{\Delta(q^{1-\alpha})}{q^{1-\alpha}} + \mathcal{O}(\epsilon^2)\right) \\
&\quad \times \left(1 + \epsilon m\omega(1-\alpha) - \epsilon m\alpha\frac{\Delta q}{q} + \epsilon m\frac{\Delta(fq^{1-\alpha})}{fq^{1-\alpha}}\mathcal{O}(\epsilon^2)\right) \\
&= f\left(1 + \epsilon m\left(-\frac{\Delta(q^{1-\alpha})}{q^{1-\alpha}} + \frac{\Delta(fq^{1-\alpha})}{fq^{1-\alpha}}\right) + \mathcal{O}(\epsilon^2)\right) \\
&= f + \epsilon m\left(2\frac{\nabla q^{1-\alpha}}{q^{1-\alpha}}\cdot\nabla f + \Delta f\right) + \mathcal{O}(\epsilon^2) \\
&= f + \epsilon m(2(1-\alpha)\nabla\log q \cdot \nabla f + \Delta f) + \mathcal{O}(\epsilon^2).
\end{aligned}
$$

$$(6.14)$$

Thus we obtain a weighted Laplacian,

$$L_\epsilon f = \frac{S_\epsilon f - f}{m\epsilon} = (2 - 2\alpha)\nabla\log q \cdot \nabla f + \Delta f + \mathcal{O}(\epsilon). \tag{6.15}$$

Notice that $L_\epsilon f$ is defined through a sequence of normalizations (6.12), (6.14), (6.15) of the integral operator $G_{q,\epsilon}$. As $\epsilon \to 0$, this integral operator approximates a weighted Laplacian (the order-one terms on the right-hand side of (6.15)).

When $\alpha = 0$ and the sampling density is uniform, $q = 1$, this method corresponds to the discrete graph Laplacian (Belkin & Niyogi 2003), and $L_\epsilon f = \Delta f + \mathcal{O}(\epsilon)$. The construction in (6.15), however, allows one to obtain the Laplacian even when the sampling measure is non-uniform, by choosing $\alpha = 1$. On the other hand, if we choose $\alpha = 1/2$, we obtain

$$L_\epsilon f = \nabla \log q \cdot \nabla f + \Delta f + \mathcal{O}(\epsilon) = \hat{\mathcal{L}} f + \mathcal{O}(\epsilon),$$

where $\hat{\mathcal{L}}$ is the generator (or adjoint of the Fokker–Planck operator) of the following gradient system:

$$dx = \nabla \log q(x)\, dt + \sqrt{2}\, dW_t, \tag{6.16}$$

which will lead to an interesting application (as we shall see in Example 6.5 below).

6.1.2   Discrete Approximation

In this section, we describe the discrete analog in constructing L_ϵ. The key to this approach is the intuition that continuous notions such as functions and operators have discrete representations in the basis of delta functions centered on each of the data points. Given a data set $\{x_i\}_{i=1}^N \subset \mathcal{M} \subset \mathbb{R}^n$, sampled independently from a sampling measure with density $q(x)$, a function f is represented by a vector $\vec{f} = (f(x_1), f(x_2), \ldots, f(x_N))^\top$.

In practice, one can choose a Gaussian kernel,

$$h\left(\frac{\|x - y\|^2}{\epsilon}\right) = K_\epsilon(x, y) = \exp\left(-\frac{\|x - y\|^2}{4\epsilon}\right), \tag{6.17}$$

such that h is an exponentially decaying function of $\|x - y\|$ as required in Theorem 6.1. With this choice, notice that $m = m_0/m_2 = 1$ where m_0 and m_2 are defined in Theorem 6.1. Subsequently, the integral operator,

$$\epsilon^{d/2} G_{\epsilon,q} f(x_i) := \int_\mathcal{M} K_\epsilon(x_i, y) f(y) q(y) dV(y),$$

is represented by a matrix–vector multiplication between the $N \times N$ matrix, $K_{ij} = K_\epsilon(x_i, x_j)$ and the N-dimensional vector, $\vec{f}$. With these definitions, $K\vec{f}$ is a vector of length N whose ith component is given as

$$\frac{1}{N}\left(K\vec{f}\right)_i = \frac{1}{N}\sum_{j=1}^N K_{ij}\vec{f}_j = \frac{1}{N}\sum_{j=1}^N K_\epsilon(x_i, x_j) f(x_j) \xrightarrow{N \to \infty} \epsilon^{d/2} G_\epsilon f(x_i),$$

where the limit follows from interpreting the summation as a Monte Carlo integral. Thus, the matrix K maps functions defined on $\{x_i\}$ to functions defined on $\{x_i\}$. In this sense, we can think of K as an operator written in the basis of delta functions $\{\delta_{x_i}\}$ on the data set. Notice that, when the data is not uniformly distributed on $\mathcal{M}$, the operator is biased by the sampling measure $q(y)$. This same bias applies to inner products, if f, g are functions on $\mathcal{M}$ and $\vec{f}, \vec{g}$ are the corresponding discrete representations evaluated at $\{x_i\}$, then the dot product has the following interpretation:

$$\frac{1}{N}\vec{f} \cdot \vec{g} = \frac{1}{N}\sum_{i=1}^N f(x_i) g(x_i) \xrightarrow{N \to \infty} \int_\mathcal{M} f(y) g(y) q(y) dV(y) := \langle f, g \rangle_q,$$

where the inner product is defined over $L^2(\mathcal{M}, q)$.

Given the kernel in (6.17), we construct a discrete approximation to L_ϵ as follows.

- Estimate q_ϵ in (6.11) at the training data x_i with

$$q_\epsilon(x_i) = \frac{1}{N} \sum_{j=1}^{N} K_\epsilon(x_i, x_j).$$

- Apply the right normalization in (6.12) by computing

$$\hat{K}_\epsilon(x_i, x_j) = \frac{K_\epsilon(x_i, x_j)}{q_\epsilon(x_i)^\alpha q_\epsilon(x_j)^\alpha}. \tag{6.18}$$

- Approximate (6.13) as

$$\hat{q}_\epsilon(x_i) = \frac{1}{N} \sum_{j=1}^{N} \hat{K}_\epsilon(x_i, x_j).$$

- Define $S_\epsilon = \hat{K}_\epsilon(x_i, x_j)/\hat{q}_\epsilon(x_i)$. Notice that the term $q_\epsilon(x_i)^\alpha$ in (6.18) does not affect S_ϵ since the same term should appear in $\hat{q}_\epsilon(x_i)$. Finally, the discrete approximation to the weighted Laplacian (depending on the choice of α) is given by $L_\epsilon = (S_\epsilon - \mathcal{I}_N)/\epsilon$.

Numerically, the matrix K_ϵ is $N \times N$, so the memory requirement becomes large as the number of data points N increases. However, since the kernel is exponentially decaying, we can replace $K_\epsilon(x_i, x_j)$ by zero for x_i that is sufficiently far away from x_j. Numerically, this is typically done by using a k-nearest-neighbors algorithm which evaluates K_ϵ on each point x_i and its nearest k neighbors. Notice that this matrix construction is not symmetric because x_j may belong to the set of k nearest neighbors of x_i, but x_i need not necessarily be in the set of k nearest neighbors to x_j. For practical purposes, it is more convenient to have a symmetric K_ϵ and, in our numerical results below, we replace it with $(K_\epsilon + K_\epsilon^\top)/2$, which will give similar results when ϵ is small enough that the truncated entries are already very close to zero.

If we define an $N \times N$ matrix K with components $K_{ij} := \hat{K}_\epsilon(x_i, x_j)$ and an $N \times N$ diagonal matrix D with components $D_{ii} := \hat{q}_\epsilon(x_i)$, then the discrete approximation to the weighted Laplacian $L_\epsilon = \epsilon^{-1}(D^{-1}K - \mathcal{I}_N)$ is not a symmetric matrix. To solve such a large eigenvalue problem, it is convenient to consider solving a symmetric eigenvalue problem of the following matrix:

$$\hat{L} = D^{1/2} L_\epsilon D^{-1/2} = \epsilon^{-1}(D^{-1/2} K D^{-1/2} - \mathcal{I}_N). \tag{6.19}$$

Let $\hat{L}U = U\Lambda$, where the columns of U are the eigenvectors of $\hat{L}$ and the diagonal components of Λ are the associated eigenvalues. Define $\Phi = D^{-1/2}U$, then

$$L_\epsilon \Phi = D^{-1/2} \hat{L} D^{1/2} \Phi = D^{-1/2} \hat{L} U = D^{-1/2} U \Lambda = \Phi \Lambda.$$

This means that the columns of Φ are the eigenvectors of L_ϵ and the diagonal components of Λ are the associated eigenvalues.

Define $\Phi = (\vec{\varphi}_0, \vec{\varphi}_1, \ldots, \vec{\varphi}_M)$. Then each column vector, $\vec{\varphi}_j$, approximates the eigenfunction evaluated on the data points that are sampled with density q; that is, the ith component of $\vec{\varphi}_j \in \mathbb{R}^N$ is a discrete approximation to $\varphi_j(x_i)$. Since the eigenfunctions are orthonormal in $L^2(\mathcal{M}, q)$, we have

$$1 = \|\varphi_j\|_q^2 = \int_{\mathcal{M}} \varphi_j^2(x) q(x) dV(x) \approx \frac{1}{N} \sum_{i=1}^{N} \varphi_j^2(x_i) = \frac{1}{N} \vec{\varphi}_j^\top \vec{\varphi}_j,$$

which suggests that one should normalize columns of Φ such that $\vec{\varphi}_j^\top \vec{\varphi}_j = N$.

When the Laplace–Beltrami operator, Δ, is constructed (that is, by setting $\alpha = 1$), since Δ is self-adjoint with respect to $L^2(\mathcal{M})$ and negative-definite, its eigenfunctions $\varphi_j(x)$ form an orthonormal basis of $L^2(\mathcal{M})$ with eigenvalues ordered as follows: $0 = \lambda_0 \geq \lambda_1 \geq \lambda_2 \geq \ldots$. The *heat kernel* for Δ is defined as the function $S_\epsilon(x, y)$ that satisfies

$$e^{\epsilon \Delta} f(x) = \int_{\mathcal{M}} S_\epsilon(x, u) f(u) dV(u),$$

for all f, which implies that $S_\epsilon(x, y) = e^{\epsilon \Delta} \delta_y(x)$. The *diffusion distance* between x and y is defined as an average of the difference between transition probabilities starting from x to y over all intermediate points u. Specifically,

$$D_\epsilon(x, y)^2 := \|S_\epsilon(x, \cdot) - S_\epsilon(y, \cdot)\|_{L^2(\mathcal{M})}^2,$$

where $S_\epsilon(x, y)$ represents the transition probability of the passage of a Brownian particle from x to y for time length ϵ. Since we can write

$$S_\epsilon(x, y) = e^{\epsilon \Delta} \delta_y(x) = \sum_{j=0}^{\infty} \langle e^{\epsilon \Delta} \delta_y, \varphi_j \rangle \varphi_j(x) = \sum_{j=0}^{\infty} e^{\lambda_j \epsilon} \varphi_j(y) \varphi_j(x),$$

the diffusion distance becomes

$$D_\epsilon(x, y)^2 = \int_{\mathcal{M}} \sum_{j=1}^{\infty} e^{2\lambda_j \epsilon} (\varphi_j(x) - \varphi_j(y))^2 \varphi_j(u)^2 \, dV(u)$$

$$= \sum_{j=1}^{\infty} e^{2\lambda_j \epsilon} (\varphi_j(x) - \varphi_j(y))^2,$$

where the difference of the terms with index $j = 0$ vanishes since $\varphi_0(x) = 1$ and $\lambda_0 = 0$. This suggests that the diffusion distance can be approximated by a Euclidean distance between two M-dimensional vectors in the diffusion coordinates. In particular,

$$D_\epsilon(x, y)^2 \approx \|\Psi_{\epsilon, M}(x) - \Psi_{\epsilon, M}(y)\|_{\mathbb{R}^M}^2 \qquad (6.20)$$

for large enough M, where

$$\Psi_{\epsilon, M}(x) := (e^{\lambda_1 \epsilon} \varphi_1(x), e^{\lambda_2 \epsilon} \varphi_2(x), \ldots, e^{\lambda_M \epsilon} \varphi_M(x)) \in \mathbb{R}^M. \qquad (6.21)$$

The operator $\Psi_{\epsilon,M}\colon \mathcal{M} \to \mathbb{R}^M$ as defined in (6.21) is called the *diffusion map* (Coifman & Lafon 2006). With appropriate choices of ϵ and M, the diffusion map is an isometric embedding (in the sense of (6.20)). The diffusion map, which represents the data $x \in \mathcal{M}$ on the diffusion coordinates as defined in (6.21), is a nonlinear manifold learning algorithm.

6.2   Generalization with Variable-Bandwidth Kernels

In practical applications, we often have sparse samples near the tail of the distribution, which suggests that the data might not necessarily lie on a compact manifold as assumed in Theorem 6.1. In classical kernel density estimation problems, this issue can be overcome with variable-bandwidth kernels of the form

$$K_\epsilon(x,y) = \exp\left(-\frac{\|x-y\|^2}{4\epsilon\rho(x)\rho(y)}\right), \tag{6.22}$$

where the choice of bandwidth function $\rho(x)$ is critical for accurate estimation of the tails of the distribution and in regions of sparse sampling (Terrell & Scott 1992, Sain & Scott 1996).

In the diffusion maps construction, the limiting operator using the variable-bandwidth kernel was first established in Ting *et al.* (2010). Subsequently, the first rigorous error bounds for this construction were reported in Berry & Harlim (2016*d*). Practically, the main result in Berry & Harlim (2016*d*) suggests that the construction of $L^S_{\epsilon,\alpha}$,

$$K^S_\epsilon(x_i,x_j) = \exp\left\{-\frac{\|x_i-x_j\|^2}{4\epsilon\rho(x_i)\rho(x_j)}\right\}, \qquad q^S_\epsilon(x_i) = \sum_{j=1}^N \frac{K_\epsilon(x_i,x_j)}{\rho(x_i)^d},$$

$$K^S_{\epsilon,\alpha}(x_i,x_j) = \frac{K^S_\epsilon(x_i,x_j)}{q^S_\epsilon(x_i)^\alpha q^S_\epsilon(x_j)^\alpha}, \qquad q^S_{\epsilon,\alpha}(x_i) = \sum_{j=1}^N K^S_{\epsilon,\alpha}(x_i,x_j),$$

$$\hat{K}^S_{\epsilon,\alpha}(x_i,x_j) = \frac{K^S_{\epsilon,\alpha}(x_i,x_j)}{q^S_{\epsilon,\alpha}(x_i)}, \qquad L^S_{\epsilon,\alpha}(x_i,x_j) = \frac{\hat{K}^S_{\epsilon,\alpha}(x_i,x_j)-\delta_{ij}}{\epsilon\rho(x_i)^2},$$

converges to

$$\mathcal{L}_{\alpha,\rho}f := \Delta f + 2(1-\alpha)\nabla f \cdot \frac{\nabla q}{q} + (d+2)\nabla f \cdot \frac{\nabla \rho}{\rho} \tag{6.23}$$

in probability.

By choosing the bandwidth function to be inversely proportional to the sampling density, $\rho = q^\beta + \mathcal{O}(\epsilon)$, we increase the bandwidth in the areas of sparse sampling and decrease it in the areas of dense sampling. With this bandwidth function, the convergence rate is given as follows (see Berry & Harlim (2016*d*) for the detailed proof):

$$L_{\epsilon,\alpha} f(x_i) = \Delta f(x_i) + c_1 \nabla f \cdot \frac{\nabla q}{q} + \mathcal{O}\left(\epsilon, \frac{q(x_i)^{(1-d\beta)/2}}{\sqrt{N}\epsilon^{2+d/4}}, \frac{\|\nabla f(x_i)\|q(x_i)^{-c_2}}{\sqrt{N}\epsilon^{1/2+d/4}}\right),$$

with $c_1 = 2 - 2\alpha + d\beta + 2\beta$ and $c_2 = 1/2 - 2\alpha + 2d\alpha + d\beta/2 + \beta$.

The key to applying this result is in choosing α and β. The first consideration is the desired operator, which is controlled by c_1, and solving for β. The second consideration is that on a non-compact manifold q may become arbitrarily close to zero. In order to bound the error terms on a non-compact manifold, the exponents in the error components must satisfy $(1 - d\beta)/2 > 0$ and $c_2 < 0$. Intuitively, we expect $\beta < 0$ to have the best results since this increases the bandwidth in areas of sparse sampling and decreases it in areas of dense sampling. Some natural choices for β are $-1/2$, $-1/d$, and $-1/(d/2+1)$. One advantage of the choice $\beta = -1/2$ is that we find $c_1 = 1 - 2\alpha - d/2$ and so simply by taking α large enough we can guarantee $c_1 > 0$ even when the dimension is unknown. This is important for gradient flow systems where the fundamental properties (such as the invariant measure) are dramatically altered if $c_1 < 0$. In the numerical example below, we will set $\beta = -1/2$. If one is interested in approximating the generator of the gradient system in (6.16), for which $c_1 = 1$, then $\alpha = -d/4$. On the other hand, if one is interested in estimating the Laplacian, for which $c_1 = 0$, then $\alpha = 1/2 - d/4$. Of course, one can also obtain the Laplacian by choosing $\beta = 0$ and $\alpha = 1$, which implies using the fixed bandwidth and recovers the asymptotic expansion in (6.15).

Notice that the construction of $L_{\epsilon,\alpha}^S$ is not symmetric due to the normalization by $q_{\epsilon,\alpha}^S$ and ρ^2. However, as in the fixed-bandwidth construction, one can define an appropriate similarity transformation such that solving the eigenvalue problem for $L_{\epsilon,\alpha}^S$ amounts to solving a related symmetric eigenvalue problem. In particular, let $D_{ii} := q_{\epsilon,\alpha}^S(x_i)$ and $P_{ii} := \rho(x_i)$ be diagonal $N \times N$ matrices and define the symmetric matrix $K_{ij} := K_{\epsilon,\alpha}^S(x_i, x_j)$. Let $L_{ij} := L_{\epsilon,\alpha}^S(x_i, x_j)$ be the desired normalized Laplacian matrix. Note that $L = P^{-2}(D^{-1}K - \mathcal{I})/\epsilon$ and, since P and D are diagonal, we can form the conjugation of L by the diagonal matrix $S = PD^{1/2}$ to find the symmetric matrix

$$\hat{L} = SLS^{-1} = \frac{1}{\epsilon}(S^{-1}KS^{-1} - P^{-2}).$$

In order to find the eigenvectors of L, we first solve the eigendecomposition of $\hat{L} = \hat{U}\Lambda\hat{U}^\top$, and then, on setting $U = S^{-1}\hat{U}$, we have

$$LU = S^{-1}\hat{L}SU = S^{-1}\hat{L}SS^{-1}\hat{U} = S^{-1}\hat{L}\hat{U} = S^{-1}\Lambda\hat{U} = \Lambda U,$$

since S is diagonal. Thus, columns of U are the desired eigenvectors of L with eigenvalues given by the diagonal components of Λ. Computing eigenvalues of $\hat{L}$ directly might not be numerically feasible when ϵ is small. One way to circumvent this issue is to exploit the fact that

$$\lim_{\epsilon \to 0}(\mathcal{I} + \epsilon\hat{L})^{1/\epsilon} = e^{\hat{L}},$$

which allows one to approximate the eigenvalues of $\hat{L}$ with $\lambda_k \approx \log(\xi_k^{1/\epsilon})$, where ξ_k are eigenvalues of $\mathcal{I} + \epsilon \hat{L}$.

Notice that $U^\top S^2 U = \mathcal{I}$ since $\hat{U}$ is an orthonormal matrix. Since we want the eigenfunctions to be orthonormal in $L^2(\mathcal{M}, p_{\text{eq}})$, that is,

$$1 = [U^\top S^2 U]_{kk} = \frac{1}{N} \sum_{i=1}^{N} \varphi_k^2(x_i) S_{ii}^2 \approx \int_{\mathcal{M}} \varphi_k^2(x) p_{\text{eq}}(x) dV(x),$$

it is clear that $S_{ii}^2 = p_{\text{eq}}(x_i)/q(x_i)$ is an appropriate choice for the Monte Carlo approximation above to be consistent. Since the sampling density is estimated by $q(x_i) \approx q_{\epsilon,\alpha}^S(x_i)$, we can estimate the equilibrium density by $p_{\text{eq}}(x_i) = S^2(i,i)q(x_i)$.

In the implementation with the fixed-bandwidth kernel in (6.17), one only needs to specify the parameter ϵ. Notice that, in the variable-bandwidth kernel, one also needs to specify the bandwidth function ρ and the intrinsic dimension of the manifold d. For the bandwidth function, since the result assumes only $\rho = q^\beta + \mathcal{O}(\epsilon)$, we do not require that the sampling density be exactly known. For practical applications we may use any kernel density estimation method to find an order-ϵ approximation of q for the purposes of defining the bandwidth function ρ. Next, we will briefly discuss one way to specify ϵ and d.

6.2.1   Automatic Specification of ϵ and d

In this section, we discuss an automated method for tuning the parameters ϵ and d that is based on the idea originally suggested in Coifman *et al.* (2008). It was noted in Coifman *et al.* (2008) that, for a fixed-bandwidth kernel in (6.17), in the limit as $\epsilon \to 0$ the kernel approaches zero, and in the limit as $\epsilon \to \infty$ the kernel approaches one for all pairs of data points. Moreover, they noted that, when ϵ is well tuned, the kernel localizes the data set so that

$$S(\epsilon) = \frac{1}{N^2} \sum_{i,j} K_\epsilon(x_i, x_j) \approx \frac{1}{\text{vol}(\mathcal{M})} \int_{\mathcal{M}} \int_{T_x \mathcal{M}} K_\epsilon(x,y) dy \, dV(x)$$

$$= \int_{\mathcal{M}} \frac{(4\pi\epsilon)^{d/2}}{\text{vol}(\mathcal{M})} dV(x) = (4\pi\epsilon)^{d/2}, \tag{6.24}$$

where d is the dimension of the manifold and $T_x\mathcal{M} \cong \mathbb{R}^d$ is the tangent space at x. When ϵ is very large, $S(\epsilon)$ will approach 1, whereas when ϵ is very small, $S(\epsilon)$ will approach $1/N$. Coifman *et al.* (2008) suggested that we can choose ϵ by evaluating $S(\epsilon)$ for a large range of values and searching for the region where $\log(S(\epsilon))$ grows linearly with respect to $\log(\epsilon)$. In the region of linearity, $\log(S(\epsilon)) = (d/2)\log(\epsilon) + (d/2)\log(4\pi)$ and the maximal value of the slope is $d/2$.

In several examples (see Figures 6 and 7 in Berry & Harlim (2016*d*)), it was shown that the maximum of the slope $d\log(S(\epsilon))/d\log(\epsilon)$ is numerically close to $1/2$ for a one-dimensional circle and to 1 for data sampled from a two-dimensional sphere. These empirical results suggest that it may be possible to estimate the dimension of the manifold as two times the maximum value of the slope, $d = 2 \times \max\{d\log(S(\epsilon))/d\log(\epsilon)\}$. Furthermore, one can choose ϵ to be the value corresponding to the maximum slope. Since to employ the variable-bandwidth kernel one requires knowledge of the intrinsic dimension, one can use a fixed bandwidth kernel to estimate the dimension prior to applying a variable-bandwidth kernel in the diffusion maps algorithm.

Alternatively, one can also specify the dimension using the method derived from the scaling laws established in Berry & Harlim (2016b). We should note that there are other methods for estimating the intrinsic dimension (Hein & Audibert 2005, Little *et al.* 2009). To close this section, we include a numerical example comparing estimates from the variable-bandwidth kernels with and without using the automated ϵ and d tuning.

Example 6.4   Let $x_i \sim \mathcal{N}(0, \sigma^2)$, where $\sigma^2 = 1/25$. Here, the sampling distribution is $q(x) \propto \exp(-x^2/(2\sigma^2))$. In this example, we set $\{x_i\}_{i=1}^{N}$, where $N = 10{,}000$ random samples, so the manifold is simply the real line, $\mathbb{R}$, and the intrinsic dimension is $d = 1$.

In this example, our goal is to apply the diffusion maps algorithm with the variable-bandwidth kernel (with $\alpha = -d/4, \beta = -1/2$) to estimate the eigenfunctions of the weighted Laplacian that is associated with the generator of the Ornstein–Uhlenbeck process, $\mathcal{L} = -(x/\sigma^2)\partial/\partial x + \partial^2/\partial x^2$. For this simple example, one can verify that the eigenvalues of $\mathcal{L}$ are given by $\lambda_k = -k/\sigma^2$ and the associated eigenfunctions are simply the normalized Hermite polynomials

$$\varphi_k(x) = \frac{1}{\sqrt{k!}}(-1)^k e^{\frac{x^2}{2\sigma^2}} \frac{d^k}{dx^k}\left(e^{-\frac{x^2}{2\sigma^2}}\right). \tag{6.25}$$

In Figure 6.1, we compare the first 10 eigenvalues estimated using the variable-bandwidth construction by specifying (1) both $\epsilon = 10^{-5}$ and $d = 1$, (2) only $\epsilon = 10^{-5}$, and (3) neither of these two parameters. In cases (2) and (3), we use the automatic specification for d by matching the maximum slope of $\log(S(\epsilon))$, where $S(\epsilon)$ is defined in (6.24). Also, for case (3), we use the ϵ associated with this maximum slope. Both for case (2) and for case (3), the estimated dimension is 0.9909, which is close to the true intrinsic dimension $d = 1$. For case (3), the estimated $\epsilon = 8.76 \times 10^{-6}$. In Figure 6.2, we compare the estimates of the first three eigenfunctions with the analytical formula given in (6.25).

In plotting these eigenfunctions, sometimes the estimates (the eigenvectors) can be scaled differently, since eigenvectors are non-unique. That is, if $\vec{x}$ is an eigenvector of A, then $\alpha\vec{x}$ is also an eigenvector of A for any $\alpha \neq 0$. Therefore, for visual comparison we rescale the estimates by the scaling factor obtained through regressing the true and the estimated eigenfunctions. When the eigenvalues are repeated, the numerical approximations to the eigenfunctions corresponding to repeated eigenvalues can be any orthogonal transformation of the true eigenfunctions with the given eigenvalue. The same regression strategy is used to find the orthogonal transformation for visual comparison.

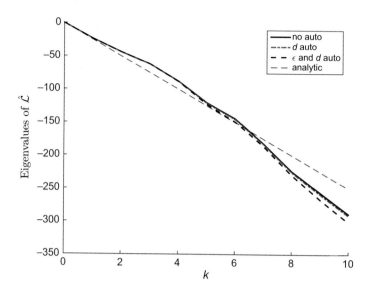

Figure 6.1 The 10 leading eigenvalues of $\hat{\mathcal{L}}$, the generator of the Ornstein–Uhlenbeck process in Example 6.4.

Note that, while this example compares the estimates for the eigenvalues and eigenfunctions, the theory discussed in the previous section does not imply spectral convergence. Instead, the asymptotic expansion in (6.23) yields pointwise convergence in probability, so the estimates are sensitive to the samples. For the spectral convergence result, see the recent results by Berry & Sauer (2016).

6.3   Nonparametric Probabilistic Modeling

In this section, we describe a nonparametric probabilistic modeling approach using the data-driven eigenfunctions estimated by the diffusion maps algorithm. In particular, we will construct a nonparametric model for the diffusion process $x(t) \in \mathcal{M} \subset \mathbb{R}^n$, which satisfies

$$dx = a(x)dt + b(x)dW_t, \quad x(0) = x_0 \sim p_0(x). \qquad (6.26)$$

Here, W_t denotes the standard Wiener process, $a(x)$ denotes the vector field, and $b(x)$ denotes the diffusion tensor, all of which are defined on the manifold $\mathcal{M} \subset \mathbb{R}^n$ such that the solutions of this SDE exist and the associated density function $p(x,t)$ solves the Fokker–Planck equation,

$$\frac{\partial p}{\partial t} = \text{div}_x \left(-ap + \frac{1}{2} \nabla (bb^\top)p \right) := \mathcal{L}^* p, \quad p(x,0) = p_0(x), \qquad (6.27)$$

such that $p(x,t) \to p_{\text{eq}}(x)$ as $t \to \infty$, where p_{eq} denotes the unique equilibrium density which satisfies $\mathcal{L}^* p_{\text{eq}} = 0$. This ergodicity assumption implies that the

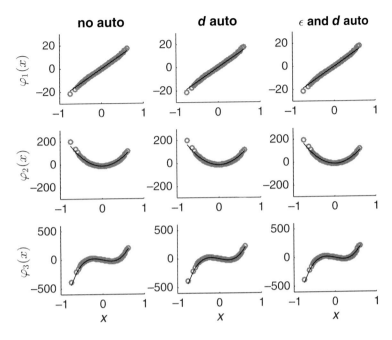

Figure 6.2 Estimates of the Hermite polynomials of order one to three, which are eigenfunctions of the generator of the Ornstein–Uhlenbeck process in Example 6.4.

manifold $\mathcal{M}$ is the attractor of the dynamical system in (6.26). The goal of *nonparametric probabilistic modeling* is to approximate $p(x,t)$ without knowing the model either in (6.26) or in (6.27). Instead, we assume that we are given only a time series of $x_i := x(t_i) \in \mathcal{M} \subset \mathbb{R}^n$ with a sampling measure that is exactly the equilibrium measure, $q(x) = p_{\mathrm{eq}}(x)$. Before discussing the nonparametric method, let us first review several related properties of the weighted Laplacian estimated by the diffusion maps algorithm.

In particular, given the data $x_i \sim p_{\mathrm{eq}}(x)$, we employ the diffusion maps algorithm to estimate the operator

$$\hat{\mathcal{L}} = \nabla \log(p_{\mathrm{eq}}) \cdot \nabla + \Delta, \tag{6.28}$$

which is the generator of gradient flow in (6.16). This operator is self-adjoint with respect to $L^2(\mathcal{M}, p_{\mathrm{eq}})$. The self-adjointness can be verified by noting that, for any pair of functions $f, g \in L^2(\mathcal{M}, p_{\mathrm{eq}})$, we have

$$\begin{aligned}
\langle \hat{\mathcal{L}} f, g \rangle_{p_{\mathrm{eq}}} &= \langle \nabla \log(p_{\mathrm{eq}}) \cdot \nabla f, g \rangle_{p_{\mathrm{eq}}} + \langle \Delta f, g p_{\mathrm{eq}} \rangle \\
&= \langle \nabla \log(p_{\mathrm{eq}}) \cdot \nabla f, g \rangle_{p_{\mathrm{eq}}} - \langle \nabla f, \nabla(g p_{\mathrm{eq}}) \rangle \\
&= \langle \nabla p_{\mathrm{eq}} \cdot \nabla f, g \rangle - \langle \nabla f, \nabla g \rangle_{p_{\mathrm{eq}}} - \langle \nabla f, g \nabla p_{\mathrm{eq}} \rangle \\
&= -\langle \nabla f, \nabla g \rangle_{p_{\mathrm{eq}}}, \tag{6.29}
\end{aligned}$$

which also means that $\langle f, \hat{\mathcal{L}}g\rangle_{p_{\mathrm{eq}}} = -\langle \nabla f, \nabla g\rangle_{p_{\mathrm{eq}}}$. Furthermore, the equality in (6.29) implies that $\hat{\mathcal{L}}$ is not positive, that is, $\langle \hat{\mathcal{L}}f, f\rangle_{p_{\mathrm{eq}}} = -\|\nabla f\|_{p_{\mathrm{eq}}} \leq 0$ for all $f \in L^2(\mathcal{M}, p_{\mathrm{eq}})$. Assuming that the operator $\hat{\mathcal{L}}$ has a discrete spectrum, the eigenfunctions φ_j form an orthonormal basis of $L^2(\mathcal{M}, p_{\mathrm{eq}})$.

While $\hat{\mathcal{L}}$ is self-adjoint with respect to the weighted Hilbert space $L^2(\mathcal{M}, p_{\mathrm{eq}})$, it is not self-adjoint with respect to the unweighted space $L^2(\mathcal{M})$ and the adjoint of $\hat{\mathcal{L}}$ with respect to $L^2(\mathcal{M})$ is

$$\hat{\mathcal{L}}^* = -\mathrm{div}(\nabla\log(p_{\mathrm{eq}})\cdot) + \Delta,$$

and we find that

$$\begin{aligned}
\hat{\mathcal{L}}^*(f p_{\mathrm{eq}}) &= -\mathrm{div}\Big(f p_{\mathrm{eq}} \nabla\log(p_{\mathrm{eq}}) - \nabla(f p_{\mathrm{eq}})\Big) \\
&= -\mathrm{div}\Big(f\,\nabla p_{\mathrm{eq}} - \nabla(f p_{\mathrm{eq}})\Big) \\
&= \mathrm{div}\Big(p_{\mathrm{eq}}\nabla f\Big) = \nabla p_{\mathrm{eq}} \cdot \nabla f + p_{\mathrm{eq}}\,\Delta f \\
&= p_{\mathrm{eq}}\hat{\mathcal{L}}f,
\end{aligned}$$

which immediately implies that $\hat{\mathcal{L}}^*(\varphi_j p_{\mathrm{eq}}) = p_{\mathrm{eq}}\hat{\mathcal{L}}\varphi_j = \lambda_j\varphi_j p_{\mathrm{eq}}$. That is, $\varphi_j p_{\mathrm{eq}}$ are eigenfunctions of the operator $\hat{\mathcal{L}}^*$ which means that they are also eigenfunctions of $e^{t\hat{\mathcal{L}}^*}$. From the orthonormality of φ_j, it is clear that $\langle \varphi_i p_{\mathrm{eq}}, \varphi_j p_{\mathrm{eq}}\rangle_{p_{\mathrm{eq}}^{-1}} = \langle \varphi_i, \varphi_j\rangle_{p_{\mathrm{eq}}} = \delta_{ij}$.

Given these eigenfunctions, let the solutions of the Fokker–Planck equation in (6.27) be in the following form:

$$p(x, t) = e^{t\mathcal{L}^*}p_0(x) = \sum_{k=0}^{\infty} c_k(t)\varphi_k(x)p_{\mathrm{eq}}(x). \tag{6.30}$$

Here, we represent the solutions in the space spanned by the data-driven basis functions obtained via the diffusion maps algorithm. To draw an analogy with the classical theory of linear PDEs, we typically represent solutions of linear PDEs with Fourier series when the domain of the solutions is periodic. In fact, if the manifold is a one-dimensional circle $\mathcal{M} = S^1$ and the data are uniformly distributed, then the diffusion maps algorithm (with appropriate normalization) estimates eigenfunctions of the Laplace–Beltrami operator on this domain, and these eigenfunctions are exactly the Fourier bases as shown in Example 1.3. With this perspective, the representation in (6.30) is a generalization of Fourier series to data-driven basis functions. The striking difference is that we do not have explicit expression for $\varphi_k(x)$ and $p_{\mathrm{eq}}(x)$ as functions of x. Instead we have vectors $\vec{\varphi}$ and $\vec{p}_{eq}$ whose ith components are discrete estimates of $\varphi_k(x_i)$ and $p_{\mathrm{eq}}(x_i)$, respectively. This is the first key idea of the nonparametric modeling approach.

By substituting (6.30) into the Fokker–Planck equation in (6.27) and applying the Galerkin method, that is, requiring the residual to be orthogonal to the basis functions $\varphi_k p_{eq}$ with respect to $\langle \cdot, \cdot \rangle_{p_{eq}^{-1}}$, we obtain a system of differential equations with solutions given by

$$
\begin{aligned}
c_k(t) &= \langle e^{t\mathcal{L}^*} p_0, \varphi_k p_{eq} \rangle_{p_{eq}^{-1}} \\
&= \langle p_0, e^{t\mathcal{L}} \varphi_k \rangle \\
&= \left\langle \sum_{j=0}^{\infty} c_j(0) \varphi_j p_{eq}, e^{t\mathcal{L}} \varphi_k \right\rangle \\
&= \sum_{j=0}^{\infty} \langle \varphi_j, e^{t\mathcal{L}} \varphi_k \rangle_{p_{eq}} c_j(0).
\end{aligned}
\tag{6.31}
$$

Computationally, we apply a finite summation up to mode M in (6.30) and, if M is too small, then the Gibbs phenomenon will reduce the accuracy of the approximation as in the standard spectral method.

With a finite truncation, equation (6.31) can be written in a compact form as a matrix–vector multiplication, $\vec{c}(t) = A\vec{c}(0)$, where the kth component of $\vec{c}(t) \in \mathbb{R}^{M+1}$ is $c_k(t)$, and the components of the matrix $A \in \mathbb{R}^{(M+1) \times (M+1)}$ are

$$
A_{kj} = \langle \varphi_j, e^{t\mathcal{L}} \varphi_k \rangle_{p_{eq}}.
\tag{6.32}
$$

The second crucial idea for the nonparametric modeling is in approximating the matrix A, since we assume that the Fokker–Planck operator $\mathcal{L}^*$ is unknown. Before discussing this approximation, let us give an example where A can be specified explicitly.

Example 6.5 If the underlying process is indeed a gradient flow with isotropic diffusion as in (6.16), then we have a trivial nonparametric model with an analytic expression for the matrix A. In this very special situation, the adjoint of the Fokker–Planck operator in (6.27) is the generator $\mathcal{L} = \hat{\mathcal{L}}$, which can be approximated using the diffusion maps algorithm, such that $\hat{\mathcal{L}}\varphi_j(x) = \lambda_j \varphi_j(x)$. In this case, it is clear that the matrix A is diagonal, since

$$
A_{kj} = \langle \varphi_j, e^{t\hat{\mathcal{L}}} \varphi_k \rangle_{p_{eq}} = \langle \varphi_j, e^{\lambda_k t} \varphi_k \rangle_{p_{eq}} = e^{\lambda_k t} \langle \varphi_j, \varphi_k \rangle_{p_{eq}} = e^{\lambda_k t} \delta_{jk}.
$$

This simply means that the system of ODEs obtained by representing the solutions of

$$
\frac{\partial p}{\partial t} = \mathcal{L}^* p = \hat{\mathcal{L}}^* p = -\mathrm{div}(\nabla \log(p_{eq})p) + \Delta p
\tag{6.33}
$$

with the series in (6.30) is linear and diagonal,

$$
\frac{dc_k}{dt} = \lambda_k c_k.
$$

In this example, the solutions to the Fokker–Planck equation in (6.33) are given by (6.30), where the coefficients $c_k(t) = e^{\lambda_k t} c_k(0)$ and the basis functions $\varphi_k p_{eq}$ can be obtained without knowing $\mathcal{L}$ and $\mathcal{M}$. This is the essence of *nonparametric probabilistic modeling*. In practice, all we need is the discrete estimates of the eigenfunctions and the associated eigenvalues of $\hat{\mathcal{L}}$. For nonparametric uncertainty quantification applications on this class of dynamical systems, we refer readers to Berry & Harlim (2015), which also discusses a nonlinear filtering approach and a method to quantify the nonlinear response statistics of perturbed potentials.

In general, when the underlying SDE in (6.26) is not gradient flows with isotropic diffusion, the generator $\mathcal{L} \neq \hat{\mathcal{L}}$. In this case, we need to approximate the matrix A. In order to estimate the components of A, we need to approximate $e^{t\mathcal{L}} \varphi_i$ in (6.32). From Dynkin's formula (Øksendal 2003), we see that, for $f \in C^2(\mathcal{M})$, where $\mathcal{M}$ is compact, we can express the solutions of the backward Kolmogorov equation

$$\frac{\partial u}{\partial t} = \mathcal{L}u, \quad u(x, t_i) = f(x_i)$$

for the Itô diffusion in (6.26) as

$$e^{\tau \mathcal{L}} f(x_i) = u(x, t_{i+1}) = \mathbb{E}_{x_i}[f(x_{i+1})], \quad (6.34)$$

for $\tau = t_{i+1} - t_i > 0$. Here, $\mathbb{E}_{x_i}$ denotes the expectation conditional to the state x_i. The equation (6.34) suggests that $f(x_{i+1})$ is an unbiased estimator for $e^{\tau \mathcal{L}} f(x_i)$. This fact motivates the idea behind the *diffusion forecast* (Berry *et al.* 2015), which approximates the semigroup of the generator $\mathcal{L}$ by the shift operator (also known as the Koopman operator when x is deterministic)

$$e^{\tau \mathcal{L}} f(x_i) \approx f(x_{i+1}) := S_\tau f(x_i),$$

where S_τ is defined as the shift operator which operates on functions $f \in L^2(\mathcal{M}, p_{eq}) \cap C^2(\mathcal{M})$. With this choice, the components of the matrix A can be numerically estimated as

$$A_{kj} = \langle \varphi_j, e^{\tau \mathcal{L}} \varphi_k \rangle_{p_{eq}} \approx \langle \varphi_j, S_\tau \varphi_k \rangle_{p_{eq}} = \tilde{A}_{kj}.$$

Numerically, we can approximate $\tilde{A}_{kj}$ with a Monte Carlo integral,

$$\tilde{A}_{kj} \approx \hat{A}_{kj} := \frac{1}{N-1} \sum_{i=1}^{N-1} \varphi_j(x_i) \varphi_k(x_{i+1}). \quad (6.35)$$

With this approximation, notice that the solutions of the Fokker–Planck equation in (6.27) are approximated nonparametrically with the representations in (6.30), (6.31), and (6.35). All we need are the eigenfunctions φ_k of the operator (6.28), which are obtained via the diffusion maps algorithm. Notice that, to construct A in (6.35), we need the time series x_i. The error in approximating A_{kj} is given in the following theorem.

Theorem 6.6 *Let $x(t_i) = x_i$ be a time series of i.i.d. samples of the equilibrium measure of the Itô diffusion process in (6.26); that is, $x_i \sim p_{\mathrm{eq}}(x)$ and $\tau = t_{i+1} - t_i > 0$. Let $\varphi_k(x) \in H^2(\mathcal{M}, p_{\mathrm{eq}})$ be the eigenfunctions of the generator (6.28), where $\mathcal{M}$ is a compact manifold embedded in $\mathbb{R}^n$. Assume also that $\|b\| \leq b_0$, where b_0 is a constant. Then the error in approximating $A_{kj} = \langle \varphi_j, e^{\tau \mathcal{L}} \varphi_k \rangle_{p_{\mathrm{eq}}}$ with $\hat{A}_{kj} = (1/(N-1)) \sum_{i=1}^{N-1} \varphi_j(x_i) \varphi_k(x_{i+1})$ is on the order of $\tau^{-1/2} N^{-1/2}$ in probability.*

Proof Let $f \in H^2(\mathcal{M}, p_{\mathrm{eq}})$. Then, by the Itô formula, we have

$$df = \mathcal{L}f \, dt + \nabla f^\top b \, dW_t,$$

or, in integral form,

$$f(x_{i+1}) = f(x_i) + \int_{t_i}^{t_{i+1}} \mathcal{L}f \, ds + \int_{t_i}^{t_{i+1}} \nabla f^\top b \, dW_s. \tag{6.36}$$

Taking the expectation conditional on x_i, we have

$$\mathbb{E}_{x_i}[f(x_{i+1})] = f(x_i) + \int_{t_i}^{t_{i+1}} \mathbb{E}_{x_i}[\mathcal{L}f] ds. \tag{6.37}$$

On subtracting (6.37) from (6.36), using (6.34), we obtain

$$S_\tau f(x_i) = f(x_{i+1}) = e^{\tau \mathcal{L}} f(x_i) + \int_{t_i}^{t_{i+1}} Bf \, ds + \int_{t_i}^{t_{i+1}} \nabla f^\top b \, dW_s, \tag{6.38}$$

where we define $Bf = \mathcal{L}f - \mathbb{E}_{x_i}[\mathcal{L}f]$. We take $g \in H^2(\mathcal{M}, p_{\mathrm{eq}})$. Then we have

$$\langle g, S_\tau f \rangle_{p_{\mathrm{eq}}} = \langle g, e^{\tau \mathcal{L}} f \rangle_{p_{\mathrm{eq}}} + \left\langle g, \int_{t_i}^{t_{i+1}} \nabla f^\top b \, dW_s \right\rangle_{p_{\mathrm{eq}}} + \left\langle g, \int_{t_i}^{t_{i+1}} Bf \, ds \right\rangle_{p_{\mathrm{eq}}},$$

where the inner products are realized by the Monte Carlo integral with respect to the sampling measure of the data set. Since Bf is bounded in $L^2(\mathcal{M}, p_{\mathrm{eq}})$ for any function $f \in H^2(\mathcal{M}, p_{\mathrm{eq}})$, the last term is on the order of τ. By the Cauchy–Schwarz inequality, we find that

$$\left| \left\langle g, \int_{t_i}^{t_{i+1}} \nabla f^\top b \, dW_s \right\rangle_{p_{\mathrm{eq}}} \right| \leq \|g\|_{p_{\mathrm{eq}}} \left\| \int_{t_i}^{t_{i+1}} \nabla f^\top b \, dW_s \right\|_{p_{\mathrm{eq}}}.$$

By the Itô isometry and asymptotic expansion in τ, we have

$$\left\| \int_{t_i}^{t_{i+1}} \nabla f^\top b \, dW_s \right\|_{p_{\mathrm{eq}}}^2 = \lim_{N \to \infty} \frac{1}{N} \sum_{i=1}^{N} \left(\int_{t_i}^{t_{i+1}} \nabla f^\top b \, dW_s \right)^2 \tag{6.39}$$

$$= \lim_{N \to \infty} \frac{1}{N} \sum_{i=1}^{N} \int_{t_i}^{t_{i+1}} (\nabla f^\top b)^2 \, ds$$

$$= \lim_{N \to \infty} \frac{1}{N} \sum_{i=1}^{N} (\nabla f(x_i)^\top b(x_i))^2 \tau + \mathcal{O}(\tau^2)$$

$$= \tau \|\nabla f^\top b\|_{p_{\mathrm{eq}}}^2 + \mathcal{O}(\tau^2),$$

which implies that

$$\left| \left\langle g, \int_{t_i}^{t_{i+1}} \nabla f^\top b\, dW_s \right\rangle_{p_{eq}} \right| \leq \sqrt{\tau} \|g\|_{p_{eq}} \|\nabla f^\top b\|_{p_{eq}} \leq \sqrt{\tau} b_0 \|g\|_{p_{eq}} \|\nabla f\|_{p_{eq}},$$

where we used the assumption that b is bounded from above by the constant b_0. From the Courant–Rayleigh minimax principle, it is clear that φ_j is the minimizer of $\|\nabla f\|_{p_{eq}} = -\langle \mathcal{L}f, f\rangle_{p_{eq}}$. The minimum value is given by $\|\nabla \varphi_j\| = -\lambda_j > 0$, where φ_j is orthogonal to $\text{span}\{\varphi_0, \ldots, \varphi_{j-1}\}$. This fact motivates the choice of representing the solutions on the basis of eigenfunctions of $\hat{\mathcal{L}}$. On replacing $g = \varphi_j$ and $f = \varphi_k$, we obtain

$$\tilde{A}_{kj} - A_{kj} = \langle \varphi_j, S_\tau \varphi_k \rangle_{p_{eq}} - \langle \varphi_j, e^{\tau \mathcal{L}} \varphi_k \rangle_{p_{eq}} \leq -\sqrt{\tau} b_0 \lambda_k + \mathcal{O}(\tau).$$

Define $\hat{A}_{kj} = (1/(N-1)) \sum_{i=1}^{N-1} \varphi_j(x_i) \varphi_k(x_{i+1})$. The mean of each component in the sum is

$$\mathbb{E}[\mathbb{E}_{x_i}(\varphi_j S_\tau \varphi_k)] = \lim_{N\to\infty} \frac{1}{N-1} \sum_{i=1}^{N-1} \varphi_j(x_i) \mathbb{E}_{x_i}[S_\tau \varphi_k(x_i)]$$

$$= \lim_{N\to\infty} \frac{1}{N-1} \sum_{i=1}^{N-1} \varphi_j(x_i) e^{\tau \mathcal{L}} \varphi_k(x_i) = A_{kj}.$$

By Jensen's inequality, we have

$$\mathbb{E}[(\varphi_j S_\tau \varphi_k - A_{kj})^2] \leq (\mathbb{E}[\varphi_j S_\tau \varphi_k] - A_{kj})^2 = (\tilde{A}_{kj} - A_{kj})^2$$
$$\leq \tau b_0^2 \lambda_k^2 + \mathcal{O}(\tau^2),$$

which means that $\mathbb{E}[(\hat{A}_{kj} - A_{kj})^2] \leq \tau b_0^2 \lambda_k^2 N^{-1} + \mathcal{O}(\tau^2 N^{-1})$. Assuming that the x_i are i.i.d., the Chebyshev inequality implies that

$$\mathbb{P}(|\hat{A}_{kj} - A_{kj}| > \epsilon) \leq \frac{\tau b_0^2 \lambda_k^2}{\epsilon^2 N} + \mathcal{O}(\tau^2 N^{-1} \epsilon^{-2}).$$

For convergence in probability, the leading term in the right-hand side has to be strictly less than one, which means that the error $\epsilon = \mathcal{O}(\tau^{1/2} N^{-1/2})$ in probability. $\square$

The error estimate in the theorem above requires i.i.d. samples, which can be realized only when τ is larger than the decaying timescale of the dynamical system. However, if we have enough data (large N), we can offset the error for large $\tau > 0$. In fact, under appropriate conditions, a sufficiently large number of data points N guarantees the convergence of the solutions.

Theorem 6.7   *Let $p(x, \tau) \in L^2(\mathcal{M}, p_{eq}^{-1})$ for all $t \geq 0$ be the solutions of (6.27) with a bounded diffusion tensor, b, and assume that $\mathcal{M}$ is compact. Assume also that $\hat{\mathcal{L}}$ in (6.28) has eigenvalues λ_j with smooth eigenfunctions φ_j. Let*

$$\hat{p}(x, \tau) = \sum_{k=0}^{M} \hat{c}_k(\tau) \varphi_k(x) p_{eq}(x),$$

be the approximate solutions from the diffusion forecasting method, that is,
$\hat{c}_k(\tau) = \sum_{j=0}^{M} \hat{A}_{kj} c_j(0)$, *with $\hat{A}$ defined as in (6.35) using data $\{x_i\}_{i=1}^{N}$ with*
$\tau = t_{i+1} - t_i$. *Then there exists a sufficiently large $M > 0$ and a constant $C > 0$*
such that

$$\mathbb{E}\left[\|(p(\cdot, \tau) - \hat{p}(\cdot, \tau))^2\|_{p_{\mathrm{eq}}^{-1}}^2\right] \leq C \frac{\tau}{N}.$$

Proof By Parseval's identity,

$$\|(p - \hat{p})^2\|_{p_{\mathrm{eq}}^{-1}}^2 = \sum_{k=0}^{M} (c_k(\tau) - \hat{c}_k(\tau))^2 + \sum_{k=M+1}^{\infty} c_k^2(\tau)$$

$$= \sum_{j,k=0}^{M} (A_{kj} - \hat{A}_{kj})^2 c_j^2(0) + \sum_{k=M+1}^{\infty} c_k^2(\tau).$$

Using the result from the previous theorem, $\mathbb{E}[(\hat{A}_{kj} - A_{kj})^2] \leq \tau b_0^2 \lambda_k^2 N^{-1}$, we
obtain

$$\mathbb{E}\left[\|(p - \hat{p})^2\|_{p_{\mathrm{eq}}^{-1}}^2\right] \leq \frac{\tau b_0^2}{N} \sum_{j,k=0}^{M} \lambda_k^2 c_j(0)^2 + \sum_{k=M+1}^{\infty} c_k^2(\tau).$$

Since $p(x, \tau) \in L^2(\mathcal{M}, p_{\mathrm{eq}}^{-1})$, by the Parseval's identity, $\sum_{k=0}^{\infty} c_k^2(\tau) < \infty$, which
implies that $c_k \to 0$ as $k \to \infty$, which means that one can choose $M > 0$ large
enough that $\sum_{k=M+1}^{\infty} c_k^2(\tau)$ is smaller than τ/N and the proof is complete. □

Since $\|\vec{c}(0)\|_2^2 < \infty$, as $N \to \infty$, the error decreases, assuming that the
eigenfunctions φ_k can be estimated precisely. While a large M can be chosen
to suppress the truncation error, the term $\sum_{k=0}^{M} \lambda_k^2$ can be large since it is an
increasing function of M. Therefore, the error can be controlled either by using
data with better resolution, i.e., smaller time lags, $\tau = t_{i+1} - t_i$, or by using a
sufficiently large data set, or both.

For solutions at longer times, we can iterate A to obtain $\vec{c}(t + n\tau) = A^n \vec{c}(t)$,
where c_j is the jth component of $\vec{c}$. We should note that, since we assume that
the diffusion process in (6.26) is ergodic, the largest eigenvalue of $e^{\tau\mathcal{L}}$ is equal
to 1, with constant eigenfunction $\mathbb{1}(x)$. Note that

$$\langle e^{\tau\mathcal{L}} \varphi_k, \mathbb{1} \rangle_{p_{\mathrm{eq}}} = \sum_j \langle e^{\tau\mathcal{L}} \varphi_k, \varphi_j \rangle_{p_{\mathrm{eq}}} \langle \varphi_j, \mathbb{1} \rangle_{p_{\mathrm{eq}}} = \sum_j A_{kj} \langle \varphi_j, \mathbb{1} \rangle_{p_{\mathrm{eq}}},$$

where the left-hand side can be written as $\langle e^{\tau\mathcal{L}} \varphi_k, \mathbb{1} \rangle_{p_{\mathrm{eq}}} = \langle \varphi_k, e^{\tau\mathcal{L}^*} p_{\mathrm{eq}} \rangle =$
$\langle \varphi_k, p_{\mathrm{eq}} \rangle = \langle \varphi_k, \mathbb{1} \rangle_{p_{\mathrm{eq}}}$, using the fact that p_{eq} is an eigenfunction of $e^{\tau\mathcal{L}^*}$ with
eigenvalue 1. As a consequence, we have $\sum_j A_{kj} \langle \varphi_j, \mathbb{1} \rangle_{p_{\mathrm{eq}}} = \langle \varphi_k, \mathbb{1} \rangle_{p_{\mathrm{eq}}}$, which
means that the largest eigenvalue of A is also 1, corresponding to eigenvector
$[\vec{e}_1]_j = \langle \mathbb{1}, \varphi_j \rangle_{p_{\mathrm{eq}}}$, i.e., $A\vec{e}_1 = \vec{e}_1$. Here, $\vec{e}_1$ denotes a vector that is 1 on the first
component and zero otherwise. Therefore,

$$\lim_{n \to \infty} \vec{c}(t + n\tau) = \lim_{n \to \infty} A^n \vec{c}(t) = \vec{e}_1.$$

This means that the solutions (6.30) will converge to the equilibrium density,

$$\lim_{t\to\infty} p(x,t) = \lim_{n\to\infty} \sum_j c_j(t+n\tau)\varphi_j(x)p_{\mathrm{eq}}(x) = \mathbb{1}(x)p_{\mathrm{eq}}(x) = p_{\mathrm{eq}}(x). \quad (6.40)$$

Numerically, the largest eigenvalue of the estimated $\hat{A}$ can be greater than one due to the presence of finite samples in the Monte Carlo integral. To overcome this issue, one can ensure the stability by normalizing any eigenvalue with norm greater than one to a unit norm. With this numerical correction, the nonparametric forecast will produce a consistent equilibrium density as shown in (6.40), by design.

Example 6.8   Consider the following two-dimensional system of SDEs:

$$\begin{aligned}
\frac{du}{dt} &= \frac{1}{2}uv - d\Lambda_{11}u + (1 - d\Lambda_{12})v + S_{11}\dot{W}_1 + S_{12}\dot{W}_2, \\
\frac{dv}{dt} &= -\frac{1}{2}u^2 + (-1 - d\Lambda_{12})u - d\Lambda_{22}v + S_{12}\dot{W}_1 + S_{22}\dot{W}_2
\end{aligned} \quad (6.41)$$

where the nonlinear terms conserve energy and W_i denotes white noise. The model in this example is identical to that of Example 5.7. Exactly as before, we set $d = 1/2$, $S = \Lambda^{1/2}$ with

$$\Lambda = \begin{pmatrix} 1 & 1/4 \\ 1/4 & 1 \end{pmatrix}.$$

We simulate the solutions of this model with the Euler–Maruyama scheme with time discretization $\tau = 0.01$. Using $N = 40{,}000$ data points $x = (u, v)$, we construct 1000 basis functions $\varphi_k(x)$. In Figure 6.3, we show a few basis functions obtained from the diffusion maps algorithm with the variable-bandwidth kernel (with $\alpha = -d/4, \beta = -1/2$). Notice that φ_1 looks very similar to the leading principal component depicted in Figure 5.5. While the POD produces another principal component which is perpendicular to the leading principal component in the sense of the vector dot product, the diffusion maps algorithm produces basis functions (see Figure 6.3) that are orthonormal in the sense of $L^2(\mathcal{M}, p_{\mathrm{eq}})$.

In the numerical implementation of the diffusion forecast, the evolution of $\vec{c}(t)$ might not preserve the normalization of the corresponding density, due to the finite approximation. Since the normalization constant is given by

$$\begin{aligned}
Z &= \int_{\mathcal{M}} p(x,t)dV(x) = \sum_k c_k(t) \int_{\mathcal{M}} \varphi_k(x)p_{\mathrm{eq}}(x)dV(x) \\
&= \sum_k c_k(t)\langle 1, \varphi_k\rangle_{p_{\mathrm{eq}}},
\end{aligned} \quad (6.42)$$

one can precompute $\langle 1, \varphi_k\rangle_{p_{\mathrm{eq}}} \approx (1/N)\sum_{i=1}^N \varphi_k(x_i)$ and normalize $p(x)$ by setting it to be $p(x)/Z$, where Z is computed using (6.42).

In Figure 6.4, we show the evolution of a Gaussian initial density specified at a random initial state that is not on the training period with variance 0.05. As a reference, we also show the corresponding point measure with 2000 initial

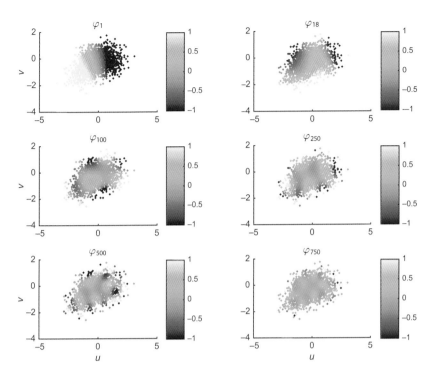

Figure 6.3 Basis functions $\varphi_k(x)$ (eigenfunctions of $\hat{\mathcal{L}}$ corresponding to the equilibrium measure of (6.41)).

conditions sampled from the same Gaussian distribution, where the measure is evolved by solving an ensemble of initial value problems with the perfect model in (6.41). We will call these solutions the *ensemble forecasts*. Notice the consistency between the two distributions at all times.

If the quantity of interest is a functional $A(x) \in L^1(\mathcal{M}, p)$, then we can obtain

$$\mathbb{E}[A(X)](t) = \int_{\mathcal{M}} A(x)p(x,t)dV(x) = \sum_k c_k(t) \int_{\mathcal{M}} A(x)\varphi_k(x)p_{\mathrm{eq}}(x)dV(x),$$

$$= \sum_k c_k(t)\langle A, \varphi_k \rangle_{p_{\mathrm{eq}}}$$

by precomputing $\langle A, \varphi_k \rangle_{p_{\mathrm{eq}}} \approx (1/N) \sum_{i=1}^{N} A(x_i)\varphi_k(x_i)$. For quantifying uncertainties, we are interested in the first kth-order moments, $A(x) = x^k$. In Figure 6.5, we show for comparison the evolution of the first four lowest-order uncentered moments as functions of time. In this figure, the moments of the diffusion forecast are computed using the 1000 basis functions estimated from 40,000 data points. On the other hand, the moments of the ensemble forecasts are the empirical averages of 100,000 solutions evolved using the true dynamics. Notice that, although there are slight disagreements between these moments, especially regarding the fourth-order moment, the patterns of these statistical forecasts are highly correlated.

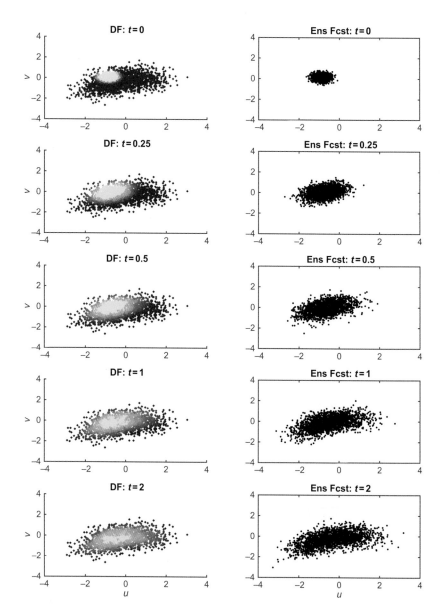

Figure 6.4 Evolution of probability densities (time increases downward); diffusion forecasting method (DF, left column), ensemble forecasting (Ens Fcst, right column).

6.4   Estimation of Initial Densities

To implement nonparametric probabilistic modeling in real applications, one needs to specify the initial density $p_0(x)$ in (6.30) from the given data. This requirement is crucial when we have no access to the initial density $p_0(x)$. In this section, we will discuss two methods for specifying the initial conditions.

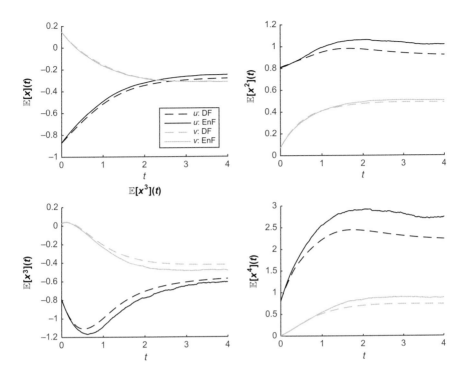

Figure 6.5 The first four lowest-order uncentered moments as functions of time: diffusion forecast (DF, dashes); ensemble forecast (EnF, solid).

The first method is the Nyström extension technique, which specifies the initial densities of noiseless data. This method was introduced in Harlim & Yang (2017). The second method is a Bayesian filtering, which specifies the initial density from noisy data. This method was introduced in Berry & Harlim (2016a).

In general, consider specifying initial densities from the observations

$$y_n = x_n + \eta_n, \tag{6.43}$$

where x_n does not belong to the training data set and η_n denotes measurement noises of arbitrary distribution.

6.4.1 Nyström Extension

When the observations are noiseless, the initial density is given by $p_0(x) = p(x|y_n) = \delta(x - y_n)$, such that the coefficients are

$$c_k(t_n) = \langle p(\cdot|y_n), \varphi_k \rangle = \int_{\mathcal{M}} \delta(x - y_n)\varphi_k(x)dV(x) = \varphi_k(y_n). \tag{6.44}$$

Practically, this requires one to evaluate φ_k on a new data point y_n that does not belong to the training data set, $\{x_i\}_{i=1,\dots,N}$.

One way to do this evaluation is with the Nyström extension (Nyström 1930), which can be formulated using the basic theory of reproducing kernel Hilbert space (RKHS) (Aronszajn 1950). In our particular application, let $L^2(\mathcal{M}, p_{eq})$ be an RKHS with a symmetric positive kernel $\hat{\mathcal{T}}\colon \mathcal{M} \times \mathcal{M} \to \mathbb{R}$ that is defined such that the components of $\hat{T} := \mathcal{I}_N + \epsilon \hat{L} \in \mathbb{R}^{N \times N}$, where $\hat{L}$ is defined as in (6.19), are given by the kernel function evaluated at the training data, $\hat{T}_{ij} := \hat{\mathcal{T}}(x_i, x_j)$. Let $T := \mathcal{I}_N + \epsilon L_\epsilon$ be the conjugate matrix of $\hat{T}$ with $L_\epsilon := D^{-1/2} \hat{L} D^{1/2}$ and a diagonal matrix D with components $D_{ii} := \hat{q}_\epsilon(x_i)$ as defined in (6.19). Recall that, if the diagonal matrix Λ and the orthonormal matrix U satisfy the eigendecomposition $\hat{T}U = U\Lambda$, then the columns of $\Phi = D^{-1/2}U$ are eigenvectors of L_ϵ, that is, $L_\epsilon \Phi = \Phi \Lambda$.

For convenience, we also define a function $\mathcal{T}\colon \mathcal{M} \times \mathcal{M} \to \mathbb{R}$ such that the components of the non-symmetric matrix T are given by $T_{ij} := \mathcal{T}(x_i, x_j) = \hat{q}_\epsilon^{-1/2}(x_i)\hat{\mathcal{T}}(x_i, x_j)\hat{q}_\epsilon^{1/2}(x_j)$. Then, for any function $f \in L^2(\mathcal{M}, p_{eq})$, the Moore–Aronszajn theorem states that one can evaluate f at $a \in \mathcal{M}$ with the inner product $f(a) = \langle f, \hat{\mathcal{T}}(a, \cdot)\rangle_{p_{eq}}$. In our application, the extension of φ_k on the new observation y_n can be approximated as

$$
\begin{aligned}
\varphi_k(y_n) &= \hat{q}_\epsilon^{-1/2}(y_n)u_k(y_n) \\
&= \hat{q}_\epsilon^{-1/2}(y_n)\langle u_k, \hat{\mathcal{T}}(y_n, \cdot)\rangle_{p_{eq}} \\
&\approx \hat{q}_\epsilon^{-1/2}(y_n)\frac{1}{N}\sum_{i=1}^{N} \hat{\mathcal{T}}(y_n, x_i)u_k(x_i) \\
&= \hat{q}_\epsilon^{-1/2}(y_n)\frac{1}{N}\sum_{i=1}^{N} \hat{\mathcal{T}}(y_n, x_i)\hat{q}_\epsilon^{1/2}(x_i)\varphi_k(x_i) \\
&= \frac{1}{N}\sum_{i=1}^{N} \mathcal{T}(y_n, x_i)\varphi_k(x_i).
\end{aligned}
\tag{6.45}
$$

In (6.45), we have defined $u_j(x_i)$ as the ijth component of the matrix U which satisfies $\hat{T}U = U\Lambda$ and used the fact that the eigenvectors of T are defined via the conjugation formula $\Phi = D^{-1/2}U$, whose components are given by $\varphi_k(x_i) = \hat{q}^{-1/2}(x_i)u_k(x_i)$. In summary, the estimation of the coefficients in (6.44) requires the construction of an N-dimensional vector whose ith component is defined as $\mathcal{T}(y_n, x_i)$. This vector is constructed using the same diffusion maps procedure as that described in Section 6.1.2 on pairs of training and new data points, x_i and y_n, respectively.

6.4.2   Bayesian Filtering

When the observed data in (6.43) are corrupted by noises, one can define a likelihood function based on the distribution of the noises. For example, suppose that the noises are i.i.d. Gaussian, $\eta_n \sim \mathcal{N}(0, R)$. In this case, a likelihood function can be specified explicitly as

$$
p(y_n|x) \propto \exp\left(-\frac{1}{2}(y_n - x)^\top R^{-1}(y_n - x)\right).
\tag{6.46}
$$

In the case when the parametric likelihood function is not known, one can also construct data-driven nonparametric likelihood functions using embeddings of the conditional distribution formulated in Song *et al.* (2009, 2013). See also Berry & Harlim (2017) for nonparametric likelihood functions constructed using the diffusion coordinates.

Given a likelihood function, e.g., (6.46), we can estimate the initial density as a posterior density of the following Bayes formula (Berry & Harlim 2016*a*):

$$p_0(x) = p(x|y_n) \propto p(x)p(y_n|x). \tag{6.47}$$

Numerically, the prior density $p(x)$ is represented by an N-dimensional vector whose ith component approximates $p(x_i)$. The prior density is obtained from the diffusion forecast construction through the representation in (6.30). The likelihood function is also represented by an N-dimensional vector whose ith component is the value of the likelihood function evaluated at the training data, $p(y_n|x_i)$. Taking the component-wise product of these two vectors, we obtain an N-dimensional vector whose ith component is the desired posterior density $p(x_i|y)$, up to the normalization constant Z. We estimate the normalization factor, Z, using a Monte Carlo integral,

$$Z = \frac{1}{N} \sum_{i=1}^{N} \frac{p(x_i)p(y_n|x_i)}{p_{\text{eq}}(x_i)} \approx \int_{\mathcal{M}} p(x)p(y_n|x)dV(x).$$

On dividing the product $p(x_i)p(y_n|x_i)$ by Z we recover the posterior density. The only assumption on the posterior density is that it is well approximated in the truncated basis $\{\varphi_j\}_{j=1}^{M}$, which intuitively implies that the posterior density is smooth and not very highly oscillatory.

Notice that the Bayesian filtering described here represents the prior density with data-adapted nonparametric smooth basis functions. This is an alternative both to MCMC, which represents the prior density with a point measure, and to the EnKF, which represents the prior density with a Gaussian measure.

Example 6.9 Now, let's revisit Example 6.8 with initial conditions specified using the two methods discussed above.

In Figure 6.6, we compare the mean estimates obtained from the Nyström extension and the Bayesian filtering with the truth at the verification time interval that contains 9600 data points that do not overlap with the training data. For the Bayesian filtering, the observations are corrupted by Gaussian noises with variance $R = 0.01$. Qualitatively, the mean estimates from these two methods look very similar to the truth. Quantitatively, the Nyström extension mean estimates are more accurate with RMSE $= 0.0352$, than those of the Bayesian filtering, with RMSE $= 0.1021$, which is not surprising since the Bayesian filtered initial conditions are estimated from noisy data.

In Figure 6.7, we show the lead forecasts with a one-standard-deviation error bar, for four randomly chosen verification interval periods. Here, we use the mean estimates to forecast the true state variable. For the ensemble forecast, we

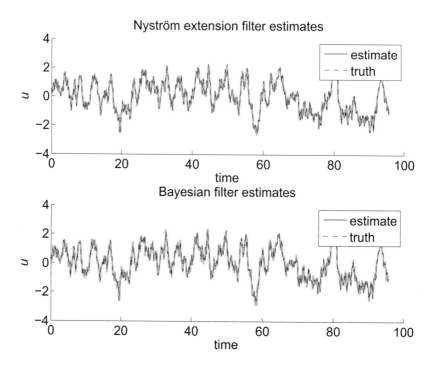

Figure 6.6 Filter estimates and truth for 9600 data points that do not overlap with the training data.

use the perfect initial conditions with zero uncertainty, which implies that all of the initial ensemble members are exactly the truth, so the forecast uncertainties are completely intrinsic. For the diffusion forecasts, we use the initial densities obtained from the Bayesian filtering technique above. Notice the consistency in the forecast mean and variance of these two schemes, the diffusion forecasts and the ensemble forecasts. We neglect showing the forecasting results that are based on the initial conditions obtained from the Nyström extension in order to avoid presenting cumbersome figures. We refer interested readers to Harlim & Yang (2017) for more extensive numerical tests on this method.

In Figure 6.8, we show the RMSE and the correlation between the mean forecast and the truth as functions of the lead time. Here we also include the persistent forecast, which simply uses the initial condition as the state estimate at future times. From these results, we conclude that the forecasting skill of the nonparametric model is almost identical to that of the ensemble forecasting method which uses the full model.

As a final remark, we should point out that a different set of basis functions for diffusion forecasting has been proposed in Harlim & Yang (2017). These basis functions are constructed using a QR factorization on columns of the matrix $T = I_N + \epsilon L_\epsilon$, where L_ϵ is the discrete representation of $\hat{\mathcal{L}}$, defined in Section 6.1.2.

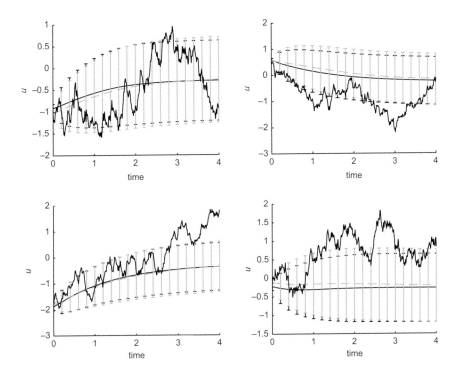

Figure 6.7 The lead forecasts with a standard deviation error bar compared with the truth at four different time windows. The data in these verification windows do not overlap with the training data. Diffusion forecast (black with error bar); ensemble forecast (gray with error bar); truth (black solid).

These basis functions were designed to avoid solving a large eigenvalue problem, which is computationally demanding as the amount of data becomes large. With the QR basis functions, it has been found that the diffusion forecasting skill is superior to those with eigenbases in forecasting deterministic dynamics. For the stochastic dynamics, the new basis improves the forecasting skill compared with using a small number of eigenbases.

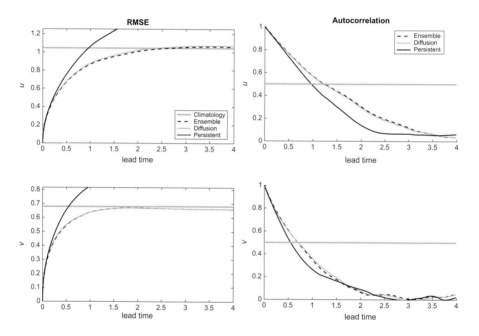

Figure 6.8 The lead forecast RMSE and correlation statistics, averaged over forecasts of the 9600 initial conditions from the Bayesian filtering.

Appendix A. Elementary Probability Theory

This appendix reviews the basic notion of probability theory that is used in the book.

Definition A.1   Let Ω be a sample space; that is, a space of all possible outcomes of an experiment. An element $\omega \in \Omega$ is called a *sample* (or experimental outcome). An event is a subset of Ω.

Example A.2 $A = \{2, 4, 6\}$ is the event that an even number turns up when a die is rolled.

Definition A.3 (σ-algebra)   We want to assign probabilities to events that are subsets of Ω, more precisely to a field $\mathcal{F}$ that satisfies the following criteria.

1. $\emptyset \in \mathcal{F}, \Omega \in \mathcal{F}$.
2. If $A \in \mathcal{F}$, then $A^c \in \mathcal{F}$.
3. If $\mathcal{A} = \{A_1, A_2, \ldots\}$ is a finite or countable collection in $\mathcal{F}$, then any union and intersection of elements in $\mathcal{A}$ is in $\mathcal{F}$.

Any field $\mathcal{F}$ that satisfies these three conditions is called a σ-algebra.

Example A.4   If one is interested in whether an even number or an odd number occurs when a die is rolled, then $\mathcal{F} = \{\emptyset, \Omega, \{1, 3, 5\}, \{2, 4, 6\}\}$ is a σ-algebra. On the other hand, $\mathcal{F} = \{\emptyset, \Omega, \{1, 3, 5\}, \{2, 4, 6\}, \{1\}\}$ is *not* a σ-algebra, since $\{1\}^c = \{2, 3, 4, 5, 6\} \notin \mathcal{F}$.

Definition A.5   A probability measure $\mathbb{P}$ is a function $\mathbb{P} \colon \mathcal{F} \to \mathbb{R}$, defined on any events $A \in \mathcal{F}$ such that the following statements hold.

1. $\mathbb{P}(\Omega) = 1$.
2. $\mathbb{P}(A) \geq 0$.
3. If $\{A_1, A_2, \ldots\}$ is a finite or countable collection of disjoint events, i.e., $A_j \in \mathcal{F}$ and $A_i \cap A_j = \emptyset$ for every $i \neq j$, then

$$\mathbb{P}\left(\bigcup_{j \geq 1} A_j\right) = \sum_{j \geq 1} \mathbb{P}(A_j).$$

The triple $(\Omega, \mathcal{F}, \mathbb{P})$ is called a *probability space*.

Definition A.6   A random variable is a function $X : \Omega \to \mathbb{R}$.
We can define the probability of a random variable $X = x$ as

$$\mathbb{P}(X = x) := \mathbb{P}(\omega \in \Omega : X(\omega) = x),$$

or, in general,

$$\mathbb{P}(X \in A) := \mathbb{P}(\omega \in \Omega : X(\omega) \in A).$$

Example A.7   Let a random variable X be a sum of two dice. Then $\mathbb{P}(X = 11) = \mathbb{P}(\{5, 6\}) + \mathbb{P}(\{6, 5\}) = 2/36$.

Definition A.8   Let X be a random variable. We define a cumulative distribution function (which sometimes is called a distribution) as

$$F_X(x) := \mathbb{P}(X \le x) = \mathbb{P}(\omega \in \Omega : X(\omega) \le x).$$

F_X is monotone, nondecreasing with

$$\lim_{x \to -\infty} F_X(x) = 0 \text{ and } \lim_{x \to \infty} F_X(x) = 1.$$

Definition A.9   A random variable X is continuous if there exists a density function $p_X(x)$ such that

$$F_X(x) = \int_{-\infty}^{x} p_X(y) dy, \quad x \in \mathbb{R}.$$

This definition implies that the density $p_X(x) = dF_X(x)/dx$ exists almost everywhere, which means that F_X is absolutely continuous with respect to the Lebesque measure. This condition suggests that, for continuous random variables, $\mathbb{P}(X(\omega) = x) = 0$. To see this, notice that

$$\mathbb{P}(X(\omega) = x) = \lim_{\epsilon \to 0} \mathbb{P}(x - \epsilon < X(\omega) \le x)$$
$$= F_X(x) - \lim_{\epsilon \to 0} F_X(x - \epsilon)$$
$$= F_X(x) - F_X(x^-) = 0.$$

Also, since F_X is monotonically increasing, it is clear that $p_X(x) \ge 0$ and $\int_{\mathbb{R}} p_X(x) dx = 1$.

Example A.10   An email occurs at random in time interval $\Omega = [0, T]$ with probability $\mathbb{P}(t_1 \le \omega \le t_2) = (t_2 - t_1)/T$, $t_1, t_2 \in \Omega$. Define $X(\omega) = \omega$.

- If $x > T$, then $F_X(x) = \mathbb{P}(\{X(\omega) \le x\}) = \mathbb{P}(\Omega) = 1$.
- If $0 \le x \le T$, then $\{X(\omega) \le x\} = \{0 \le \omega \le x\}$, so $F_X(x) = \mathbb{P}(0 \le \omega \le x) = x/T$.
- If $x < 0$, then $\{X(\omega) \le x\} = \emptyset$, so $F_X(x) = 0$.

In summary, we have

$$F_X(x) = \begin{cases} 0, & \text{if } x < 0, \\ x/T, & \text{if } 0 \le x \le T, \\ 1, & \text{if } x > T, \end{cases}$$

whose density is

$$p_X(x) = \begin{cases} 0, & \text{if } x < 0, \\ 1/T, & \text{if } 0 < x < T, \\ 0, & \text{if } x > T. \end{cases}$$

Notice that p_X is undefined at 0 and 1, since F_X is not differentiable at these points.

Definition A.11 (Expectation)   Consider a random variable X with density $p_X(x)$. Let $g(x)$ be a continuous function defined on the range of X, thus

$$\mathbb{E}[g(X)] = \int_{\mathbb{R}} g(x) p_X(x) dx.$$

In particular, the following statements hold.

- If $g(x) = x$, then $\mathbb{E}[X] = \int_{\mathbb{R}} x p_X(x) dx$ is the first-order moment (mean).
- If $g(x) = x^n$, $n > 1$, then $\mathbb{E}[X^n] = \int_{\mathbb{R}} x^n p_X(x) dx$ is the nth-order uncentered moment.
- $\mathbb{E}[(X - \mathbb{E}(X))^2] := \text{Var}(X)$ is the variance (or the centered second-order moment) of X.
- $\sigma(X) := \sqrt{\text{Var}(X)}$ is the standard deviation of X.

Definition A.12 (Gaussian or normal distribution)   A random variable $X \in \mathbb{R}$ is Gaussian if its density function is defined as

$$p_X(x) = \frac{1}{\sqrt{2\pi\sigma^2}} e^{-\frac{(x-\mu)^2}{2\sigma^2}}.$$

We denote the Gaussian random variable as $X \sim \mathcal{N}(\mu, \sigma^2)$.

One can verify that $\mathbb{E}(X) = \mu$ and $\text{Var}(X) = \sigma^2$. In fact, one can also show that

$$\mathbb{E}[(X - \mathbb{E}(X))^n] = \begin{cases} 0, & \text{if } n \text{ is odd}, \\ 1 \cdot 3 \cdot 5 \cdots (n-1)\sigma^n, & \text{if } n \geq 2 \text{ is even}. \end{cases}$$

So, knowing μ and σ is sufficient to characterize the Gaussian distribution.

Definition A.13 (Joint and marginal distributions)   The continuous random variables $X_1, \ldots, X_n$ are jointly distributed if they are defined on the same probability space. One can characterize this random variable with a joint distribution function,

$$F_{X_1, \ldots, X_n}(x_1, \ldots, x_n) := \mathbb{P}(X_1 \leq x_1, \ldots, X_n \leq x_n),$$

or with a joint density function that satisfies,

$$F_{X_1, \ldots, X_n}(x_1, \ldots, x_n) := \int_{-\infty}^{x_1} \cdots \int_{-\infty}^{x_n} p_{X_1, \ldots, X_n}(x_1, \ldots, x_n) dx_1 \cdots dx_n,$$

if one exists. If $m < n$, the marginal density of $X_1, \ldots, X_m$ is defined as

$$p_{X_1, \ldots, X_m}(x_1, \ldots, x_m) := \int_{-\infty}^{\infty} \cdots \int_{-\infty}^{\infty} p_{X_1, \ldots, X_n}(x_1, \ldots, x_n) dx_{m+1} \cdots dx_n.$$

Definition A.14 (Expectation)   Let $Y = f(X_1, \ldots, X_n)$, then

$$\mathbb{E}[Y] = \int_{\mathbb{R}^n} f(x_1, \ldots, x_n) p_{X_1, \ldots, X_n}(x_1, \ldots, x_n) dx_1 \cdots dx_n.$$

In particular, the following statements hold.

- $\mathbb{E}[X_k^\alpha X_l^\beta]$ are the higher moments of order $\alpha + \beta$.
- The covariance is defined as

$$\mathrm{Cov}(X_k, X_l) := \mathbb{E}\big[(X_k - \mathbb{E}[X_k])(X_l - \mathbb{E}[X_l])\big]$$
$$= \mathbb{E}\big[X_k X_l\big] - \mathbb{E}\big[X_k\big]\mathbb{E}\big[X_l\big].$$

- The variance and standard deviation are defined as $\mathrm{Var}(X_k) := \mathrm{Cov}(X_k, X_k)$ and $\sigma(X_k) := \sqrt{\mathrm{Var}(X_k)}$, respectively.

Definition A.15 (Correlation coefficient)   The correlation coefficient of two random variables, X_k and X_l, is defined as

$$\rho(X_k, X_l) = \frac{\mathrm{Cov}(X_k, X_l)}{\sigma(X_k)\sigma(X_l)}.$$

By the Cauchy–Schwarz inequality (or by the Hölder inequality), $\mathrm{Cov}(X_k, X_l)^2 \leq \mathrm{Var}(X_k)\mathrm{Var}(X_l)$, which implies that $0 \leq |\rho(X_k, X_l)| \leq 1$.

Definition A.16 (Uncorrelated)   Two random variables, X_k and X_l, are uncorrelated if their second moments are finite and $\mathrm{Cov}(X_k, X_l) = 0$, which together trivially imply $\rho(X_k, X_l) = 0$.

Lemma A.17 $|\rho(X_k, X_l)| = 1$ *if and only if* $X_k = aX_l + b$, *where* a, b *are fixed constants.*

Proof   To see this, note that $\sigma(X_k) = \pm a\sigma(X_l)$ and $\mathrm{Cov}(X_k, X_l) = a\,\mathrm{Var}(X_l)$, and use the definition of ρ. $\square$

Definition A.18 (Independent)   Two random variables X and Y are independent if, for all $x \in X, y \in Y$,

$$F_{X,Y}(x, y) = F_X(x)F_Y(y),$$
$$p_{X,Y}(x, y) = p_X(x)p_Y(y).$$

If X and Y are independent, then, for integrable functions $f(x)$ and $g(y)$, we have

$$\mathbb{E}[f(X)g(Y)] = \mathbb{E}[f(X)]\mathbb{E}[g(Y)].$$

Theorem A.19   *Independence of two variables implies that they are uncorrelated, but the converse is not true.*

Proof   ($\Rightarrow$) Let X and Y be independent, so that $\mathrm{Cov}(X, Y) := \mathbb{E}[(f(X)g(Y)] = \mathbb{E}[f(X)]\mathbb{E}[g(Y)] = 0$, since $f(x) = x - \mathbb{E}[X]$ and $g(y) = y - \mathbb{E}[Y]$.
($\Leftarrow$) Let $Y = \sin(2\pi X)$ and $Z = \cos(2\pi X)$, where $X \sim U[0, 1]$. Thus $\mathbb{E}[Y] = \mathbb{E}[Z] = 0$ and $\mathrm{Cov}(Y, Z) = \mathbb{E}[YZ] = 0$. So, Y and Z are uncorrelated but they are not independent, since $Y^2 + Z^2 = 1$. $\square$

Definition A.20 (Conditional distribution)   Given two events A and B, we define the conditional distribution of event A given the event B as

$$\mathbb{P}(A|B) = \frac{\mathbb{P}(A \cap B)}{\mathbb{P}(B)},$$

where $\mathbb{P}(B) > 0$.

From this definition, it is clear that, if A and B are independent, $\mathbb{P}(A|B) = \mathbb{P}(A)$. Now let X and Y be random variables with a joint distribution, $F_{X,Y}$. We seek the distribution (and density) of X given $Y = y$. For continuous random variables, let $A = \{X(\omega) \le x\}$ and $B = \{y < Y(\omega) \le y + \epsilon\}$, and assume that $p_Y(y) > 0$. Then we have

$$F_{X|B}(x|B) = \mathbb{P}(X(\omega) \le x|B) = \mathbb{P}(A|B) = \frac{\mathbb{P}(A \cap B)}{\mathbb{P}(B)}$$

$$= \frac{\mathbb{P}(X(\omega) \le x, y < Y(\omega) \le y + \epsilon)}{\mathbb{P}(y < Y(\omega) \le y + \epsilon)}$$

$$= \frac{F_{X,Y}(x, y + \epsilon) - F_{X,Y}(x, y)}{F_Y(y + \epsilon) - F_Y(y)}.$$

On multiplying the right-hand side by $(1/\epsilon)/(1/\epsilon)$ and taking $\epsilon \to 0$, we obtain

$$F_{X|Y}(x|y) = \frac{\partial F_{X,Y}(x, y)/\partial_y}{dF_y(y)/dy} = \frac{\int_{-\infty}^{x} p_{X,Y}(x, y)dx}{p_Y(y)}.$$

Taking a derivative with respect to x, we obtain the conditional density of X given $Y(\omega) = y$,

$$p_{X|Y}(x|y) = \frac{p_{X,Y}(x, y)}{p_Y(y)},$$

for all x, y such that $p_Y(y) > 0$.

From the definition of the conditional density, it is easy to deduce the following theorem.

Theorem A.21 (Bayes)

$$p_{X|Y}(x|y) = \frac{p_{X,Y}(x, y)}{p_Y(y)}$$

$$= \frac{p_{X,Y}(x, y)}{\int_{\mathbb{R}} p_{X,Y}(x, y)dx}$$

$$= \frac{p_{Y|X}(y|x)p_X(x)}{\int_{\mathbb{R}} p_{Y|X}(y|x)p_X(x)dx}.$$

Since the denominator is constant, sometimes, we write Bayes' theorem as

$$p_{X|Y}(x|y) \propto p_{Y|X}(y|x)p_X(x).$$

Definition A.22 (Convergence almost surely)   A sequence of random variables $\{X_n\}$ converges almost surely to X, $X_n \overset{\text{a.s.}}{\to} X$, if, for all $\epsilon > 0$, $\lim_{n \to \infty} \mathbb{P}(|X_n - X| < \epsilon) = 1$.

Definition A.23 (Convergence in probability)   A sequence of random variable $\{X_n\}$ converges in probability to X, $X_n \overset{\text{P}}{\to} X$, if, for all $\epsilon > 0$, $\mathbb{P}(|X_n - X| > \epsilon) \to 0$ as $n \to \infty$.

Definition A.24 (Mean-square convergence)   A sequence of random variable $\{X_n\}$ converges in L^2 (or in the mean-square sense) to X, $X_n \overset{\text{m.s.}}{\to} X$, if, for all $\epsilon > 0$, $\mathbb{E}[(X_n - X)^2] \to 0$ as $n \to \infty$.

By Chebyshev's inequality, it is clear that $X_n \overset{\text{m.s.}}{\to} X$ implies $X_n \overset{\text{P}}{\to} X$.

Definition A.25 (Convergence in distribution)   A sequence of random variables $\{X_n\}$ converges in distribution to X, $X_n \overset{\text{d}}{\to} X$, if $\lim_{n \to \infty} F_{X_n}(x) = F_X(x)$ at all x where $F_X(x)$ is continuous.

Theorem A.26   *If $X_n \overset{\text{a.s.}}{\to} X$, then $X_n \overset{\text{P}}{\to} X$. If $X_n \overset{\text{P}}{\to} X$, then $X_n \overset{\text{d}}{\to} X$.*

Theorem A.27 (Central limit theorem)   *Let X_i be i.i.d. random variables with $\mathbb{E}[X_i] = \mu$ and $\text{Var}[X_j] = \sigma^2 < \infty$. Let $Y_n = \sum_{j=1}^{n} X_j$. Then*

$$Z_n = \frac{Y_n - n\mu}{\sigma\sqrt{n}} \overset{\text{d}}{\to} \mathcal{N}(0,1). \tag{A.1}$$

Appendix B. Stochastic Processes

This appendix reviews selective topics on stochastic processes that are relevant for the book.

Definition B.1 A stochastic process $X_t \colon \Omega \to E$ is a family of random variables parameterized by $t \in T$. To be more precise, a stochastic process is a collection of random variables $X = \{X_t, t \in T\}$ such that, for each fixed $t \in T$, X_t is a random variable that takes a component of a probability space $(\Omega, \mathcal{F}, \mathbb{P})$ to $(E, \mathcal{G})$. Here, E is the state space of stochastic process X and $\mathcal{G}$ is the σ-algebra of E.

One can also think of $X_t(\omega)$ as a function $X \colon \Omega \times T \to E$, where, for each t, $X_t(\cdot)$ is a random variable and, for each realization $\omega \in \Omega$, $X_\cdot(\omega)$ is a realization of the process.

One often associates E as the state space and the parameter space T as a temporal space. The following statements give the standard classification of stochastic processes.

- If both E and T are discrete, X is a discrete parameter chain.
- If E is discrete and T is continuous, X is a continuous parameter chain.
- If E is continuous and T is discrete, X is a random sequence.
- If both E and T are continuous, X is a stochastic process.

In Appendix A, we define a real-valued random variable with $E = \mathbb{R}$ and $\mathcal{G} = \mathcal{B}(\mathbb{R})$.

Example B.2 (Random walk) Flip a coin such that $\Omega = \{h, t\}$ with $\mathbb{P}(\{h\}) = p$ and $\mathbb{P}(\{t\}) = q = 1 - p$. Define a random variable

$$W_n(\omega) = \begin{cases} +\Delta x, & \text{if } \omega = h, \\ -\Delta x, & \text{if } \omega = t, \end{cases} \tag{B.1}$$

so $\mathbb{P}(W_n(\omega) = +\Delta x) = p$ and $\mathbb{P}(W_n(\omega) = -\Delta x) = q$.

Let X_n be the position at instant n before the execution of a step at that instant. Assume $X_0 = 0$ and

$$X_n = \sum_{i=0}^{n-1} W_i, \tag{B.2}$$

so $\{X_n\}_{n\in\mathbb{Z}^+}$ is a discrete parameter chain and $X_n\colon \Omega' \to \Delta t\,\mathbb{Z}$, where $\Omega' = \{htth\ldots\}$ is a discrete space of countable realizations of flipping coins and the state space is a discrete lattice $E = \Delta t\,\mathbb{Z}$.

The Probability law

Let $\{X_t\}_{t\in T}$ be a stochastic process. For any finite set $t_1,\ldots,t_n \in T$, we can characterize the stochastic process X_t by a finite-dimensional distribution $F(x_{t_i},\ldots,x_{t_n})$ for all $t_1,\ldots,t_n \in T$. Specifying the probability law of X_t is equivalent to finding $F(x_{t_1},\ldots,x_{t_n})$ or the associated density $p(x_{t_1},\ldots,x_{t_n})$ for all finite sets of $t_1,\ldots,t_n \in T$. In particular, we use the following definition.

Definition B.3　We define

- $p(x_t) := p_{X_t}(x_t)$ to be the density of random variable X_t for any t,
- $p(x_t, x_\tau) := p_{X_t, X_\tau}(x_t, x_\tau)$ to be the joint density of X_t and X_τ at any t, τ,
- $p(x_t|x_\tau) = p(x_t, x_\tau)/p(x_\tau) := p_{X_t|X_\tau=x_\tau}(x_t)$ to be the conditional density of X_t given $X_\tau = x_\tau$ for any t, τ.

In applications, it is usually difficult to specify the probability law (density). Instead, one tries to sample (or estimate) their statistics, such as those in the following definition.

Definition B.4　The first- and second-order statistics of the continuous state space stochastic process X_t are as follows.

- The mean, $\mu_X(t) := \mathbb{E}[X_t] = \int_E x_t p(x_t)\,dx_t$. For discrete state space, one replaces the integral with a discrete sum over the components of E.
- The autocovariance function,

$$R_X(t,s) = \mathbb{E}[(X_t - \mu_X(t))(X_s - \mu_X(s))].$$

Note that the covariance function of X_t is defined as $R_X(t,t)$.

Example B.5　Let $X_t = a + bt$, $t \geq 0$, where (a,b) is a joint Gaussian distribution. Take finite instances, $t_1,\ldots,t_n \in T$, such that

$$\vec{w} = \begin{pmatrix} X_{t_1} \\ \vdots \\ X_{t_n} \end{pmatrix} = \begin{pmatrix} 1 & t_1 \\ \vdots & \vdots \\ 1 & t_n \end{pmatrix} \begin{pmatrix} a \\ b \end{pmatrix} = A\vec{z},$$

so $\vec{w} \sim \mathcal{N}(A\mu_{\vec{z}}, AC_{\vec{z}}A^\top)$ and the probability law is characterized by the density function

$$p(\vec{w}) = (2\pi)^{-n/2}|AC_{\vec{z}}A^\top|^{-1/2}\exp\left(-\frac{1}{2}(\vec{w} - A\mu_{\vec{z}})^\top (AC_{\vec{z}}A^\top)^{-1}(\vec{w} - A\mu_{\vec{z}})\right).$$

In this example we can compute the first- and second-order statistics without knowing the probability law:

$$\mu_X(t) = \mathbb{E}[a] + \mathbb{E}[b]t,$$
$$R_X(t,s) = \mathbb{E}[a^2] + \mathbb{E}[ab](t+s) + \mathbb{E}[b^2]ts - (\mathbb{E}[a] + \mathbb{E}[b]t)(\mathbb{E}[a] + \mathbb{E}[b]s)$$
$$= \mathbb{E}[a^2] - \mathbb{E}[a]^2 + (\mathbb{E}[ab] - \mathbb{E}[a]\mathbb{E}[b])(t+s) + (\mathbb{E}[b^2] - \mathbb{E}[b]^2)ts.$$

Definition B.6   A stochastic process is called centered if its mean is zero.

Definition B.7   A stochastic process X_t is mean-square (m.s.-)continuous if $\lim_{\epsilon \to 0} \mathbb{E}[(X_{t+\epsilon} - X_t)^2] = 0$.

Theorem B.8   *A centered stochastic process $\{X_t\}_{t \in T}$ is m.s.-continuous if and only if R_X is continuous on $T \times T$.*

Proof   ($\Rightarrow$) Suppose X_t is m.s.-continuous. Then

$$|R_X(t + \epsilon, s + \nu) - R_X(t, s)| = |\mathbb{E}[X_{t+\epsilon}X_{s+\nu}] - \mathbb{E}[X_t X_s]|$$
$$= |\mathbb{E}[(X_{t+\epsilon} - X_t)(X_{s+\nu} - X_s)]|$$
$$+ |\mathbb{E}[(X_{t+\epsilon} - X_t)X_s]| + |\mathbb{E}[X_t(X_{s+\nu} - X_s)]|.$$

By the Cauchy–Schwarz inequality, we have

$$|R_X(t + \epsilon, s + \nu) - R_X(t, s)| \leq \mathbb{E}[(X_{t+\epsilon} - X_t)^2]^{1/2}\mathbb{E}[(X_{s+\nu} - X_s)^2]^{1/2}$$
$$+ \mathbb{E}[(X_{t+\epsilon} - X_t)^2]^{1/2}\mathbb{E}[X_s^2]^{1/2}$$
$$+ \mathbb{E}[X_t^2]^{1/2}\mathbb{E}[(X_{s+\nu} - X_s)^2]^{1/2}.$$

Since X_t is m.s.-continuous, it is clear that

$$\lim_{(\epsilon, \nu) \to (0,0)} |R_X(t + \epsilon, s + \nu) - R_X(t, s)| = 0.$$

($\Leftarrow$) Trivial. $\square$

Definition B.9   A stochastic process $\{X_t\}_{t \in T}$ is strictly stationary if its probability law is similar to that of $\{X_{t+\tau}\}_{t \in T}$ for any $\tau \in T$. That is,

$$p(x_{t_1}, \ldots, x_{t_n}) = p(x_{t_1 + \tau}, \ldots, x_{t_n + \tau}).$$

If $p(x_{t_k}) = p(x_{t_k + \tau})$ for any $\tau \in T$, then $p(x_t)$ is independent of time, so $\mu_X(t)$ is constant (also independent of time). Also, if $p(x_{t_k}, x_{t_l}) = p(x_{t_k + \tau}, x_{t_l + \tau})$ for any $\tau \in T$, then $R_X(t, s) = R_X(t - s, 0) := R_X(t - s)$.

Definition B.10   A stochastic process $\{X_t\}_{t \in T}$ is weakly stationary (or stationary in the wide sense, w.s.s.) if it has finite second-order moments with constant mean and a covariance function that satisfies $R_X(t, s) = R_X(t - s)$.

From these definitions, it is clear that a strictly stationary process with a finite second moment is also stationary in the wide sense. The converse, however, is not true: a weakly stationary process is not necessary a strictly stationary process.

Brownian motion
Let $W_t \in \mathbb{R}$ represent the position of a particle at time $t \geq 0$. We call W_t a Brownian motion if it satisfies the following criteria.

- $W_0 = 0$.
- $W_t \sim \mathcal{N}(0, t)$. Implicitly, we define $\mathbb{E}[W_t] = 0$, $\mathbb{E}[W_t^2] = t$.

- Independence; that is, given $t_1 < t_2 < t_3 < t_4$, $W_{t_2} - W_{t_1}$ is independent with respect to W_{t_1} and to $W_{t_4} - W_{t_3}$. This means that $\mathbb{E}[W_t W_s] = \mathbb{E}[(W_t - W_s)W_s] + \mathbb{E}[W_s^2] = s$ if $s < t$, so, by symmetry, $\mathbb{E}[W_t W_s] = \min(t,s)$.
- Stationary increment; that is, the distribution of $W_t - W_s$ does not change in time. In particular, for $s < t$, $W_t - W_s$ has the same distribution as $W_{t-s} - W_0$, namely $W_t - W_s \sim \mathcal{N}(0, t-s)$.

From this definition, we deduce the following statements.

- Although W_t has stationary increments, by definition it is not stationary in the wide sense (the variance grows linearly as a function of t).
- Brownian motion is m.s.-continuous; that is,

$$\lim_{t \to s} \mathbb{E}[(W_t - W_s)^2] = \lim_{t \to s} |t - s| = 0.$$

- However, it is not m.s.-differentiable; that is,

$$\lim_{t \to s} \mathbb{E}\left[\left(\frac{W_t - W_s}{t - s}\right)^2\right] = \lim_{t \to s} |t - s|^{-1} = \infty.$$

Multidimensional Brownian motion is known as the Wiener process.

Example B.11 (Recall the random-walk example.) Let X_n be the position at instant n before the execution of a step at that instant. Assume $X_0 = 0$ and

$$X_n = \sum_{i=0}^{n-1} Y_i, \tag{B.3}$$

where $\mathbb{P}(Y_i = +1) = \mathbb{P}(Y_i = -1) = 1/2$. So Y_i is i.i.d. with $\mathbb{E}[Y_i] = 0$ and $\mathbb{E}[Y_i^2] = 1$. Let's rescale the time increment to $\Delta t = 1/n$ and define $W_{k\Delta t} = \sqrt{\Delta t} X_k$, for $k = 0, 1, 2, \ldots$. When $k = 1$, we have $W_{\Delta t} = \sqrt{\Delta t} X_1 = X_1/\sqrt{n}$. So, on every Δt, the size of jump is $\sqrt{\Delta t} = 1/\sqrt{n}$. By the central limit theorem, the distribution of $W_1 = X_n/\sqrt{n} \xrightarrow{d} \mathcal{N}(0,1)$ as $n \to \infty$. If we repeat the same argument with $\Delta t = t/n$, then $W_t = \sqrt{t} X_n/\sqrt{n}$. Define $A_i = \sqrt{t} Y_i$, such that $\mathbb{E}[A_i] = 0$ and $\mathbb{E}[A_i^2] = t$. By the central limit theorem, we obtain $W_t = \sum_{i=0}^{n-1} A_i/\sqrt{n} \xrightarrow{d} \mathcal{N}(0,t)$ as $n \to \infty$.

White noise

A Gaussian white noise $\dot{W}_t$ is defined as independent identically distributed with

$$\mathbb{E}[\dot{W}_t] = 0,$$
$$\mathbb{E}[\dot{W}_t \dot{W}_s] = \delta(t - s), \tag{B.4}$$

where $\delta(x)$ is a Dirac delta distribution; that is, $\delta(x) = 0$ for all $x \neq 0$ and $\int_{\mathbb{R}} \delta(x)dx = 1$. Note that, for any continuous function f,

$$\int_0^t f(x)\delta(x - s)dx = \begin{cases} f(s), & \text{if } 0 < s < t, \\ 0, & \text{if } s = t. \end{cases} \tag{B.5}$$

   Although the Wiener process is not differentiable anywhere, one can sometimes think of white noise as the "derivative" of the Wiener process (or Brownian motion) with the following definition:

$$dW_t := \dot{W}_t \, dt. \tag{B.6}$$

With this definition we can see that, for $W_0 = 0$,

$$\mathbb{E}[W_t] = \mathbb{E}\left[\int_0^t dW_s\right] = \mathbb{E}\left[\int_0^t \dot{W}_s \, ds\right] = \int_0^t \mathbb{E}[\dot{W}_s] ds = 0$$

and

$$\begin{aligned}
\mathbb{E}[W_t^2] &= \mathbb{E}\left(\int_0^t dW_s \int_0^t dW_u\right) \\
&= \int_0^t \int_0^t \mathbb{E}\left(dW_s \, dW_u\right) \\
&= \int_0^t \int_0^t \mathbb{E}[\dot{W}_s \dot{W}_u] ds \, du \\
&= \int_0^t \int_0^t \delta(s-u) ds \, du = t,
\end{aligned}$$

and these statistics are consistent with the definition of the Wiener process.

The Itô Isometry

With the definition above, we can evaluate the stochastic integral of functions f and g with respect to the Wiener process in the following sense:

$$\begin{aligned}
\mathbb{E}\left[\left(\int_0^t f(s)dW_s\right)\left(\int_0^t g(u)dW_u\right)\right] &= \int_0^t \int_0^t \mathbb{E}[\dot{W}_s \dot{W}_u] f(s) g(u) ds \, du \\
&= \int_0^t \int_0^t \delta(s-u) f(s) g(u) ds \, du \\
&= \int_0^t f(s) g(s) ds, \tag{B.7}
\end{aligned}$$

which is known as the *Itô isometry*. In particular, when $f = g$, we obtain

$$\mathbb{E}\left[\left(\int_0^t f(s)dW_s\right)^2\right] = \int_0^t f(s)^2 \, ds.$$

The Ornstein–Uhlenbeck Process

Consider a real-valued linear stochastic differential equation

$$du = -\gamma u \, dt + \sigma \, dW_t, \tag{B.8}$$

where $\gamma, \sigma > 0$ and dW_t is a Gaussian white noise. Given an initial condition $u(0)$, equation (B.8) can be written in integral form as

$$u(t) = e^{-\gamma t} u(0) + \sigma \int_0^t e^{-\gamma(t-s)} \, dW_s, \tag{B.9}$$

which is a stochastic process known as the Ornstein–Uhlenbeck process.

While the stochastic integral above is not easy to integrate, one can compute the following statistics. At any time $t \geq 0$, $u(t)$ is a Gaussian random variable with mean and variance given by

$$\bar{u}(t) := \mathbb{E}[u(t)] = e^{-\gamma t}\mathbb{E}[u(0)] \tag{B.10}$$

$$\mathrm{Var}[u(t)] = e^{-2\gamma t}\,\mathrm{Var}[u(0)] + \sigma^2\mathbb{E}\left[\left(\int_0^t e^{-\gamma(t-t')}\,dW_{t'}\right)^2\right]$$

$$= e^{-2\gamma t}\,\mathrm{Var}[u(0)] + \sigma^2\int_0^t e^{-2\gamma(t-s)}\,ds$$

$$= e^{-2\gamma t}\,\mathrm{Var}[u(0)] + \frac{\sigma^2}{2\gamma}(1 - e^{-2\gamma t}), \tag{B.11}$$

provided that the initial condition is Gaussian with mean $\mathbb{E}[u(0)]$ and variance $\mathrm{Var}[u(0)]$. As $t \to \infty$, the solutions are distributed according to $\mathcal{N}(0, E)$, where $E = \sigma^2/(2\gamma)$, is known as the climatological (equilibrium) variance.

Another important climatological statistic that one can compute in similar fashion is the correlation function,

$$R(\tau) = \frac{1}{E}\lim_{t \to \infty}\mathbb{E}[(u(t) - \bar{u}(t))(u(t + \tau) - \bar{u}(t + \tau))] = e^{-\gamma\tau},$$

which measures how much information in the initial conditions is carried by the variable u at time lag τ.

The decaying timescale (or decorrelation time) of this system is explicitly characterized by the damping coefficient γ:

$$T_c = \int_0^\infty R(\tau)d\tau = \frac{1}{\gamma}.$$

The Fokker–Planck Equation
Let u solve a nonlinear system of ODEs,

$$\frac{du}{dt} = f(u),$$

or SDEs

$$du = f(u)dt + \sigma(u)dW_t.$$

Let $p(u, t|w, s)$ be the (transition) density function for going from state w at time s to u at time t, where $s < t$. For the ODE case, the source of uncertainty is the sensitivity to initial conditions. Our goal is to determine the dynamical equation for $p(u, t|w, s)$, which we sometimes refer to as $p(u, t)$, suppressing the conditional dependence on w at time s. Since p is a density, we require $p > 0$, $\int_\mathbb{R} p(u, t)du = 1$.

For the ODE case, let us deduce the dynamical system using a physically relevant conservation law. In particular, let us recall the continuity equation that describes the conservation of mass of fluids. Let $v(u) \in \mathbb{R}^3$ be the velocity of fluid with density $\rho(u,t) \in \mathbb{R}$ at location $u \in \Omega$ at time t. We know that the mass is defined by the following volume integral:

$$m(t) = \int_\Omega \rho(u,t) dV.$$

The conservation of mass implies that the change of mass in Ω is equal to the fluxes across the boundary $\partial\Omega$,

$$\frac{dm}{dt} = -\int_{\partial\Omega} \rho(u,t) v(u) dS = -\int_\Omega \mathrm{div}_u(\rho(u,t) v(u)) dV,$$

using the divergence theorem. The negative sign is to ensure that outflow decreases the mass. Since the domain Ω is arbitrary, we have

$$\frac{\partial\rho}{\partial t} = -\mathrm{div}_u(\rho(u) v(u)), \tag{B.12}$$

which is known as the continuity equation. Also, if $v(u) = f(u) = \dot{u}$, then ρ is the probability density of u at time t, and this equation is known as the Liouville equation.

For the SDE case, we need the following result.

Definition B.12 (Itô lemma)   Let u satisfy

$$du = f(u) dt + \sigma(u) dW_t.$$

For any smooth function $h(u) \in \mathcal{C}_0^2(\mathbb{R})$ with compact support,

$$dh = h'(u) du + \frac{1}{2}\sigma^2(u) h''(u) dt$$

$$= \left(h'(u) f(u) + \frac{1}{2}\sigma^2(u) h''(u) \right) dt + h'(u)\sigma(u) dW_t.$$

In integral form, this is equivalent to

$$h(u_t) - h(u_s) = \int_s^t dh(u) = \int_s^t \left(h'(u_\tau) f(u_\tau) + \frac{1}{2}\sigma^2(u_\tau) h''(u_\tau) \right) d\tau$$

$$+ \int_s^t h'(u_\tau)\sigma(u_\tau) dW_\tau, \tag{B.13}$$

for $s < t$, where we have defined $u_t := u(t)$.

Define the conditional expectation of a functional $A(u)$ given $u_s = w$ as

$$\mathbb{E}[A] = \int_\mathbb{R} A(u) \, p(u,t|w,s) du = \int_\mathbb{R} A(u) \, p(u,t) du,$$

where we define $p(u,t) := p(u,t|w,s)$ to shorten the notation. Taking this expectation on (B.13), we obtain

$$\int_\mathbb{R} h(u) p(u,t) du - h(w) = \int_s^t \int_\mathbb{R} \left(h'(u) f(u) + \frac{1}{2}\sigma^2(u) h''(u) \right) p(u,\tau) du \, d\tau.$$

Taking the derivative with respect to t and using the fundamental theorem of calculus, we have

$$\int_{\mathbb{R}} h(u) \frac{\partial}{\partial t} p(u,t) du = \int_{\mathbb{R}} \left(h'(u) f(u) + \frac{1}{2} \sigma^2(u) h''(u) \right) p(u,t) du. \quad \text{(B.14)}$$

Upon applying integration by parts to the first component on the right-hand side of (B.14), we obtain

$$\int_{\mathbb{R}} h'(u) f(u) p(u,t) du = [h(u) f(u) p(u,t)]_{u=-\infty}^{\infty}$$

$$- \int_{\mathbb{R}} h(u) \frac{\partial}{\partial u} (f(u) p(u,t)) du$$

$$= - \int_{\mathbb{R}} h(u) \frac{\partial}{\partial u} (f(u) p(u,t)) du, \quad \text{(B.15)}$$

where the first term is zero since h has a compact support.

By a similar argument, the second component on the right-hand side of (B.14) can be expressed as

$$\int_{\mathbb{R}} \frac{1}{2} \sigma^2(u) h''(u) p(u,t) du = \int_{\mathbb{R}} h(u) \frac{1}{2} \frac{\partial^2}{\partial u^2} \left(\sigma^2(u) p(u,t) \right) du. \quad \text{(B.16)}$$

From these equations, (B.15) and (B.16), we can write (B.14) as

$$\int_{\mathbb{R}} h(u) \frac{\partial}{\partial t} p(u,t) du = \int_{\mathbb{R}} h(u) \left(-\frac{\partial}{\partial u} (f(u) p(u,t)) + \frac{1}{2} \frac{\partial^2}{\partial u^2} \left(\sigma^2(u) p(u,t) \right) \right) du.$$

Since h is an arbitrary test function, we have

$$\frac{\partial p}{\partial t} = -\frac{\partial}{\partial u} (fp) + \frac{1}{2} \frac{\partial^2}{\partial u^2} \left(\sigma^2 p \right), \quad \text{(B.17)}$$

which is a linear PDE known as the Fokker–Planck (or forward Kolmogorov) equation.

For notational convenience, we often define the differential operator

$$\mathcal{L}h = fh' + \frac{1}{2} \sigma^2 h'', \quad \text{(B.18)}$$

and denote the right-hand integral in (B.14) as

$$\langle \mathcal{L}h, p \rangle = \int_{\mathbb{R}} \left(h'(u) f(u) + \frac{1}{2} \sigma^2(u) h''(u) \right) p(u) du$$

$$= \int_{\mathbb{R}} h(u) \left(-\frac{\partial}{\partial u} (f(u) p(u)) + \frac{1}{2} \frac{\partial^2}{\partial u^2} \left(\sigma^2(u) p(u) \right) \right) du$$

$$= \langle h, \mathcal{L}^* p \rangle, \quad \text{(B.19)}$$

where we suppress the time dependence of p by writing $p(u) := p(u,t)$ and define

$$\mathcal{L}^* p = -\frac{\partial}{\partial u} (fp) + \frac{1}{2} \frac{\partial^2}{\partial u^2} (\sigma^2 p), \quad \text{(B.20)}$$

the adjoint of $\mathcal{L}$ with respect to $L^2(\mathbb{R})$. With the notation in (B.20), we can write the Fokker–Planck equation in (B.17) in compact form as

$$\frac{\partial p}{\partial t} = \mathcal{L}^* p.$$

If the initial density is positive, then $p(t)$ is positive for all $t > 0$ (by the maximum principle of parabolic PDEs). Notice that

$$\frac{d}{dt} \int_{\mathbb{R}} p\, du = \int_{\mathbb{R}} \frac{\partial p}{\partial t}\, du = \int_{\mathbb{R}} -\frac{\partial}{\partial u}(fp) + \frac{1}{2}\frac{\partial^2}{\partial u^2}\left(\sigma^2 p\right) du,$$

$$= \int_{\mathbb{R}} \frac{\partial}{\partial u}\left(-fp + \frac{1}{2}\frac{\partial}{\partial u}(\sigma^2 p)\right) du$$

$$= \left[-fp + \frac{1}{2}\frac{\partial}{\partial u}(\sigma^2 p)\right]_{u=-\infty}^{\infty} = 0.$$

Here, we are using the fact that, for p to be integrable on an unbounded domain, one expects both p and $\partial_u p$ to exponentially decay to zero as $u \to \pm\infty$ (see Pavliotis (2014)). This means that, if $\int p(u,0)du = \int p_0(u)du = 1$, then $\int p(u,t)du = 1$, for all $t > 0$.

For high-dimensional problems, one can write the Fokker–Planck equation as

$$\frac{\partial p}{\partial t} = \operatorname{div}\left(-fp + \frac{1}{2}\nabla(\sigma\sigma^\top)p\right),$$

where, if the diffusion tensor is zero, $\sigma\sigma^\top = 0$, we obtain the Liouville equation (B.12).

Appendix C. Elementary Differential Geometry

In this appendix, we give an intuitive and minimal background on the Riemannian geometry which is necessary to understand the construction of the Laplace–Beltrami operator via the diffusion maps algorithm.

Definition C.1 A topological space $(\mathcal{M}, \mathcal{O})$, where $\mathcal{O}$ denotes the topology (a collection of subsets or simply a σ-algebra of $\mathcal{M}$), is a d-dimensional topological manifold if, for every point $p \in \mathcal{M}$, there exists (1) an open set $U \subset \mathcal{M} \in \mathcal{O}$ that contains p and (2) a map $x : U \to x(U) \in \mathbb{R}^d$ such that it is invertible and both x and x^{-1} are continuous. The pair (U, x) is called a *chart* and one can think of $x = (x^1, \ldots, x^d)$ as local coordinates, where $x^j : U \to \mathbb{R}$.

Intuitively, a manifold is a topological space that is locally analogous to a Euclidean space at each point. A manifold is smooth if the transition maps $x_p \circ x_q^{-1} : \mathbb{R}^d \to \mathbb{R}^d$ between the local coordinates restricted to the overlapping domain of the two charts (U, x_p) and (V, x_q) are C^∞ for any pair $p, q \in \mathcal{M}$.

Definition C.2 (directional derivative) Let $\gamma : \mathbb{R} \to \mathcal{M}$ be a C^1 curve on a d-dimensional manifold such that $\gamma(0) = p \in \mathcal{M}$. We can define the velocity of γ at p as a linear map $v_{\gamma,p} : C^\infty(\mathcal{M}) \to \mathbb{R}$ as

$$v_{\gamma,p}(f) = (f \circ \gamma)'(0),$$

which is a directional derivative along γ.

In local coordinates (with respect to a local chart (U, x)), we can write

$$v_{\gamma,p(f)} = (f \circ x^{-1} \circ x \circ \gamma)'(0) = \left((f \circ x^{-1}) \circ (x \circ \gamma) \right)'(0)$$

$$= \sum_{i=1}^{d} (x^i \circ \gamma)'(0) \partial_i (f \circ x^{-1})((x \circ \gamma)(0))$$

$$= \sum_{i=1}^{d} (x^i \circ \gamma)'(0) \partial_i (f \circ x^{-1})(x(p))$$

$$:= \dot{\gamma}_x^i(0) \left(\frac{\partial}{\partial x^i} \right)_p f,$$

where we have used the Einstein summation convention in the last equality and defined $\dot{\gamma}_x^i(0) := (x^i \circ \gamma)'(0)$ and $(\partial/\partial x^i)_p f := \partial_i (f \circ x^{-1})(x(p))$. Notice that

$(\partial/\partial x^i)_p$ is not the usual Euclidean partial derivative since the domain of f is $\mathcal{M}$. Since f is arbitrary, we can express the velocities in local coordinates as

$$v_{\gamma,p} = \dot{\gamma}_x^i(0) \left(\frac{\partial}{\partial x^i} \right)_p,$$

where $\dot{\gamma}_x^i(0)$ represents the components of the velocity in the direction of $(\partial/\partial x^i)_p$.

Definition C.3 (tangent space) A collection of tangent vectors (velocities) is a tangent space $T_p\mathcal{M} := \{v_{\gamma,p} : \gamma \in C^1 \text{ intersects } p\}$.

One can show that $T_p\mathcal{M}$ is indeed a vector space with respect to scalar addition and multiplication. One can also show that the direction $(\partial/\partial x^i)_p$ is a chart-induced basis of the tangent space of $\mathcal{M}$ at p. To see this, notice that, if

$$a^i \left(\frac{\partial}{\partial x^i} \right)_p = 0, \tag{C.1}$$

then

$$a^i \left(\frac{\partial}{\partial x^i} \right)_p x^j = a^i \, \partial_i (x^j \circ x^{-1})(x(p)) = a^i \delta_i^j = a^j = 0, \tag{C.2}$$

which means that the $(\partial/\partial x^i)_p$ are linearly independent. We will often use the notation $X_p \in T_p\mathcal{M}$, with local coordinate representation $X_p = X_p^i(\partial/\partial x^i)_p$.

Definition C.4 (Riemannian manifold) We define the Riemannian manifold as a smooth manifold equipped with a Riemannian metric g; that is, a family of positive definite symmetric bilinear functions $g_p \colon T_p\mathcal{M} \times T_p\mathcal{M} \to \mathbb{R}$ that varies smoothly with $p \in \mathcal{M}$.

In local coordinates $x = (x^1, \ldots, x^d)$, the component of the metric g at each point p is defined as

$$g_{ij}(p) := g_p \left(\left(\frac{\partial}{\partial x^i} \right)_p, \left(\frac{\partial}{\partial x^j} \right)_p \right).$$

In our discussion in Chapter 6, we will be particularly interested in d-dimensional Riemannian manifolds embedded in $\mathbb{R}^n$, that is, $\mathcal{M} \subset \mathbb{R}^n$. Implicitly, this implies that there exists an embedding[1] function $\iota \colon \mathcal{M} \hookrightarrow \mathbb{R}^n$ such that the Riemannian metric inherited by $\mathcal{M}$ from the ambient space, $\mathbb{R}^n$, is defined as

$$g_p(u, v) = \langle D\iota(p)u, D\iota(p)v \rangle_{\mathbb{R}^n} = u^\top D\iota(p)^\top D\iota(p)v,$$

where $u, v \in T_p\mathcal{M}$. Equivalently, this definition means that ι is an isometric embedding since it preserves the metric. In local coordinates, $g_{ij}(p) = \left(D\iota(p)^\top D\iota(p) \right)_{ij}$.

---

[1] A function ι is an embedding if it is a homeomorphism onto its image $\iota(\mathcal{M}) \subseteq \mathbb{R}^n$.

Example C.5 Let $\mathcal{M} \subset \mathbb{R}^3$ be a plane parameterized by x^1, x^2, defined with an embedding function $\iota(x^1, x^2) = (x^1, x^2, x^1 + x^2 + 1)^\top$. So the manifold is the plane $z = x + y + 1$. Then, for any $p \in \mathcal{M}$,

$$D\iota(p) = \begin{pmatrix} 1 & 0 \\ 0 & 1 \\ 1 & 1 \end{pmatrix}$$

and

$$g_p(u, v) = u^\top \begin{pmatrix} 2 & 1 \\ 1 & 2 \end{pmatrix} v,$$

for $u, v \in T_p\mathcal{M} \cong \mathbb{R}^2$ and for any p.

The Riemannian metric inherited from the ambient space $\mathbb{R}^3$ is simply a weighted Euclidean metric as expected, since the manifold is just a plane. The length of a tangent vector $u = (1, 1)^\top$ is given by $g(u, u)^{1/2} = \sqrt{6}$. In the ambient space $D\iota(1, 1)^\top = (1, 1, 2)^\top$ and the length is given by the standard Euclidean metric, $\|(1, 1, 2)\| = \sqrt{1^2 + 1^2 + 2^2} = \sqrt{6}$.

Example C.6 Let an ellipse $\mathcal{M} \subset \mathbb{R}^2$ be parameterized by $t \in [0, 2\pi)$. So, for any $p \in \mathcal{M}$, in local coordinates $x(p) = t \in [0, 2\pi)$. Consider an embedding $\iota(t) = (a \cos(t), b \sin(t))^\top$. In this case, the Riemannian metric induced by the ambient space is $g_p(u, v) = g_{x^{-1}(t)}(u, v) = u^\top(a^2 \sin^2(t) + b^2 \cos^2(t))v$, where $u, v \in T_p\mathcal{M} \cong \mathbb{R}$ and the metric component is given by $g_{11}(p) = g_{11}(x^{-1}(t)) = a^2 \sin^2(t) + b^2 \cos^2(t)$.

Definition C.7 Let $\mathcal{M} \subset \mathbb{R}^m$. A function $f \colon \mathcal{M} \to \mathbb{R}$ is an element of an inner product space $L^2(\mathcal{M})$ if

$$\int_\mathcal{M} f^2(p) dV(p) < \infty,$$

where dV is the volume form inherited by $\mathcal{M}$ from the ambient space.

In a local coordinate system (U, x), we can write $dV(p) = \sqrt{|g|} dx$, such that

$$\int_\mathcal{M} f(p) dV(p) = \int_{x(U)} (f \circ x^{-1})(x^1, \dots, x^d) \sqrt{|g|} dx.$$

Essentially, this is a generalization of the change of variables for integrals in the standard calculus to Riemannian manifolds. In particular, let $\phi^{-1}(G) \subset \mathbb{R}^d$ be the preimage of $G \subset \mathbb{R}^d$ under the coordinate transformation ϕ. The integral of $F \colon \mathbb{R}^d \to \mathbb{R}$ over the domain $G \subset \mathbb{R}^n$ (if it exists) can be written as

$$\int_G F(x) dx = \int_{\phi^{-1}(G)} (F \circ \phi)(y) |\det(\partial_y \phi)| dy.$$

Example C.8 Consider the ellipse in Example C.6. Suppose we want to compute the arc length of the ellipse. Given the embedding function ι, the length can be computed with

$$L = \int_0^{2\pi} \|\iota'(t)\| dt = \int_0^{2\pi} \sqrt{a^2 \sin^2(t) + b^2 \cos^2(t)} dt = \int_0^{2\pi} \sqrt{|g|} dt.$$

Example C.9 Consider the unit sphere $\mathcal{M} = S^2 \subset \mathbb{R}^3$ with the standard parameterization $\theta \in (0, \pi), \varphi \in (0, 2\pi)$. Here, the embedding is given by

$$\iota(\theta, \varphi) = (\sin\theta\cos\varphi, \sin\theta\sin\varphi, \cos\theta)^\top.$$

For this case, it is easy to check that the induced Riemannian metric is given by

$$g_{x^{-1}(\theta,\varphi)}(u, v) = u^\top \begin{pmatrix} 1 & 0 \\ 0 & \sin^2\theta \end{pmatrix} v, \quad u, v \in T_{x^{-1}(\theta,\varphi)}\mathcal{M},$$

and the corresponding volume form is

$$dV = \sin\theta \, d\theta \, d\phi.$$

In Chapter 6, we will be particularly interested in the Laplace–Beltrami operator $\Delta_g = -\mathrm{div}_g \nabla_g$ defined on $\mathcal{M}$. To understand this operator, we need to define the gradient and divergence with respect to the Riemannian metric.

Definition C.10 (gradient) The *gradient* operator ∇_g is defined as $g(\nabla_g \varphi, X) = X\varphi$.

In local coordinates, since $\nabla_g \varphi = a^j \, \partial/\partial x^j$, choosing $X = \partial/\partial x^i$, we obtain

$$\frac{\partial}{\partial x^i} \varphi = g\left(a^j \frac{\partial}{\partial x^j}, \frac{\partial}{\partial x^i}\right) = g_{ji} a^j,$$

which means that $a^j = g^{ij}(\partial/\partial x^i)\varphi$ such that

$$\nabla_g \varphi = g^{ij} \frac{\partial}{\partial x^i} \varphi \frac{\partial}{\partial x^j},$$

where we used $g^{ik} g_{kj} = \delta^i_j$. In other words, the g^{ij} are the components of the inverse of the matrix g_{ij}.

Definition C.11 (divergence) The divergence can be deduced as an adjoint of the gradient,

$$\langle -\mathrm{div}_g X, f \rangle_{L^2(\mathcal{M})} = \langle X, \nabla_g f \rangle,$$

where the inner product on the right-hand side is the global inner product on $T\mathcal{M}$.

In local coordinates, this inner product can be expressed as

$$
\begin{aligned}
\langle X, \nabla_g f \rangle &= \int_{\mathcal{M}} g(X, \nabla_g f) dV \\
&= \int_{x(U)} g\left(X^i \frac{\partial}{\partial x^i}, g^{kj} \frac{\partial}{\partial x^k} f \frac{\partial}{\partial x^j} \right) \sqrt{|g|} \, dx^1 \cdots dx^d \\
&= \int_{x(U)} X^i \frac{\partial}{\partial x^k} f g^{kj} g\left(\frac{\partial}{\partial x^i}, \frac{\partial}{\partial x^j} \right) \sqrt{|g|} dx \\
&= \int_{x(U)} X^i \frac{\partial}{\partial x^k} f g^{kj} g_{ji} \sqrt{|g|} dx \\
&= \int_{x(U)} X^i \frac{\partial}{\partial x^i} f \sqrt{|g|} dx \\
&= -\int_{x(U)} f \frac{\partial}{\partial x^i} \left(X^i \sqrt{|g|} \right) dx \\
&= -\int_{\mathcal{M}} f \frac{1}{\sqrt{|g|}} \frac{\partial}{\partial x^i} \left(X^i \sqrt{|g|} \right) dV,
\end{aligned}
$$

where we use the local coordinates with $X = X^i \partial/\partial x^i$ in the second line and the fact that $g_{ij} = g_{ji}$ and $g^{kj} g_{ji} = \delta_i^k$ in the third and fourth lines. Since f and $\mathcal{M}$ are arbitrary, in local coordinates we have

$$
\mathrm{div}_g X = \frac{1}{\sqrt{|g|}} \frac{\partial}{\partial x^i} \left(\sqrt{|g|} X^i \right).
$$

With this formulation, we can write the Laplace–Beltrami operator in local coordinates as

$$
\Delta_g f = -\mathrm{div}_g \nabla_g f = -\frac{1}{\sqrt{|g|}} \frac{\partial}{\partial x^i} \left(g^{ij} \sqrt{|g|} \frac{\partial}{\partial x^j} f \right).
$$

Example C.12   In Euclidean geometry $\mathbb{R}^d$, $g_{ij} = \delta_j^i$ and $|g| = 1$, so we obtain the standard Laplacian on $\mathbb{R}^d$, $\Delta f = -\partial^2 f/\partial x^i \, \partial x^i$. Recall that this notation is the Einstein summation convention.

Example C.13   The Laplacian on $f : S^2 \subset \mathbb{R}^3 \to \mathbb{R}$ can be written as

$$
\Delta_g f = -\frac{1}{\sin\theta} \left(\frac{\partial}{\partial\theta} \left(g^{11} \sin\theta \frac{\partial}{\partial\theta} f \right) + \frac{\partial}{\partial\varphi} \left(g^{22} \sin\theta \frac{\partial}{\partial\varphi} f \right) \right)
$$

and, since

$$
g^{-1} = \begin{pmatrix} 1 & 0 \\ 0 & 1/\sin^2\theta \end{pmatrix},
$$

we have

$$
\begin{aligned}
\Delta_g f &= -\frac{1}{\sin\theta} \left(\frac{\partial}{\partial\theta} \left(\sin\theta \frac{\partial}{\partial\theta} f \right) + \frac{\partial}{\partial\varphi} \left(\frac{1}{\sin\theta} \frac{\partial}{\partial\varphi} f \right) \right) \\
&= -\frac{1}{\sin\theta} \frac{\partial}{\partial\theta} \left(\sin\theta \frac{\partial}{\partial\theta} f \right) - \frac{1}{\sin^2\theta} \frac{\partial^2}{\partial^2\varphi} f.
\end{aligned}
$$

For notational convenience, in Chapter 6, we will construct the negative of the Laplace–Beltrami operator, $\Delta = -\Delta_g$, on Riemannian manifolds $(\mathcal{M}, g)$. With this definition, Δ is negative definite. While the basic examples in this appendix assume knowledge of the embedding function ι, the approach discussed in Chapter 6 assumes that the embedding function ι (as well as the manifold $\mathcal{M}$) is unknown.

References

Anderson, J. (2001), 'An ensemble adjustment Kalman filter for data assimilation', *Monthly Weather Rev.* **129**, 2884–2903.

Anderson, J. (2007), 'An adaptive covariance inflation error correction algorithm for ensemble filters', *Tellus A* **59**, 210–224.

Andrews, G. & Askey, R. (1985), 'Classical orthogonal polynomials', in *Polynômes orthogonaux et applications*, Springer, pp. 36–62.

Aronszajn, N. (1950), 'Theory of reproducing kernels', *Trans. Am. Math. Soc.* **68**(3), 337–404.

Bain, A. & Crisan, D. (2009), *Fundamentals of Stochastic Filtering*, Springer.

Bao, W., Jin, S. & Markowich, P. (2003), 'Numerical study of time-splitting spectral discretizations of nonlinear Schrödinger equations in the semiclassical regimes', *SIAM J. Scient. Computing* **25**(1), 27–64.

Barthelmann, V., Novak, E. & Ritter, K. (2000), 'High dimensional polynomial interpolation on sparse grids', *Adv. Comput. Math.* **12**(4), 273–288.

Belanger, P. (1974), 'Estimation of noise covariance matrices for a linear time-varying stochastic process', *Automatica* **10**(3), 267–275.

Belkin, M. & Niyogi, P. (2003), 'Laplacian eigenmaps for dimensionality reduction and data representation', *Neural Comput.* **15**(6), 1373–1396.

Bella, T., Olshevsky, V., Zhlobich, P., Eidelman, Y., Gohberg, I. & Tyrtyshnikov, E. (2010), 'A Traub-like algorithm for Hessenberg quasiseparable-Vandermonde matrices of arbitrary order,' in *Numerical Methods for Structured Matrices and Applications: The Georg Heinig Memorial Volume*, Birkhäuser Basel, pp. 127–154.

Bengtsson, T., Bickel, P. & Li, B. (2008), 'Curse of dimensionality revisited: Collapse of the particle filter in very large scale systems,' in D. Nolan & T. Speed, eds, *IMS Lecture Notes – Monograph Series in Probability and Statistics: Essays in Honor of David A. Freedman*, Vol. 2, Institute of Mathematical Sciences, pp. 316–334.

Berry, T. & Harlim, J. (2014), 'Linear theory for filtering nonlinear multiscale systems with model error', *Proc. Roy. Soc. A* 20140168.

Berry, T. & Harlim, J. (2015), 'Nonparametric uncertainty quantification for stochastic gradient flows', *SIAM/ASA J. Uncertainty Quantification* **3**(1), 484–508.

Berry, T. & Harlim, J. (2016*a*), 'Forecasting turbulent modes with nonparametric models: Learning from noisy data', *Physica D* **320**, 57–76.

Berry, T. & Harlim, J. (2016*b*), 'Iterated diffusion maps for feature identification'. *Appl. Comput. Harmon. Anal.* (in press). doi:10.1016/j.acha.2016.08.005.

Berry, T. & Harlim, J. (2016*c*), 'Semiparametric modeling: Correcting low-dimensional model error in parametric models', *J. Comput. Phys.* **308**, 305–321.

Berry, T. & Harlim, J. (2016*d*), 'Variable bandwidth diffusion kernels', *Appl. Comput. Harmon. Anal.* **40**, 68–96.

Berry, T. & Harlim, J. (2017), 'Correcting biased observation model error in data assimilation', *Monthly Weather Rev.* **145**(7), 2833–2853.

Berry, T. & Sauer, T. (2013), 'Adaptive ensemble Kalman filtering of nonlinear systems', *Tellus A* **65**, 20331.

Berry, T. & Sauer, T. (2016), 'Consistent manifold representation for topological data analysis'. https://arxiv.org/abs/1606.02353

Berry, T., Giannakis, D. & Harlim, J. (2015), 'Nonparametric forecasting of low-dimensional dynamical systems', *Phys. Rev. E* **91**, 032915.

Bickel, P., Li, B. & Bengtsson, T. (2008), 'Sharp failure rates for the bootstrap filter in high dimensions', in *IMS Lecture Notes – Monograph Series: Essays in Honor of J. K. Gosh'*, Vol. 3, Institute of Mathematical Sciences, pp. 318–329.

Bishop, C., Etherton, B. & Majumdar, S. (2001), 'Adaptive sampling with the ensemble transform Kalman filter part I: The theoretical aspects', *Monthly Weather Rev.* **129**, 420–436.

Brezis, H. (2010), *Functional Analysis, Sobolev Spaces and Partial Differential Equations*, Springer.

Cameron, R. & Martin, W. (1947), 'The orthogonal development of non-linear functionals in series of Fourier–Hermite functionals', *Annals of Mathematics* **48**(2), 385–392.

Chorin, A. & Hald, O. (2013), 'Estimating the uncertainty in underresolved nonlinear dynamics', *Math. Mech. Solids* **19**(1), 28–38.

Chorin, A., Hald, O. & Kupferman, R. (2000), 'Optimal prediction and the Mori–Zwanzig representation of irreversible processes', *Proc. Nat. Acad. Sci.* **97**(7), 2968–2973.

Chorin, A., Hald, O. & Kupferman, R. (2002), 'Optimal prediction with memory', *Physica D: Nonlinear Phenomena* **166**(3), 239–257.

Chorin, A., Lu, F., Miller, R., Morzfeld, M. & Tu, X. (2016), 'Sampling, feasibility, and priors in data assimilation', *Discrete Continuous Dynam. Syst.* **36**(8), 4227–4246.

Christen, J. & Fox, C. (2005), 'MCMC using an approximation', *J. Comput. Graphical Statist.* **14**(4), 795–810.

Coifman, R. & Lafon, S. (2006), 'Diffusion maps', *Appl. Comput. Harmon. Anal.* **21**, 5–30.

Coifman, R., Shkolnisky, Y., Sigworth, F. & Singer, A. (2008), 'Graph Laplacian tomography from unknown random projections', *IEEE Trans. Image Processing* **17**(10), 1891–1899.

Dashti, M. & Stuart, A. (2017), 'The Bayesian approach to inverse problems', in *Handbook of Uncertainty Quantification*, Springer.

De La Chevrotière, M. & Harlim, J. (2017*a*), 'A data-driven method for improving the correlation estimation in serial ensemble Kalman filters', *Monthly Weather Rev.* **145**(3), 985–1001.

De La Chevrotière, M. & Harlim, J. (2017*b*), 'Data-driven localization mappings in filtering the monsoon-Hadley multicloud convective flows'. *Mon. Wea. Rev.* (in press). doi:10.1175/MWR-D-17-0381.1.

Dee, D., Cohn, S., Dalcher, A. & Ghil, M. (1985), 'An efficient algorithm for estimating noise covariances in distributed systems', *IEEE Trans. Automatic Control* **30**(11), 1057–1065.

Dee, D. & da Silva, A. (1998), 'Data assimilation in the presence of forecast bias', *Q. J. Roy. Meteorol. Soc.* **124**, 269–295.

Doucet, A., de Freitas, N. & Gordon, N. (2001), 'Sequential monte carlo methods in practice. series statistics for engineering and information science'.

Dunik, J., Straka, O., Kost, O. & Havlik, J. (2017), 'Noise covariance matrices in state-space models: A survey and comparison of estimation methods? Part I'. *Int. J. Adapt. Control Signal Process* **31** (11), 1505–1543.

Evensen, G. (1994), 'Sequential data assimilation with a nonlinear quasi-geostrophic model using Monte Carlo methods to forecast error statistics', *J. Geophys. Research* **99**, 10143–10162.

Friedland, B. (1969), 'Treatment of bias in recursive filtering', *IEEE Trans. Automatic Control* **14**, 359–367.

Friedland, B. (1982), 'Estimating sudden changes of biases in linear dynamical systems', *IEEE Trans. Automatic Control* **27**, 237–240.

Gamerman, D. & Lopes, H. (2006), *Markov Chain Monte Carlo: Stochastic Simulation for Bayesian Inference*, second edition, Chapman & Hall/CRC Texts in Statistical Science, Taylor & Francis.

Gaspari, G. & Cohn, S. E. (1999), 'Construction of correlation functions in two and three dimensions', *Q. J. Roy. Meteorol. Soc.* **125**(554), 723–757.

Gershgorin, B., Harlim, J. & Majda, A. (2010), 'Test models for improving filtering with model errors through stochastic parameter estimation', *J. Comput. Phys.* **229**(1), 1–31.

Ghanem, R. & Spanos, P. (2003), *Stochastic Finite Elements: A Spectral Approach*, Courier Corporation.

Golub, G. H. & Welsch, J. W. (1969), 'Calculation of Gauss quadrature rules', *Math. Comput.* **23**, 221–230.

González-Tokman, C. & Hunt, B. R. (2013), 'Ensemble data assimilation for hyperbolic systems', *Physica D: Nonlinear Phenomena* **243**(1), 128–142.

Gottwald, G., Crommelin, D. & Franzke, C. (2017), 'Stochastic climate theory', in *Nonlinear and Stochastic Climate Dynamics*, Cambridge University Press, pp. 209–240.

Haario, H., Laine, M., Mira, A. & Saksman, E. (2006), 'DRAM: Efficient adaptive MCMC', *Statist. Comput.* **16**(4), 339–354.

Haken, H. (1975), 'Analogy between higher instabilities in fluids and lasers', *Phys. Lett. A* **53**(1), 77–78.

Hamill, T. M., Whitaker, J. S. & Snyder, C. (2001), 'Distance-dependent filtering of background error covariance estimates in an ensemble Kalman filter', *Monthly Weather Rev.* **129**(11), 2776–2790.

Härdle, W., Müller, M., Sperlich, S. & Werwatz, A. (2012), *Nonparametric and Semiparametric Models*, Springer.

Harlim, J. (2017), 'Model error in data assimilation', *Nonlinear and Stochastic Climate Dynamics*, Cambridge University Press, pp. 276–317.

Harlim, J. & Li, X. (2015), 'Parametric reduced models for the nonlinear Schrödinger equation', *Phys. Rev. E.* **91**, 053306.

Harlim, J., Mahdi, A. & Majda, A. (2014), 'An ensemble Kalman filter for statistical estimation of physics constrained nonlinear regression models', *J. Comput. Phys.* **257A**, 782–812.

Harlim, J. & Yang, H. (2017), 'Diffusion forecasting model with basis functions from QR-decomposition'. *J. Nonlinear Sci.* (2017). doi:10.1007/s00332-017-9430-1.

Hein, M. & Audibert, J.-Y. (2005), 'Intrinsic dimensionality estimation of submanifolds in R^d', in *Proceedings of the 22nd International Conference on Machine Learning, ICML '05*, ACM, pp. 289–296. http://doi.acm.org/10.1145/1102351.1102388

Heiss, F. & Winschel, V. (2008), 'Likelihood approximation by numerical integration on sparse grids', *J. Econometrics* **144**(1), 62–80.

Higdon, D., Lee, H. & Holloman, C. (2003), 'Markov chain Monte Carlo-based approaches for inference in computationally intensive inverse problems', in *Bayesian Statistics 7: Proceedings of the Seventh Valencia International Meeting*, Oxford University Press, pp. 181–197.

Houtekamer, P. & Mitchell, H. (1998), 'Data assimilation using an ensemble Kalman filter technique', *Monthly Weather Rev.* **126**, 796–811.

Hunt, B., Kostelich, E. & Szunyogh, I. (2007), 'Efficient data assimilation for spatiotemporal chaos: A local ensemble transform Kalman filter', *Physica D* **230**, 112–126.

Hwang, M. & Seinfeld, J. H. (1972), 'Observability of nonlinear systems', *J. Optimization Theory Appl.* **10**(2), 67–77.

Kaipio, J. & Somersalo, E. (2006), *Statistical and Computational Inverse Problems*, Springer.

Kalman, R. & Bucy, R. (1961), 'New results in linear filtering and prediction theory', *Trans. AMSE J. Basic Eng.* **83D**, 95–108.

Karlin, S. (2014), *A First Course in Stochastic Processes*, Academic Press.

Kelly, D., Law, K. & Stuart, A. (2014), 'Well-posedness and accuracy of the ensemble Kalman filter in discrete and continuous time', *Nonlinearity* **27**(10), 2579–2603.

Kennedy, M. & O'Hagan, A. (2001), 'Bayesian calibration of computer models', *J. Roy. Statist. Soc.: Series B (Statist. Methodol.)* **63**(3), 425–464.

Kwiatkowski, E. & Mandel, J. (2015), 'Convergence of the square root ensemble Kalman filter in the large ensemble limit', *SIAM/ASA J. Uncertainty Quantification* **3**(1), 1–17. http://dx.doi.org/10.1137/140965363

Lawler, G. (2006), *Introduction to Stochastic Processes*, CRC Press.

Lax, P. (2007), *Linear Algebra and Its Applications*, Wiley.

Le Maître, O. P. & Knio, O. M. (2010), *Spectral Methods for Uncertainty Quantification: With Applications to Computational Fluid Dynamics*, Springer.

Lee, Y. & Majda, A. (2016), 'State estimation and prediction using clustered particle filters', *Proc. Nat. Acad. Sci.* 201617398.

Little, A., Jung, Y.-M. & Maggioni, M. (2009), 'Multiscale estimation of intrinsic dimensionality of data sets', in *Manifold Learning and Its Applications: Papers from the AAAI Fall Symposium*, AAAI, pp. 26–33.

Lorenz, E. (1963), 'Deterministic nonperiodic flow', *J. Atmosph. Sci.* **20**, 130–141.

Lorenz, E. (1969), 'Atmospheric predictability as revealed by naturally occurring analogues', *J. Atmosph. Sci.* **26**(4), 636–646.

Lorenz, E. (1996), 'Predictability – a problem partly solved', in *Proceedings of Seminar on Predictability, held at ECMWF on 4–8 September 1995*, pp. 1–18.

Lu, F., Lin, K. & Chorin, A. (2017), 'Data-based stochastic model reduction for the Kuramoto–Sivashinsky equation', *Physica D: Nonlinear Phenomena* **340**, 46–57.

Majda, A. & Grooms, I. (2014), 'New perspectives on superparameterization for geophysical turbulence', *J. Comput. Phys.* **271**, 60–77.

Majda, A. & Harlim, J. (2012), *Filtering Complex Turbulent Systems*, Cambridge University Press.

Majda, A. & Harlim, J. (2013), 'Physics constrained nonlinear regression models for time series', *Nonlinearity* **26**, 201–217.

Majda, A. & Qi, D. (2016*a*), 'Improving prediction skill of imperfect turbulent models through statistical response and information theory', *J. Nonlinear Sci.* **26**(1), 233–285.

Majda, A. & Qi, D. (2016*b*), 'Strategies for reduced-order models for predicting the statistical responses and uncertainty quantification in complex turbulent dynamical systems', submitted to *SIAM Review*.

Majda, A. & Tong, X. (2016), 'Robustness and accuracy of finite ensemble kalman filters in large dimensions', *Comm. Pure Appl. Math.* (in press). doi:10.1002/cpa.21722.

Mandel, J., Cobb, L. & Beezley, J. (2011), 'On the convergence of the ensemble Kalman filter', *Applications of Mathematics* **56**(6), 533–541. http://dx.doi.org/10.1007/s10492-011-0031-2

Marzouk, Y., Najm, H. & Rahn, L. (2007), 'Stochastic spectral methods for efficient Bayesian solution of inverse problems', *J. Comput. Phys.* **224**(2), 560–586.

Marzouk, Y. & Xiu, D. (2009), 'A stochastic collocation approach to Bayesian inference in inverse problems', *Commun. Comput. Phys.* **6**, 826–847.

Mattingly, J., Stuart, A. & Higham, D. (2002), 'Ergodicity for SDES and approximations: Locally Lipschitz vector fields and degenerate noise', *Stochastic Processes Appl.* **101**(2), 185–232.

Mehra, R. (1970), 'On the identification of variances and adaptive Kalman filtering', *IEEE Trans. Automatic Control* **15**(2), 175–184.

Mehra, R. (1972), 'Approaches to adaptive filtering', *IEEE Trans. Automatic Control* **17**(5), 693–698.

Ménard, R. (2010), 'Bias estimation', in *Data Assimilation*, Springer, pp. 113–135.

Mori, H. (1965), 'Transport, collective motion, and Brownian motion', *Prog. Theor. Phys.* **33**, 423–450.

Morriss, G. & Evans, D. J. (1990), *Statistical Mechanics of Nonequilbrium Liquids*, Academic Press.

Novak, E. & Ritter, K. (1996), 'High dimensional integration of smooth functions over cubes', *Numer. Math.* **75**(1), 79–97.

Nummelin, E. (1984), *General Irreducible Markov Chains and Non-Negative Operators*, Cambridge University Press.

Nyström, E. J. (1930), 'Über die praktische Auflösung von Integralgleichungen mit Anwendungen auf Randwertaufgaben', *Acta Math.* **54**(1), 185–204.

O'Kane, T. & Frederiksen, J. (2010), 'Application of statistical dynamical turbulence closures to data assimilation', *Phys. Scr.* **T142**, 014042.

Øksendal, B. (2003), *Stochastic Differential Equations: An Introduction with Applications*, Springer.

Pavliotis, G. (2014), *Stochastic Processes and Applications: Diffusion Processes, the Fokker–Planck and Langevin Equations*, Springer.

Poterjoy, J. (2016), 'A localized particle filter for high-dimensional nonlinear systems', *Monthly Weather Rev.* **144**(1), 59–76.

Reich, S. & Cotter, C. (2015), *Probabilistic Forecasting and Bayesian Data Assimilation*, Cambridge University Press.

Sain, S. & Scott, W. (1996), 'On locally adaptive density estimation', *J. Am. Statist. Ass.* **91**(436), 1525–1534.

Sapsis, T. & Majda, A. (2013), 'Blending modified Gaussian closure and non-Gaussian reduced subspace methods for turbulent dynamical systems', *J. Nonlinear Sci.* **23**(6), 1039–1071.

Smith, R. (2013), *Uncertainty Quantification: Theory, Implementation, and Applications*, Vol. 12, SIAM.

Smolyak, S. (1969), 'Quadrature and interpolation formulas for tensor products of certain classes of functions', *Dokl. Akad. Nauk SSSR* **4**, 240–243.

Solari, H., Natiello, M. & Mindlin, G. (1996), *Nonlinear Dynamics*, Institute of Physics.

Song, L., Fukumizu, K. & Gretton, A. (2013), 'Kernel embeddings of conditional distributions: A unified kernel framework for nonparametric inference in graphical models', *IEEE Signal Processing Mag.* **30**(4), 98–111.

Song, L., Huang, J., Smola, A. & Fukumizu, K. (2009), 'Hilbert space embeddings of conditional distributions with applications to dynamical systems', in *Proceedings of the 26th Annual International Conference on Machine Learning*, ACM, pp. 961–968.

Terrell, D. & Scott, D. (1992), 'Variable kernel density estimation', *Ann. Statist.* **20**, 1236–1265.

Tierney, L. (1994), 'Markov chains for exploring posterior distributions', *Ann. Statist.* **22**(4), 1701–1728.

Ting, D., Huang, L. & Jordan, M. (2010), 'An analysis of the convergence of graph Laplacians', in J. Fürnkranz & T. Joachims, eds., *Proceedings of the 27th International Conference on Machine Learning (ICML-10)*, Omnipress, pp. 1079–1086. www.icml2010.org/papers/554.pdf

Tippett, M., Anderson, J., Bishop, C., Hamill, T. & Whitaker, J. (2003), 'Ensemble square-root filters', *Monthly Weather Rev.* **131**, 1485–1490.

Tong, X., Majda, A. & Kelly, D. (2016), 'Nonlinear stability and ergodicity of ensemble based kalman filters', *Nonlinearity* **29**(2), 657–691.

Trefethen, L. (2008), 'Is Gauss quadrature better than Clenshaw–Curtis?', *SIAM Rev.* **50**(1), 67–87.

van Leeuwen, P. (2015), 'Aspects of particle filtering in high-dimensional spaces', in *Dynamic Data-Driven Environmental Systems Science*, Springer, pp. 251–262.

Wiener, N. (1938), 'The homogeneous chaos', *Am. J. Math.* **60**(4), 897–936.

Wilkinson, D. (2011), *Stochastic Modelling for Systems Biology*, second edition, Chapman & Hall/CRC Press.

Xiu, D. (2010), *Numerical Methods for Stochastic Computations: A Spectral Method Approach*, Princeton University Press.

Zhao, Z. & Giannakis, D. (2016), 'Analog forecasting with dynamics-adapted kernels', *Nonlinearity* **29**(9), 2888–2939.

Zhen, Y. & Harlim, J. (2015), 'Adaptive error covariance estimation methods for ensemble Kalman filtering', *J. Comput. Phys.* **294**, 619–638.

Zwanzig, R. W. (1961), 'Statistical mechanics of irreversiblity', in Britten, W. E., Downs, B. W. & Downs, J., *Lectures in Theoretical Physics*, Vol. 3, Interscience, pp. 106–141.

Zwanzig, R. W. (1973), 'Nonlinear generalized Langevin equations', *J. Statist. Phys.* **9**, 215–220.

Index